CW00972525

Heiress, Rebel, Vigilante, Bomber

Heiress, Rebel, Vigilante, Bomber

The Extraordinary Life of Rose Dugdale

SEAN O'DRISCOLL

SANDYCOVE

an imprint of

PENGUIN BOOKS

SANDYCOVE

UK | USA | Canada | Ireland | Australia
India | New Zealand | South Africa

Sandycove is part of the Penguin Random House group of companies
whose addresses can be found at global.penguinrandomhouse.com.

Penguin
Random House
UK

First published 2022
001

Copyright © Sean O'Driscoll, 2022

The moral right of the author has been asserted

Set in 13.5/16pt Garamond MT Std
Typeset by Jouve (UK), Milton Keynes
Printed and bound in Great Britain by Clays Ltd, Elcograf S.p.A.

The authorized representative in the EEA is Penguin Random House Ireland,
Morrison Chambers, 32 Nassau Street, Dublin D02 YH68

A CIP catalogue record for this book is available from the British Library

ISBN: 978–1–844–88555–8

To Seán Óg, may he grow up in an Ireland at peace

Contents

CONTENTS

Prologue

They enter the powder room of Buckingham Palace for a final review. Yardley's Feather Finish cream powder; Goya's Kiss Again lipstick, applied slowly in the mirror with a pucker of the lips; Elizabeth Arden's Blue Grass perfume, dabbed from tiny bottles in purses.

Rose adjusts her dress, fitted by Worth of London. It is white, and shoulderless, in keeping with the style of the 1958 season.

She looks in the mirror. She knows that this is not the world she wants to inhabit; that there is, as she will put it decades later, 'another world, somewhere', where she could be herself.

Rose greets her friend Meg Poole, who has arrived with her father and Lady Kilmuir, the wife of the Lord Chancellor. Because of her status, Lady Kilmuir was allowed to bring Meg up a back stairway, avoiding the long queue of debutantes waiting to enter the palace. ('I was wearing a blue dress,' Meg will remember. 'It was the style of that year, this hideous balloon bulge at the bottom, it truly was ghastly. And we all HAD to have long gloves to the elbow. I remember thinking, I will never wear these again.')

Rose adjusts her dress. Underneath is a girdle of great complexity. She adjusts her hair; the girls share mints.

When the debutantes emerge smiling, bemedalled royal

chaperones are waiting: middle-aged men who fought in the war, and who volunteer for royal ceremonies. The young women walk down the corridor in silence. This is a last chance for Rose to mentally rehearse the curtsey learned at Madame Vacani's school of dance on Brompton Road in Knightsbridge, where hundreds of girls were sent each year to learn how to comport themselves before royalty.

The chaperones lead them into the reception room and the debutantes sit on long rows of golden chairs. Meg and Rose whisper to each other. Most of the girls are dressed in white, signifying their virginal status for the husband-hunting season that lies ahead of them. (Meg would recall: 'Uniformed footmen came in to make sure we were not messing about, to frighten us, but we were too nervous to do anything.')

In Rose's hands are two cards. The first reads, 'To be presented'. She hands it to a servant, who takes it with a smile.

The palace guards, silent and bearing long axes, swing open the door. She enters the ballroom. 'Miss Rose Dugdale,' a guard announces.

She walks, with poise learned in finishing school and refined by Madame Vacani, to the centre of the room. There she turns to face the Queen and her consort, Prince Philip. The royal couple sit on thrones inside an Indian shamiana. Rose smiles. She throws out her chest, bustles her dress and with outstretched arms sinks to the ground and curtseys.

The Queen smiles and nods. Rose rises, Prince Philip nods, she does another swan-dive curtsey for him. She is now blessed to begin 'the season' – the year-long list of dinner parties, dances, horse shows and balls that mark her out as an upper-class virgin waiting to be plucked.

The Buckingham Palace curtsey is what Jessica Mitford, in

Hons and Rebels, calls the 'specific, upper-class version of the puberty rite'. It is also an acknowledgement that one is not of the very highest class; that, in order to maximize one's chances of ending up with a suitable husband, a house in the country and some babies, one is willing to bend to the ground before royalty.

After the ceremony, Rose is led to the Green Dining Room, to be reunited with her father, who stands with a rictus smile and hugs her. She can loosen her posture and have the traditional post-curtsey chocolate cake.

('I didn't stay long and neither did Rose,' Meg recalls. Meg went to the Turf Club to celebrate with her father. They had oysters and champagne. 'I had a bad oyster. Have you ever had a bad oyster? It's a fairly abysmal and unique experience.')

She and her father were due to go to the Old Vic theatre, where the Queen was also due to attend a performance, but on the way there Meg started feeling unwell. 'My father ordered the chauffeur to take me straight home. Luckily, I was sick only when I got home. My father went on to the event and met the Queen. He told her that his daughter was one of the debutantes earlier that day. The Queen joked that she thought her head was going to fall off from all that nodding.'

The Queen would never have to do it again. The Lord Chamberlain had announced that debutantes would no longer be presented at court.

Britain was changing. It was losing its colonies one by one, and barely a year had passed since the loss of the Suez Canal. There was a growing sense that the upper class was losing control – not just of Suez, or India, or Ireland, but also of the lower orders in Britain itself. John Osborne's searing play *Look Back in Anger*, about a young woman who escapes the upper class to live with a left-wing radical, expressed a grow-ing hostility to Britain's fossilized traditions and class structure.

Rose was unaware of the tidal wave of change that was about to hit Britain – she knew only that the debutante season didn't *feel* right and that society didn't feel right. She wanted to escape what lay ahead – the Tory husband, the stifling dinner parties, the perfectly mannered children. She agreed to endure the debutante season on one condition: that she be allowed to apply to Oxford University.

1. The Perfect Candidate

Rose Dugdale was born at Yarty, her family's Devon estate, in March 1941. She was christened Bridget Rose – the Irish forename oddly prescient, in a family without Irish roots. She was always known as Rose, and she believes this may have been a decision made by her father, who gave nicknames to his other children: 'Puss' for Caroline, and 'Fatty' for baby James. 'I was lucky, in a way, that he called me Rose, compared to the nicknames the other two got,' she says.

Shortly after her birth, her father, Lieutenant Colonel Eric Dugdale, was called in to Montgomery's campaign to drive the Nazis out of North Africa, eventually suffering a shrapnel wound to the leg and being discharged.

While her husband was away at war, Rose's mother, Carol Dugdale, kept a gun under the bed, in case the Germans should invade. She intended to fight them off, and if that didn't work, she would shoot herself and her family.

Rose recalls that her mother grew her own vegetables during the war but perhaps didn't wholly embrace the logic of thrift in a time of scarcity. She was an amateur painter, and Eric was amazed to learn that she'd destroyed canvases of paintings she did not like: he could not understand why she didn't reuse them to help the war effort. Carol bought a cow for the girls during the war because it looked pretty, but it gave little milk.

Carol Dugdale was born Caroline Timmis. She grew up in Matson House, a mansion in Gloucestershire, which was held in trust for her and her siblings. She attended the Slade

School of Art in London and became good friends with the novelist Rebecca West and the painter Teddy Wolfe.

In 1925, aged twenty-two, she married a 23-year-old stockbroker named John Mosley, the younger brother of Oswald Mosley, a young politician who would go on to become the leader of British fascism. The wedding was held at St Margaret's Church in the Palace of Westminster.

Carol and John lived first at 83 Sloane Street in Chelsea and later moved to 21 Milner Street nearby. They produced two sons: Tim John Oswald Mosley, who was born in April 1926, and Simon James Mosley, born a year later.

The family lived for a time near Horsham in West Sussex, in a house which John Mosley had inherited from his Uncle Tat. According to Oswald Mosley's memoir, *My Life*, it was a tiny 'medieval doll's house', where John was bothered by fascists in the 1930s: they wrote slogans on the long garden wall in support of Oswald. 'My genial relations with my brother survived even this test,' Oswald wrote.

John Mosley's vice was women, not fascism. 'He was a bit of a cad,' says a member of the family, speaking on condition of anonymity. 'He would be at the club, drinking champagne, and liked to do press-ups to show off. I gather there were many affairs, in an era when there were affairs but it was not talked about.'

Divorce records show that Carol's solicitor, Frank Caola, got an investigator to follow her husband – revealing that he spent two nights at the Charing Cross Hotel in July 1935 with a woman who booked in under the name Mrs Kitty Rose. Carol filed for divorce immediately.

Further investigations by Mr Caola revealed that Kitty Rose was in fact Edna King of 43 St James's Terrace in Regent's Park. A court clerk erased the name Kitty Rose from the divorce documentation and wrote 'Edna King' in red pen above it. Hoping to avoid scandal, John and Carol unsuccessfully sought to have the divorce hearings moved to Middlesex.

John agreed to a divorce on the condition that he could live in perpetuity at one of the homes she owned. He moved into 9 Wilbraham Place, Sloane Square, and within a few months married a Romanian woman. Meanwhile, the Mosley name fell further and further into disrepute as Britain and Germany edged closer to war. John Mosley would later move to France and, according to a family member, drifted out of the lives of his two sons.

Finding herself divorced, and the mother of two children named Mosley, Carol would have had cause for doubt about her remarriage prospects. Being a divorcee meant not being allowed to present a daughter at Buckingham Palace during debutante season and being cut off from the oxygen of establishment dinner parties.

With two very young children, Carol 'was aware of how difficult it was for her and she was very anxious to marry someone', according to a family member. She received a marriage proposal from the gay music critic Eddy Sackville-West and 'came close to accepting'. Sackville-West was upper class (and later a hereditary member of the House of Lords), a former Etonian, a novelist, a member of the Bloomsbury set of artists and best friend to Sir Alfred Beit, one of Britain's great art collectors. He lived at Knole, one of the largest houses in Britain, located on 1,000 acres of forest and farmland in Kent. The house, a former archbishop's palace with modern wings attached, has over four hundred rooms under seven acres of roofs.

A member of the Mitford family, who were also married into the Mosleys, introduced Carol to Eric Dugdale through a friend. 'Into her life came this military man, good natured, kind and very wealthy,' a relative says. 'He wanted a family . . . and Carol came with a family. It seems that maybe both found something they were looking for in the other.'

Most of Eric's income came from his membership of a syndicate, a group of so-called 'Names' from Britain's wealthiest families who had accepted an invitation to be underwriters for Lloyd's of London, the insurance brokers. Carol's parents 'thought that John Mosley was a lot of fun, but not a good husband, while Eric was a very good husband', the family member says. 'Eric was normality, stability and calm and looked after Simon and Tim and was very kind and fair to them.'

The two Mosley children came to live with the Dugdale family in St Leonard's Terrace in Chelsea. Eric and Carol had three children together – Caroline, Rose and James – and the two families were raised together after Eric purchased the townhouse next door.

Carol suffered post-partum depression after Rose's birth, and her half-brothers helped to look after her: Simon sometimes changed her nappies, Tim would walk her to the park.

St Leonard's Terrace was – as it still is – one of the most desirable streets in London, looking out on to the vast grounds and gardens of the Royal Hospital Chelsea and the cricket pitches of Burton Court public park. To the left, just around the corner from the Dugdale family's two five-storey townhouses, lay the 11-acre Duke of York's barracks with its wide, green lawns.

Life in St Leonard's Terrace was traditional, even by upper-class standards of the time. Rose and her sister, Caroline, were required to wear formal dresses for dinner, and to curtsey when introduced to guests.

The Dugdale children were expected to excel at music. Rose played the piano, her sister the violin. Their younger brother was the singer. Rose would later say that Mozart was an early favourite and stayed with her all her life, as did her childhood love of Rachmaninov's piano concertos and Bach's fugues.

The family attended church every Sunday at the Chelsea Hospital chapel, Rose's and Caroline's hair immaculately brushed, in matching ribbons. They looked like a pair of sisters from a Renoir painting, the writer Fiona MacCarthy recalled. 'And I didn't want to be a Renoir painting,' Rose would later insist. 'We couldn't even run, because Mother would tell us to stop.'

At Yarty, the 600-acre family estate in Devon, Rose had a pony called Eros and played often with her father's two hunting dogs. By the age of five, she could ride Eros around a paddock and attempt tiny jumps.

Meg Poole recalls: 'Rose was such a beautiful little thing. She was more confident and outgoing than her older sister. I know that her parents had high hopes for her, especially her father.'

Aged five, Rose was enrolled in Miss Ironside's School for Girls in Kensington. The school was founded and run by sisters Rene and Nelly Ironside. Neither Rene nor Nelly ever married, and both dedicated their lives to education.

'Rene was always proper,' recalls her grand-niece, Virginia Ironside, who attended the school with Rose. 'Everything was about improvement. Shoulders back, stand up straight, speak clearly, learn, improve oneself. She was thin and had very long ear lobes. She was very disapproving and seemed something of a headmistress parody. She had a very dry sense of humour but appeared humourless. Nelly was round and fun, and fixed windows and did all the repairs around the school.'

Virginia Ironside's father, who was tutored by his Aunt Rene, recalled her as 'a person who had no interest in pleasure for little children – it was all improvement. Even if you were given a present, it was an improving present.'

Virginia remembers Miss Ironside's as a large, impractical family house that was not suited to education. 'Being at Rene's was like being at a school in the 1920s, or having a governess. It was a school not of its time. I was trapped in an education of another age, in the same house from three years old to sixteen.'

At the school, a girl's comportment and posture were viewed as essential elements of character. 'Every morning Rene stood in the hall to say good morning to every pupil,' Virginia recalls. 'And you had to look her in the eye when you said good morning, too. She would stand, perfectly erect, with her serious face, dressed often in a tartan or powder-blue or burgundy suit. Underneath would be a blouse with an Edwardian neck. She would wear lisle stockings, and shoes with a thin strap with a button. Old-fashioned diamond earrings would hang from the long lobes of her ears.' Virginia remembers Rene's constant correction of pupils' and teachers' posture. One teacher said: 'She once came in when I was stretched out in front of the class. Later she took me aside and said: "Never slouch, always sit up when you teach."'

Virginia went on, 'But handwriting was her particular thing. One of the lessons that she taught, apart from simple music lessons and reading, was known then as "scriptwriting". It was always italic and always had to be done with Osmiroid pens. Most of the schoolbooks we had had frontispieces with wonderful black-and-red lettering, with woodcut illustrations.'

With such a focus on improvement, there was little room for comfort. 'There were two lavatories for 140 children and no staff room,' Virginia Ironside recalls. 'Christmas there was not much fun. What was good about Rene was her absolute commitment to education and learning. At that time, there was a woman selling lavender on the street outside by singing a song: "Who will buy my lavender?" or something like that, it was like something from Dickens, and it had been very common in nineteenth-century London. Rene invited the woman in and asked her to sing her song to every class because there were not many women like this left in London.

'There was no punishment as such; there didn't need to be. I was talking in class one time and I was sent down to Rene's office. She had this stare and she said: "Well, I hope this is the last time you are sent down to me!" You were reduced to a puddle. I wish prisons could have that effect.'

Rene disapproved of trivialities such as comic books. Virginia remembers visiting her grand-aunts in Scotland and being refused a comic for the long train journey back to London. 'I was dying for a comic, but Rene refused and instead gave me a book on Norman architecture. Just before the train took off, Nelly burst through the door and threw some comics on the table. "If you must have the lurid things, there they are," she said, and stormed out.'

Almost all of the teachers at Miss Ironside's were, like Rene and Nelly, middle-aged and unmarried. Meg Poole, who joined Miss Ironside's with Rose, remembers Rene as having 'an interesting way of hiring staff – she hired people she felt needed help'. Virginia Ironside, similarly, says that the teachers were 'all desperate people, all washed up. Some were drinking, some were crazy. They were an odd bunch of single women.'

The girls had elocution and speech lessons with Miss Pocock.

'I'm afraid, in those days, it was all received English. People in Scotland and everywhere else were expected to speak like the upper class and Miss Pocock was faced with us – we all had posh accents, so she didn't mess with that, but she gave us poetry to learn,' says Meg Poole.

One of the most beloved teachers was Stella Kelvin, a Jewish pianist who had fled the Nazis in the 1930s. 'She was an Austrian refugee who lived in Elvaston Place with my great-aunts, in a tiny bedroom with a piano and a little cooker where she brewed up gruel,' remembers Virginia Ironside. 'Stella worked illegally as a music teacher. She lived, slept and taught all in one room. She was an overpowering woman, with a fine, handsome face, masses of baggy clothes, swathes of white hair pulled into a bun, and long skirts to hide dreadful, swollen legs. She was an absolutely terrifying woman, liable to throw the wildest of rages, and a very odd, emotional, middle-European presence in such a very English, Presbyterian household.

'It was only later that I realized I had been taught by a genius. She could easily have been a concert pianist in Vienna. She herself had been taught by Theodor Leschetizky, who had himself been taught by Czerny, who was taught by Beethoven.

'Her whole room seemed to smell of Austria. She had those heart-shaped biscuits covered in icing in her room at all times. It tasted ghastly but was pleasant to see. If you hit a wrong note, you got a chop across the hand. She truly loved music and wanted children to love it too.'

Rose, with her long blonde hair and love of music, was a favourite of Miss Kelvin's. Piano was a great passion and she was known for doing duets with her brother, James, both in the school and at St Leonard's Terrace, according to Fiona MacCarthy.

Miss Staynes, the English and Latin teacher, was younger than the rest and another favourite. 'She was twenty-eight when she arrived, and everyone else was in their sixties,' recalls Virginia Ironside. 'I remember her arriving in a big black hat, a belted leather jacket and a long, black velvet skirt, and there were all these dismal old people in grey. Miss Staynes arrived in a tiny bubble car, a Goggomobil, with a motorbike engine. She had her hair done up in a chignon and she wore a stole. She made English and Latin come alive, and when she took us on jaunts we all wanted to go. The film of *Julius Caesar*, the film of *Henry V*, even *The Seven Samurai*.'

Schoolmates remember Rose as having been very popular, and as someone who thrived in the disciplined atmosphere of Miss Ironside's. Meg Poole describes Rose as 'very much loved; she was very friendly and positive. She didn't hold any particularly surprising views. I knew her better after my mother met her father at a party. My mother was rather reclusive and, consequently, I was not invited to tea at the Dugdales', but when my mother saw that Mr Dugdale was more interesting than she thought, I did get an invite to the Dugdales' home and we become friends.'

In her book, *Last Curtsey: The End of the Debutantes*, Fiona MacCarthy remembers Rose and Caroline as immaculately dressed, far more so than other upper-class girls of the time. In summer, Rose and Caroline wore the family uniform of navy-blue dresses and berets. MacCarthy also remembers home and school concerts in which Caroline would play the violin and Rose the piano in identical white broderie anglaise dresses, their hair in ribbons and beautifully brushed, with their mother sternly monitoring every note. She was very surprised to enter the Dugdale house and discover that both Rose and Caroline had to curtsey to guests. Everything in the house seemed regimented – the meals, the furniture, the art, the decor.

In a photo from Caroline's tenth birthday, all of the children are in historic costume. James is dressed as Henry VIII, with fake beard and Tudor regalia; Rose is dressed as a nineteenth-century Dutch girl; Virginia Ironside as a princess from a Velázquez painting.

Fiona MacCarthy has a photo of her own birthday party at the Dorchester Hotel, with Rose's sister, Caroline, sitting beside her. A niece of the Prime Minister, Anthony Eden, sits further down the table.

The Dugdales employed a full-time French au pair, who was referred to as Mademoiselle. They kept a box at Covent Garden, where Rose invited Fiona to the ballet; they marvelled at Margot Fonteyn.

Meg Poole, who remembers going with Rose to see Richard Brinsley Sheridan's *The School for Scandal* after Rose's mother had recommended it, recalls that 'there was this formality, a terrible, terrible formality with the Dugdales, and yet there was culture, through which there was refinement'.

As Rose moved into puberty, her mother's insistence on organization and formality became a subject of fascination at Miss Ironside's. Virginia Ironside recalls: 'We would laugh when we heard descriptions from Rose's friends who were invited to their country home. They had to bring a separate set of clothes just for dining, and formal evening wear, including gloves to the elbow. It was simply peculiar, even with the formality of the times.'

Meg Poole was also struck by the way the Dugdales dressed. 'Her mother had a theory on how girls should dress in blue. The cotton dresses looked like what nurses wear on wards, this blue uniform in summer.'

At Yarty, their mother held great dinner parties, hosting both artistic friends and members of the Conservative Party establishment. According to a family member, she was friends with John Fowler, interior designer and co-founder of the influential firm Colefax and Fowler. 'She would go on shopping trips with him, to keep up with the fashions for both St Leonard's Terrace and Yarty. Her favourite designer was Elsa Schiaparelli, the Italian rival of Coco Chanel. One of her favourite Schiaparelli pieces was a rococo scrollwork jacket and dress identical to the one worn by the Duchess of Windsor as part of her wedding trousseau.' Carol's outfit was later to hang in the Manchester Art Gallery as part of a *Vogue* retrospective on the era.

Georgina Howell, a friend of Virginia's, reported back to her on an arduous weekend at the Dugdale estate. 'They had to change dresses for dinner and wear white gloves,' Virginia recalls. 'The whole day was structured around riding, talking and reading. Georgina said it was incredibly stressful to be there because it was so formal all the time . . . Everything had to be immaculate. Georgina said it was like being in the army.'

Virginia thinks this environment must have played a part in the trajectory of Rose's life. 'The Dugdale home was run with great discipline, and if you are raised in that pressured society, it would be something to rebel against. Rose was exceptionally intelligent, and people like that can be quite unstable when placed in conformity.'

At Yarty and in London, friends noticed changes in Rose after puberty. She was becoming something of a tomboy, and a number of her classmates found her attractive.

'I had a crush on Rose, as many girls did,' Virginia

Ironside recalls. 'She was so funny and charming and full of energy and visceral excitement. I can only describe her as being the perfect lead boy in a pantomime – the knee-slapping, big-smiling type. She had a beautiful, golden aura. Every girl wanted to sit with Rose with an [*imitating teenage girl*] "Oh, Rose! Sit here!"'

According to Rose, her own first crush was Henry Lennox D'Aubigné Hopkinson, who was then the Minister of State for Colonial Affairs and a frequent visitor to the country estate at Yarty. She remembers looking at him across the dining table and flicking her long blonde hair and smiling as he discussed foreign policy, under her mother's disapproving eye.

In 1956, she left Miss Ironside's, aged fifteen. In October, her sister, Caroline, had her coming-out ball in Richmond Park, an event that was reported on in the society section of *The Times*. Rose began preparing for her own social debut: there would be finishing school and trips abroad for refinement. In 1957, she travelled for almost the full school year – taking three months in Paris for 'culture', according to later records she kept of the time. The same year, she spent four months in Germany. There were also trips to Italy, Greece and Austria.

The announcement that 1958 would be the last year debutantes were presented at court led to a rush of upper-class mothers eager to get their daughters on the list. Mrs Dugdale made sure Rose was included and began preparing her for the season.

Rose was reluctant to do the debutante season at all. She was happier riding horses and shooting at Yarty, or reading. During a bout of the measles, she read *War and Peace*. 'I sat by the fire and just read the book from cover to cover,' she recalls. 'I remember being completely obsessed with the relationship between Natasha and Prince Andrei.'

Her mother hoped *War and Peace* might help win her over to the debutante season – a handsome prince, a beautiful princess. Rose eventually agreed to it, but only on condition that she be allowed to sit the Oxford entrance exam. Her parents agreed, and she enrolled in the Westminster Tutors, where women were prepped for the Oxford and Cambridge entrance exams.

Preparations for the season included getting the right dress and shoes, the right pearls, the best perfume. Parties had to be planned. In January 1959 a notice appeared in *The Times* announcing that 'Mrs Eric Dugdale will give a dance for her daughter, Miss Rose Dugdale, in London, on Thursday, July 2.' According to the April 1958 edition of *Tatler*, a proper season, with parties and travel and multiple dresses, would cost parents the equivalent of nearly £200,000 today.

There was also the matter of the official debutante photograph. The journalist, novelist and sometime society photographer Una-Mary Parker would later recall the awkwardness of Rose, the reluctant debutante, when she arrived at the studio, and her pleading and fretting mother.

'Mrs Dugdale was ambitious. She wanted her daughter to be one of the leading debutantes of the year and do all the right things and go to all the right places and meet the right young men. As soon as Rose walked into the dressing room in a white organdie dress, white gloves and a little row of pearls, and a tight perm, looking absolutely miserable and most dreadfully awkward, you realised that this girl should never have been pushed into doing something like the deb season ... She was very ungainly and unhappy about the whole thing – it was a very sticky session. I think maybe Rose should have stayed down on the farm ... you know, with the horses.'

'I didn't like having my photo taken,' Rose recalls of the event. 'I didn't like my jawline, I never have, I got it from my mother. I was stubborn and maybe I might have said some things to my mother in colourful language.' However, despite the strife, the session produced classically beautiful photos of Rose, the photographer capturing her high cheekbones and a shy smile.

After being presented at court, Rose managed to avoid much of the debutante season, including the trip to the Royal Dublin Society showjumping in Ireland, a major event for Fiona MacCarthy and others. But Rose did have her coming-out party at the River Club on the Thames, which was so close to the river that the windows had to be closed at high tide.

Debutantes danced with MPs and peers; young gentlemen danced with debutantes' mothers. Meg Poole remembers it as 'surprisingly good fun'. She had been to another debutante party at the Hurlingham Club, a Georgian building set in 42 acres in Fulham by the Thames. 'Honestly, I wanted to die at the Hurlingham Club, it was so boring. There was an old man there who was old enough to be my grandfather who latched on to me. He wouldn't let go and it was all so depressing. At Rose's party, I danced with people I knew. I remember dancing with the Conservative MP Humphry Berkeley and some of my friends. Her parents were there and it was really quite fun.'

Rose danced with Ferdinand Mount, the future *Times Literary Supplement* editor and adviser to Margaret Thatcher.

Mount remembers Rose's strong grip through her long white gloves as they danced. It was, he recalls, 'a steamy July night'. They went out to the balcony for a breather and gazed over at Battersea Power Station.

'I said something smarmy about the night and the party,' Mount recalled in his memoir, *Cold Cream*. Rose replied: 'It's a complete and utter waste of money.' Her tone wasn't indignant; she said it with a laugh. 'Already the subversive energy was visible, at this stage being defused by her irresistible merry chuckle.'

On 25 July 1959 Rose acted as godmother at the christening of George, the son of her half-brother Simon, at the Chelsea Hospital chapel, where the Dugdales attended services every Sunday. As was tradition at the time, there were two sets of godparents: Rose was joined by her other half-brother, Timothy Mosley, and by Mrs Christopher Houldsworth and Eric Dugdale, who was standing in for a family friend, the artist Lambros Orphanos.

Rose recalls being in Paris, about to go to the opera, when she heard the news: she had been accepted to Oxford to study Politics, Philosophy and Economics. It was her escape. Her father was pleased. This was what she wanted, and he was happy for her. But a family member recalls that in later years he would often advise: 'Never send your daughter to Oxford.'

Rose's formal background was being cast off, just as the 1960s were arriving. Virginia Ironside again: 'She really was the last of that very formal way of raising children. You can see how, when the world changed in the sixties, crazy and wild with students' riots and protests, Rose was simply the perfect candidate for what was to come.'

2. Clandestine Love

On Rose's first day at the all-female St Anne's College, Oxford, the five PPE students in her year had to meet their don, who would supervise them for the next three years. The don's name was Peter Ady. Rose and her classmate, Jenny Grove, wondered what he would look like.

The door swung open and a woman walked in wearing riding breeches and carrying a riding crop: she had been out with the Oxford hunt that morning. This was Peter Ady, born in Rangoon, Burma, in 1914. Her ancestry was equal parts Burmese, Scottish, French and Italian. Her mother, who had been hoping for a boy, called her Peter.

A former Oxford student, June Knowles, would later recall: 'She was extremely beautiful, dark-haired, bronze-skinned, with laughing black eyes, and when she came into a room, every male eye was on her.'

And it was not only the male eyes. A classmate of Rose's, Jenny Grove, remembers Peter's almost impossible elegance, which was very much in contrast to the other dons. 'Most of the time, the male dons shambled about in baggy trousers and almost took pride in not caring about clothes because their interests were in higher ideas, poring over some tome of classics, and clothes were seen as trivial,' she recalls. 'I had a friend at Somerville College, where everyone was so frumpy – one of the lecturers ticked off a student for wearing green eye shadow, a great intellectual sin. So Peter stood out, defiantly. She had painted fingernails and nice shoes. She was not above filing her nails while you went to see her about lectures. I remember sitting in her room and she got a phone call and said, "Yes, I'd love to come for a drive in your sports car."'

Peter Ady's family had made a fortune from a soft-drinks company in Rangoon, according to her cousin, the writer Jill Paton Walsh. While in Burma, her family lived comfortably, in the style of European expats. Peter swam at her grand-father's estate with her younger brother, Tiger, and her friends. Her father kept racehorses and let her ride his brood mares from a young age.

She was educated by nuns and received some of the high-est results in Burma in her final-year exams. At Rangoon University she earned a first-class degree in chemistry before moving to the University of London for postgraduate studies. She stayed at Gower Street, where Tiger came to visit her, bringing a Gladstone bag full of their mother's Burmese chutney with him.

Peter gained another first-class honours degree from Lady Margaret Hall in Oxford in just five terms. From 1942 to 1945 she worked on wartime economic problems at the Institute of Statistics in Oxford. After the war, with a Colonial Research Fellowship from the British government, she conducted fieldwork in Ghana and Nigeria, specializing in the cocoa market. In 1947, she was elected a fellow at what was then known as St Anne's Society in Oxford: a centre for home-schooled correspondence-course ladies. In 1952, it gained a royal charter as St Anne's College, and in 1959 – the year Rose started – it gained full college status. It lacked the historic pretentions of the older Oxford colleges. Tim Gar-dam, a former principal of St Anne's, would observe: 'It was in no sense a cloistered place, basking in a past, and its under-graduates were proud of their difference and of the fact that they did not fit in with the Oxford stereotype. It was the right college for someone like Peter Ady to make her own. [She was i]ndependent, non-conformist, intellectually rigorous, self-reliant.'

Peter was one of the two great academic pillars of St Anne's. The other was the novelist and philosopher Iris Murdoch, then in her late thirties and already gaining a reputation as one of the great minds of post-war Britain. Born into an Irish Protestant family in Dublin's north inner city, Murdoch would come to sympathize with, and occasionally try to pass herself off as, a member of the downtrodden Irish Catholic majority.

She and Peter had been lovers for many years. In 1952, Iris wrote in her diary about passionately kissing Peter in the back of her car on the way back from a party in Burcot Grange by the Thames. They went to Brittany several times together on holidays and, by the standards of the time, they wore their sexuality openly. Jill Paton Walsh remembers seeing Iris reading a book in the corner of a student bar. 'Peter walked in, came right up to her and kissed her passionately on the lips. That's the way they were.' Jill had moved into Peter's house in St Giles', Oxford, on the strict promise that she would never report anything she saw to their strictly Catholic family. She often saw Iris and Peter kissing on the steps of the house.

The relationship between Peter and Iris was complicated and they both had other partners. In 1956, Iris had married the critic John Bayley. Not long before Rose started at St Anne's, Iris had begun a relationship with Margaret Hubbard, who taught classics at St Anne's, while Peter was free to pursue an array of relationships with men and women. 'A lot of them were from the horsy set, people who hunted with hounds, that was her thing,' Jill remembers. 'I was in her back room and would be called to parties only if they were starting to sag, as a kind of way to liven things up, but I was sworn to secrecy about what I saw.'

Peter's speciality was the economies of developing countries and their trade relationship with the rich world. Her argument was that decolonization could not simply be a matter of surrendering sovereignty, withdrawing troops and leaving. It was vital, too, that new and fairer trading arrangements be established, so that the former colonizer didn't continue to exploit the former colony. For Tim Gardam, 'The economist's precision and dryness in her writing masks a dazzling, pioneering idealism about the emancipation of the post-colonial world and prefigured the debates that now shape our time.'

Peter had to struggle to get the work done by people in the developing world recognized in measurable economic terms. Her fellow Oxford economics professor Dr Maurice Scott would later explain: 'There are some who think that economic principles cannot be applied to developing countries, but she was not of that opinion and resisted the notion that many [developing country] workers were not "economic men". For her, they had good reason to do what they did.'

Every year there was a tussle when Peter flew to Burma to work as an economic adviser to the Burmese government and Oxford sought her return. 'Burma government guarantees Miss Ady returns to Oxford January 14th, just in time for term,' records one Burmese government telegram to Oxford. She was sometimes in receipt of tetchy letters from the college seeking clarification on her work abroad. One plaintive postcard from the college principal's secretary records: 'The principal has asked me to find out from you, before you go, exactly what it is you are going to do and what it should be called.' Peter sent a one-line response saying she was going to Burma for research.

Sometimes war and insurrection in Burma interrupted her research. In 1951, she wrote to the college from Rangoon: 'All records have been retarded by the insurrections . . . I could do comfortably with another month here but Oxford comes first.' At other times, she wrote back enthusiastically, as when St Anne's was to be incorporated as an official Oxford college and she had found a large table in Burma for the senior common room. She would arrange to have it shipped back. With it came a coded message of dismay that Iris Murdoch was not displaying her love while she was away. 'What news of incorporation, I wonder? I do hope it went through quietly. Tell Iris she should be keeping in touch. I feel quite cut off.'

In her early days at St Anne's, Rose was infatuated with Peter Ady and spoke of little else. She never missed one of her tutorials, which she cycled to at great speed, and she always had her assignments ready on time. In the library, she read books about Burma so she could ask intelligent questions.

Soon, Rose was by Peter's side at parties, talks and debates, and she joined the Oxford hunt so she could be with her. They would even eat with male dons in one of the other colleges. 'They walked into the dining hall and there was cheering and clapping from the students, because they never saw women dining with the male professors before,' Jenny Grove recalls.

One night, after a soirée at Peter's home, Rose leaned in and kissed her teacher. The kiss was reciprocated. Rose felt dizzy and couldn't believe it was happening. Peter led her to the bedroom. Rose had never been with a man or a woman before. Peter was a tender lover and sensed that this was Rose's first time. Afterwards, Peter stroked her hair as Rose lay on her.

'As far as either of us knew, we were not lesbians,' Rose

recalls. 'We learned in classical history classes that Greek men had relationships with each other and with women, often at the same time. We weren't trying to be feminist fundamentalists, but we were trying to just be in love.'

They had to be discreet. Jill Paton Walsh remembers a student being caught in bed with a male student in the dorms of St Anne's. The female student was expelled while the male student was only fined, seven shillings and sixpence.

Jenny moved into a house with Rose on Bedford Place, the back of which looked out on to St Anne's. With Peter now her only thought, Rose was quick to dismiss male suitors. Jenny remembers one student at Christ Church who was besotted with Rose. 'He made the mistake of sending Rose a poem and trying to impress her by telling her that he'd learned to parachute and so he knew how to land when falling from a height,' she recalls. 'The poem did not impress Rose, who was not particularly interested in poetry, but she took him up on his talk about parachute technique – so much so that she pointed to the high wall at the side of our house and urged him to jump from it.'

She and Rose had Iris Murdoch as their tutor for politics. Murdoch was researching a book about the Easter Rising that would be entirely sympathetic to Irish republicans. Jill Paton Walsh remembers calling in to Murdoch's house to tell her that she wouldn't have an essay completed on time. 'I knocked and went in. I was eager to apologize about the essay. She was coming out of the bath and was completely naked. She looked like one of those nymphs you see in paintings. She had a full figure and was really quite attractive. She had no clothes on at all and she was very nice about my lack of an essay. I blushed furiously and withdrew.'

For Rose, the coming end of the college year meant

heartache. Peter would be flying to Burma, as she did every year, to work as an adviser for the Burmese government. By now, Rose had perfected ways of staying over with Peter in her house. Sometimes, it would be after a hunt; she would linger to talk with the hunters then stay on with Peter after the others had left. At the end of the week, she would slip over to Peter's house after telling her housemates she was going to the family estate in Devon. She was learning how to be secretive, how to develop a cover story.

During Rose's first year, the Rockefeller Foundation gave Peter a grant to go to Ghana and Nigeria to complete a field study on the cocoa industry. Her expense claims, which survive in her Oxford archive, give an insight into how she operated when doing fieldwork: 'Gifts to Chiefs in Hwedien village £1 8 shillings, Akokoago village £1 6 shillings and 9 pence; Agogo village: Nil. (The Chief was away).' She hired a bicycle for a month for £2 and 8 shillings to cycle around the West African countryside looking at cocoa plantations.

Rose wrote longing letters to Peter when they were apart but was always careful not to hint at a physical relationship. 'We might have been open with each other, but you could not reveal such love in Oxford in those days, so everyone learned to speak in certain ways,' she recalls.

Jenny Grove remembers Rose, who showed little romantic interest in other students, making a pass at a male don at a party. 'I think he felt slightly unmanned by a female student making a pass at him, but that was Rose. She was tremendously popular and she liked to break boundaries.'

When college restarted after the summer, Rose rushed to see Peter, who gave her a present of a Burmese teak desk ornament. In tutorials, Rose pretended to know nothing of Peter other than as her tutor but always had pertinent and

knowing questions to ask about Burmese–British trade relations and the intricacies of Ghana's cocoa export market.

A new student arrived the same year. Her name was Devaki
Jain. Originally from northern India, she was in her mid-
twenties, older than the other students. She had left another
college where a faculty member had persistently sexually harassed her. She bonded with Peter, with whom she had a South
Asian background in common, and soon met Rose.

'Rose was beautiful,' Devaki recalls. 'She had every feature
of a golden girl – her hair was gold, her complexion was
peaches and cream, she was tall, slim and she spoke with a
perfect over-the-top English accent.' She remembers one
college student, Barbara Revans, who would tease Rose
about her upper-class background and the debutante season.
'Barbara said somewhat acidically – *"Oh! She was a deb! Look
at her – all milk and honey."* So some remarks were passed
because Rose was not only beautiful but she had the sense of
being a kind of clean, well-polished young woman.'

Jenny Grove recollects Rose's busy social life at the time.
'I remember her getting ready to go to sherry parties at Christ
Church College on a Sunday morning, putting rollers in her
hair and using a bottle of beer as a setting lotion. She'd stick
hairpins in to hold the rollers in place and when they fell out
and bounced on the floor, she'd swear roundly. She liked saying outrageous things and knew I'd be shocked, what with
my background of a convent boarding school, and I was a
bit shaken at first, but then I couldn't help laughing. Then
she'd pull on a well-cut coral-coloured suit, stuff her feet into
a pair of pointy shoes, get on her bike and pedal purpose-
fully to Christ Church.'

A new junior students' society was being set up and Rose
was elected secretary and drafted its first constitution. It was

a way for her to meet other students in their first and second year and widen her circle of friends. She began to see the power of the junior students as a distinct group. Now a well-known second-year, Rose decided to run for the position of head of the junior common room, where St Anne's students met to discuss eternal verities over cigarettes and tea. Jenny backed her, and so did Devaki. Rose campaigned energetically and was easily elected, nominating Devaki as her deputy. For Devaki, shy and uneasy at Oxford, it was the beginning of a life-long interest in politics.

Rose heard that Devaki had nowhere to go for the term break and invited her to the Dugdale home in Chelsea. 'She gave me her address and asked me if I would like to visit when her parents were out on holiday. It was in a very better-off-people's area – the houses were beautiful and complete with balconies and I remember being totally awed as I entered her house, at the meticulousness.'

Rose and Jenny sometimes went to the Oxford Union to hear the debates. The Union's membership was all male. Women could sit in the public gallery, but they could not debate. Jenny decided to get a campaign going to highlight this injustice. The Oxford Union was where many prime ministers, writers and philosophers had first learned to debate, and she and Rose wanted it open to women. Rose and Peter Ady had already broken taboos by sitting with male professors in the halls; now Rose and Jenny would take the battle to the very heart of Oxford political power.

In the autumn of 1960 Jenny started canvassing for support. She was surprised to find that there was strong sympathy for the campaign among some of the male students and that some women were uninterested. 'I remember, for example, there was one student named Caroline Trelfer, who was a big star of the Dramatic Society in St Anne's. I said, "Don't you think it's unfair that women can't take part in debates?" She said: "Oh, let the men have their little club!" She wanted nothing to do with the campaign.'

Jenny wrote to the *Telegraph*, complaining that women were only allowed to sit upstairs in the Oxford Union gallery 'in reverent silence and regard the top of the speaker's head'. This provoked angry responses in the letters page over the following days. H. K. Davies from Upminster wrote: 'Judging by Miss Jennifer Grove's letter, it would seem that women undergraduates at Oxford are today still suffering from the same illusions as they were when I was up at the University.' If women were allowed to join the Oxford Union, he said, 'the libraries and writing room would immediately lose their charm if they were filled with female giggles and perfume. We simply cannot allow the women to obtain a foothold, as, once they do, the final result will be a foregone conclusion.'

G. B. Addington Hall, a student at Queen's College, Oxford, also registered his protest, saying he had intended to support female membership of the Union when he first entered the university. 'However, I quickly . . . discovered the existence of women undergraduates capable of such un-ladylike activities as "demanding" membership and "registering protests" at exclusion from this private society.' 'Uppity' women were the sole reason he and other Union members were against female membership, he wrote. 'If Miss Jennifer Grove and others like her were not included, I feel sure that ladies would soon be accepted to full membership of the Society.'

Jenny recalls: 'In my naivety, I wrote the same letter to the *Telegraph* and *The Times*, so *The Times* called me up and said they wanted to run it, but it would have to be different, so I changed it around a bit and Rose signed her name to it too.'

In autumn 1961, a group of female Cambridge students walked into the Cambridge Union and were immediately ejected. Rose and Jenny would have to try a different route. That very day, they devised a plan: they would dress as men and sneak into the Oxford Union membership seats, breaking the nearly 140-year male-only rule. They borrowed trousers, shoes, shirts and jackets from sympathetic male students, and Rose also borrowed a pair of heavy glasses.

Jenny contacted two Oxford-based journalist-photographers and invited them to document the intervention. On Thursday, 19 October 1961, the two journalists, who worked for most of the national newspapers, followed them to an Oxford hairdresser's, where Rose asked for a male haircut.

Jenny recalls: 'Rose's hair could be combed back into a fairly convincing male style – mine much less so. The journalists solved the problem by finding a National Health Service wig maker who duly gave me a grey wig, cut it into the traditional short-back-and-sides and sprayed it brown. After that, all that was needed was to find supportive male students to lend us cavalry twill trousers, college scarves, tweed jackets and men's shoes. Rose donned thick glasses and I stuffed something into my cheeks to try to appear less feminine.'

Photos show Rose and Jenny having their hair washed and cut while the two female hairdressers smile along with them. 'One of the journalists, Rex George, phoned the London papers and put the photographs on a train to London,' Jenny says. 'Rose and I joined the crowd that was surging into the debating chamber and took our seats. When a man asked me to move so that he could climb past me, I knew my voice would give me away, so I just grunted.'

For the first time since its foundation in 1823, there were women among the men in the Oxford Union. When the debate began, Jenny and Rose could be heard shouting and heckling in deep voices at the speakers – Michael Stewart MP, a former president of the Oxford Union who was then Labour's Shadow Housing Minister, and Denzil Freeth MP, Parliamentary Secretary to the Science Minister. Their house-mate, Sarah Caudwell, watched from the public gallery.

The journalists rushed off to write up the article, and the following day Rose and Jenny were all over the national press. The *Daily Sketch* ran with the banner headline 'The Gatecrash Girls'. The article was accompanied by a photo from the hairdresser's with the caption: 'Preparing for battle: Rose Dugdale and Jennifer Grove in male disguise before gate-crashing in the Union.'

In the photos carried in all the newspapers, Rose's hair is Brylcreemed to her scalp and she is wearing a dark men's jacket several sizes too large for her. Her high cheekbones are hidden behind men's glasses.

The *Daily Express* ran the headline: 'Strangers – Disguised Girl Students Break into a Men-only Fortress'. The *Mirror* carried a large photo of Rose and Jenny at the hairdresser's with an effusively supportive article. 'It's happened! Two girls have got into the famous men-only Oxford Union Society and stayed for the whole debate. Their secret? They were disguised as men . . . The girls joined other students in inter-ruptions like "Nonsense!" and "Rubbish!"'

There would be repercussions: the *Oxford Mail* reported that both Rose and Jenny were summoned before the head of their college. The story quotes Jenny Grove as saying that the principal, Lady Mary Ogilvie, 'began by being stern and saying that the matter would have to go before the Board of Governors. But she said she was sympathetic about our wanting to get into the Union.'

The BBC interviewed Jenny in their house while Rose made them tea. This gave the college the excuse it was looking for: it suspended Jenny for a week for speaking to the media without permission.

This was not Jenny's first time making the news. The *Evening Post*, in Jenny's native Jersey, reported: 'A girl who made headlines in Jersey some time ago when she dived off an outgoing mail boat and swam back to the shore is in the news again. She is Jennifer Grove, who was rusticated last night for a week from St Anne's College, Oxford, because she invited a BBC television team into her room. The college said that this broke a ban on interviews after she dressed up as a man to get into an Oxford Union debate.'

Two days after the debate, the Oxford student newspaper, *Cherwell*, ran an opinion article with the banner headline: 'Excluded'. The student journalist Harold Lind, who would later lecture on logic at Oxford, was a big supporter of Rose and Jenny but feared the college establishment and didn't clarify in the article who had been excluded and why. He wrote: 'With the best will in the world, there is little anyone can do in the short run to alter attitudes which have often been ingrained by generations of prejudice, but at least we can take Orwell's advice and try to understand the problems of other people's prejudices by asking why and in what ways we ourselves are prejudiced.'

After a week, Jenny was allowed to return to Oxford, and she and Rose immediately restarted the campaign. 'I set about canvassing men students, making a list of all those who said they'd support us,' Jenny recalls. 'Then a week before it finally came to the vote, Rose and I put reminder slips in their pigeonholes. The reminder slips had to be typed and I wasn't good at typing, but Harold Lind offered to help. Harold had done his National Service, in the course of which he'd become a fast two-finger typist.'

College professors and administrators urged the Union to bow to the inevitable. A few months later, on Thursday, 16 February 1962, the motion was carried: for the first time in almost 140 years, women were allowed to join the Oxford Union. It meant they could debate, sit as full members and watch the debates eye to eye, use the reading room and peruse the hundreds of library books. It was a huge victory which changed British establishment politics for ever.

Rose and Jenny posed for press photographs celebrating with champagne – or what appeared to be champagne. In fact, journalists had provided a champagne bottle filled with water and fruit salts to make it look fizzy. The next day, the *Daily Mail* included a large photograph of a laughing Rose, dressed in a dark sweater and a high-collared floral blouse, pouring from the champagne bottle for Jenny and their supporters, Bernice Holroyd Rothwell and Sarah Caudwell.

The first motion on which women could debate was the Arab–Israeli conflict. Sarah Caudwell, later a famous barrister and crime writer, was the first woman to debate at the Union and emerged on stage to thunderous applause from new members Rose Dugdale and Jennifer Grove.

For Rose, the success of the campaign implanted the idea that political action was best when it was transgressive and daring. She and Jenny had crushed a very old tradition – and the victory had impressed Peter as much as anyone else.

3. The Secret

In the spring of 1962, as they were sitting together in the house in St Giles', Peter told Rose that she had been offered a secondment with the United Nations in New York working for an agency called the UN Conference on Trade and Development. The UN would provide funding for a research assistant, and Peter wanted Rose to come with her.

For Rose, this was confirmation that she wasn't just a student fling: Peter really did love her. They would go to New York together and live a full life, no longer as don and student, but as woman and woman, in love.

To help strengthen Rose's credentials for the job, Peter arranged for her to begin unprecedented research into the Radcliffe Committee, which published a very influential report on British monetary policy in 1959. Rose pored over the transcripts of the hearings to produce a guide to all the academic papers, economic reports and books referenced in the committee hearings, as well as highlighting key quotes from the participants. 'The Radcliffe Committee: A Bibliography' was published in the March 1962 edition of the *Banker Magazine*.

Peter and Rose's UN secondment wouldn't begin for another year, so Peter suggested that Rose take up a teaching placement in America and learn the ways of the country. She wrote an effusive reference in support of Rose's application to study for a master's in philosophy at Mount Holyoke, a women's college in western Massachusetts, and

Rose completed the paperwork in June 1962. Rose gave 'economic policy' as her preferred area of study, leading a Mount Holyoke staff member to write a question mark over it with the word 'Philosophy?'

Peter also arranged for Iris Murdoch, already well known to the American intelligentsia, to write a reference, and Rose was duly accepted to the master's degree programme, along with an internship position in the college's public relations department, known as the news bureau. Her duty would be to write peppy stories about the students' achievements for their hometown newspapers.

After graduating from Oxford that summer, Rose had a new MG coupé shipped to Massachusetts before flying there herself, via New York, in early August, to begin a month of training in the Mount Holyoke news bureau.

On the 22nd, the college issued a press release to the *London Times*, *Evening Standard* and *Star* newspapers announcing that 'a London girl, Miss Rose Dugdale, of St Leonard's Terrace, SW3, is now working in the News Bureau of Mount Holyoke College, South Hadley, Massachusetts. Miss Dugdale graduated from St Anne's College in 1962, with an honours degree in Politics, Philosophy and Economics. She was president of the Junior Common Room at St Anne's, and secretary of the Council of Junior Members of Oxford University, whose first constitution she drafted.' It dryly records Rose's invasion of the Oxford Union dressed as a man: 'She was also one of those involved in persuading the Union to admit women.'

Rose did not warm to Mount Holyoke. She found the American women distant, locked in their parochial cliques. 'Some of them were real snobs,' she recalls. 'They didn't want to mix outside their own little world. I didn't like the place very much. Some people were friendly, but it wasn't like Oxford. There wasn't the same spirit.'

Undergraduate Barbara Lloyd, who joined the Italian Society with Rose, remembers Mount Holyoke as rigid and parochial. 'All the women had to be unmarried. The college found out that one of the students was actually married and that was a big scandal. Why? Was she tainted? It was sort of strict, we had a curfew . . . Mount Holyoke was a backwater, that was the word. It was too small a pond for me, and for Rose, too, I suspect.'

The news bureau captured a photo of Rose, Barbara and several other students lining up to speak to the Italian Society. 'The Italian Society was run by Professor Giamatti, whom we all called Mr G, a fabulous Italian teacher who taught the course on Dante,' Barbara recalls. 'Mr G was wounded in the war and walked with a limp, and everyone adored him. He lived in a white Italian house in Mount Holyoke with carved tables, and on Fridays he would play Italian opera on his record player and we would go down there and listen to his records. He even let us have wine. He stood out in a place as quiet as Mount Holyoke.'

A philosophy professor, Richard Robin, would later tell the *Daily Express*: 'Rose, I remember, was outstanding. She spent much of her time alone and I now have regrets that I didn't try to get to know her better.' Elizabeth Green, professor of English, recalled Rose as being studious and solitary: 'Rose had brilliant prospects. She was hard-working and a natural student. Looking back, I remember her as a rather warm, likeable person. She was a loner, but there was something engaging about her.'

Rose was not entirely isolated. There was the Italian Society, and her journalism work got her away from her books. On 20 October 1963, Rose covered Martin Luther King Jr's visit to the campus for the news bureau. She was photographed taking notes as part of a group of students gathered around Dr King as he drank tea and answered questions. Dr King, who spoke in the main auditorium, was at the height of his global fame. He had made his 'I have a dream' speech before 250,000 people in Washington two months earlier and, a month before his visit, he had delivered the eulogy for four girls killed by a bomb while attending Sunday school at the 16th Street Baptist Church in Birmingham, Alabama.

Rose's Mount Holyoke master's thesis, titled 'Wittgenstein's Simples: Names and Objects', examined the philosopher's idea that language must be based on 'simples' – simple objects on which complex words and thoughts are built. According to Wittgenstein, a matter is 'simple' if it cannot be divided down any further. Her analysis deeply impressed Richard Robin, who would later recall that her master's thesis was done 'brilliantly'.

In her final summer Rose took her MG on a drive across the country with a fellow master's student. In August 1964, on her return to Mount Holyoke, Joseph D'Addario photographed her sitting on her car in a cowgirl outfit, holding a book on European history in her hand.

Rose was awarded honours for her master's thesis. After her final exam, she drove straight to New York to be with Peter, who had a UN-funded apartment on the east side of Manhattan. It was summer, the year of the so-called 'British Invasion', and The Beatles' 'She Loves You' and 'I Want to Hold Your Hand' were the two biggest-selling singles in America. Rose bought a record player for Peter.

She was granted security clearance and every day walked over to UN headquarters with Peter to research trade for developing countries. According to a later CV, the work included drafting 'reports on primary commodities, trade and growth, including writing for the UN Commodity Review'.

She helped Peter prepare a set of economic maps of Africa, analysing the resources of the continent's countries not as assets to be exploited by the West but assets with which to build their own prosperity.

Rose had everything she wanted – Peter, and a meaningful job in which she was helping the global poor. At night they drank wine and looked at the view over New York. They socialized at clubs with other UN employees. Rose was always introduced as Peter's research assistant. At weekends, they tried the bohemian, beatnik and lesbian bars on the Lower East Side.

Virginia Ironside's first novel, *Chelsea Bird*, had just been published. It told the story of a changing social scene in London – upper-class boys were now putting on mockney accents and hanging out on the King's Road, mixing with photographers, beatnik writers and models, eager to throw off the rigidity of the class system. The book was a success, and with the money she made Virginia took a trip to New York. Wanting to see her old friend Rose, she contacted James Dugdale, who was in New York at the time to visit his sister.

'He said they were going out that evening and they asked if I would like to go to the theatre. Rose showed up in some incredibly glamorous open-topped car. We went to dinner and then a Greek tragedy. Rose was so kind, she had the capacity to treat everyone the same – even if politically different and a different age. She was a golden, blessed person and she had so much energy and verve.'

*

Labour came to power in the UK in late 1964 and Barbara Castle was appointed Minister for Overseas Development. She was determined to create better trade deals for developing countries. She knew of Peter's work and wanted her in her office. Peter was hired as a senior policy adviser and Rose was taken on as Peter's research assistant. The two moved into Peter's home at 32 Ponsonby Terrace in central London.

They began work in the ministry together in 1965. Rose's office was on the top floor of the ministry building. She remembers Barbara Castle as 'very nice, and enthusiastic about our work'. Rose wrote some of the minister's speeches on aid for Africa and travelled with Peter to international conferences on behalf of the British government. They attended dinner parties together. If they were with old Oxford friends such as Iris Murdoch, they would relax and be themselves, but in the company of government officials Rose was always just the researcher.

Peter urged her to move on and get a doctorate: Rose was too smart to be a research assistant for ever; she should be a lecturer herself. Rose agreed but was concerned that this would mean being apart from Peter. By now, she had all but abandoned philosophy. Her work experience, and her life mission, was in economics, and she wanted to focus on helping the global poor. She wanted to be like Peter, not like Iris Murdoch.

With a strong reference from Peter, in 1968 she was accepted to do a doctorate in economics at Bedford College in London, where she could also teach. Peter, who by this time was back in Oxford, lecturing, let her stay at Ponsonby Terrace.

It was the first time in four years that Peter Ady would not be by her side. Rose fretted. Would Peter meet someone else? She did not have to wait long for an answer. A few months after Rose began the doctorate, Peter called her from Oxford to say that now they were away from each other, they couldn't possibly keep up a relationship. Peter would be in Burma every summer in any case and wanted to meet men and women in Oxford. She loved Rose, she said, and would always be there for her. She was not lying or trying to soften the blow. She would be there, Rose knew it. And yet Peter's integrity made the wound all the deeper. Rose was depressed for weeks, looking for answers.

Bedford College in 1968 was the home of left-wing agitation, frequent student sit-ins and demands for change. In the student politics of the time, revolutionary hyperbole was the only stable currency. Peter Ayrton, who was then a member of staff, recalls, 'I think the student scene was becoming influenced by the Red Army Faction in Germany and other European leftist guerrilla groups, which were happening in developed Western democracies like Britain. But I think Rose was more Third Worldy in her outlook and supported leftists in Argentina and Africa.'

Rose pored over Marxist and anarchist texts, stayed up all night writing letters and skipped meals. Ayrton remembers Rose as 'a very good teacher, she was loved by her students. She was very generous with her time and she had no sense of talking only to important people, she made time for everyone.'

When students created an 'alternative university' on the campus, Rose, Ayrton and a lecturer in the German department were the only staff members to defect, ignoring threats from the college. 'We were told by the dean that no staff member was allowed to teach at this student occupation,'

Ayrton recalls. 'It was something that was like a red rag to Rose.'

Around this time, Peter Ady invited Rose to meet one of her PPE students in her garden in Oxford. The student's name was Edwina Currie. Peter gave Edwina money to stay in her house in St Giles' between terms and to feed her dog, Zuleika, with sheep heads Peter stored in the fridge.

When Rose arrived, Peter and Edwina were sparring over a political point. 'And that,' Edwina Currie recalls, 'was how Rose Dugdale and I came to be eyeing each other frostily in Peter's garden over Peter's sherry – I was a Tory and Rose was a revolutionary.' Currie says, 'There was to be no chatty meeting of minds. Rose was not rude or aggressive, she just did not want to engage.'

Currie, from a far humbler background than Rose, was known as one of the best debaters at the Oxford Union, an opportunity she and other women of her generation had obtained because of Rose's rebellion against its male-only membership. Now, Rose found herself face to face with her legacy: not a revolutionary intellectual but a young female Tory with strong debating skills.

While Rose was working on her doctorate at Bedford College she and Peter Ayrton signed up for a working tour of Cuba organized by a Marxist group. They flew out with a few dozen others on a chartered plane and stayed for a while in Havana. They found a country heaving with thousands of Western students.

The British group was taken to a coffee plantation three hours outside Havana. All day long, they planted coffee beans, discussed politics and learned revolutionary songs. Their

Cuban minders invited them to divide themselves into revolutionary 'brigades'. 'We were encouraged to name our brigade,' Ayrton recalls. 'I decided to call it the Rosa Luxemburg Brigade. It came back from the Cuban leadership that that this was unacceptable – Rosa Luxemburg, an anarchist, was not in the acceptable pantheon. So we then became the Ethel and Julius Rosenberg Brigade. They were Commie spies in America, so, for the Cubans, that was considered fine.'

For many of the students it was their first taste of manual labour. 'Everyone worked in the fields in teams and I worked with a Vietnamese cadre and it was just extraordinary,' Peter Ayrton recalls. 'He was just so helpful and willing and showed me how to plant the coffee. We were pretty hopeless, as you can expect from middle-class Western intellectuals.'

Rose recalls an innocent romance with a male student from Switzerland several years her junior. They kissed but went no further.

One evening, the touring group were taken to a dancehall. Many young Communists were there to greet them and invited them to try Cuban dancing. Rose looked around. There was a large group of old people gathered outside, watching them dance. She went outside and, with no Spanish, held their hands and gestured to them to come inside. She danced with them until they all joined in with the students. 'It was a typical Rose moment,' says Ayrton. 'She was not able to communicate linguistically but, through her empathy and generosity, she was able to get everyone dancing and having a good time. I have known very few people who had that ability, but she certainly had it.'

Ayrton was told that he would no longer be allowed to work in the philosophy department at Bedford College because he had taught in the 'alternative university', but

Rose was allowed to continue her research and teaching in economics.

In 1970, with the Bedford revolutionary scene winding down, Rose gravitated to the University of Manchester, where a student occupation was demanding, among other things, a larger canteen and the overthrow of the capitalist system. Rose would later tell a documentary for the Irish-language TV station TG4, 'It's hard to explain how exciting these times were.'

In Manchester, she met a group of radical Irish students who told her of the turmoil erupting on the streets of Northern Ireland, where a large part of the Catholic nationalist population was now in rebellion against the state. 'So I went to visit Belfast,' Rose recalled, 'having not been to Ireland before, and then I became slowly aware of what was going on. From an English woman's point of view, this was a colony, and they were using the army to maintain that power. It was happening right on your doorstep, across the water in Belfast. The only question was how to get stuck in.'

Rose stayed on in Bedford until 1971 and continued to teach economics, while, according to Ayrton, questioning her students on how Marxist theory might be applied to the uprising in Northern Ireland. She wrote an essay for *Counter Course*, a collection published by Penguin the following year. The book's editor, Trevor Pateman, described it as a handbook for students 'who find that their education consists in being processed for a particular niche in the class structure of society'.

In her essay, Rose sought to align intellectual Marxism with the upheaval she saw all around her and called for new methods of teaching economics. 'Students have openly declared war on American capitalism and its tentacles of power across the continents,' she wrote, and 'are now fighting out their economics in the streets'.

She recalled that John Stuart Mill had argued that 'the ills of society can one and all be overcome by democratic decision in the light of reasoned argument'. This was liberal intellectualism, she wrote, and students were rejecting it. 'Students have begun to see the hypocrisy of "Yes, indeed society must change – we will bring about change through educational enlightenment and the victory of mature philosophical reason."'

Economic policy, when it was stripped of its well-meaning language, would always favour the ruling class. She did not urge students to drop out – indeed she had stubbornly stayed in Bedford even as other radicals such as Peter Ayrton either resigned or were removed. Indeed, she believed that students couldn't be radical until they had learned economics and 'grasped all the tools'. Once they had done this, they must take their new knowledge and make sure it was 'applied to the needs of the working class, to service the workers' revolutionary struggles'.

Before the essay was even published, Rose had moved beyond a point of no return.

4. The Revolutionary Philanthropist

In 1971, Rose Dugdale was thirty years old and, unlike most revolutionary socialists, possessed a considerable fortune. Two years earlier, the trust that her parents had set up for herself and her sister, Caroline, had been broken up. According to a statement that Eric Dugdale later made to police, Rose had come into possession of just over £75,000 worth of 'readily realizable stocks', plus 'possibly another £15,000 or £20,000' in cash. She also had a shareholding in her father's property company, Dugdale [J.F.C.] Proprietary Ltd, that was worth over £40,000. In addition, she also had several thousand pounds in the Matson Trust, which had been established by her mother. Adjusted for inflation, these assets were worth the equivalent of well over £1 million today.

Also in 1969, and with Rose's agreement, her father made her a member, or Name, of Lloyd's of London, with her contract beginning on 1 January 1970. In this capacity, Rose simply had to put her name down as an underwriter and, if Lloyd's was ever to be in financial trouble, she could be required to pay out on insurance policies from her personal resources. But the likelihood of that happening was seen as slim and her Lloyd's membership provided a steady income.

By 1971, Rose had decided that she wanted to give her fortune to the poor. 'There were many poor people who were living in dreadful conditions at the time, so it wasn't that impressive a gesture,' she says.

Rose's wealth and instinct to help the poorest found an

47

outlet in a new left-wing concept: the claimants union. If workers were to have unions, then so should those who had been left behind by the capitalist system. Rose rented an office on Broad Lane and set up the Tottenham Claimants Union, where she began offering advice and material support to the unemployed and impecunious of north London.

News quickly spread: in addition to giving advice and help in dealing with bureaucracy, the Tottenham office offered hard cash. If you couldn't pay your rent, Rose would pay it for you. If you couldn't afford coal for the winter, Rose would send a three-month supply. Gas bills, immigration documents, school supplies, groceries, cat food: if you could tell a good tale of unemployment, immigration, hardship, old age or illness, Rose would either hand out cash or pay for the supplies and have them delivered. If she felt that a family were being ill-treated by the local council or were in danger of eviction, she would take them down to the Haringey or Islington council offices and shout at officials until she got service. Soon, there were queues of people waiting to see her in the Broad Lane office.

'There were many immigrant families coming into the area,' Rose recalls. 'I couldn't exaggerate how many people were looking for help.' Idealistic young people from the colleges and the squats, eager for revolutionary justice, soon heard about the claimants union and came to volunteer.

One day, news came through that the local glass bottle plant was closing down. Workers, led by a bottler named Walter 'Wally' Heaton, staged a 'work-in' during which they refused to stop working and kept producing bottles all day. Wally was a big man – six foot four and broad-shouldered – with a wide moustache. He was handsome and could be very charming. He spoke quickly, moving his arms in the air as if conducting some imaginary orchestra.

Declassified police records show that he had previous convictions for office breaking, carrying an offensive weapon, embezzlement, assault, fraudulently consuming electricity, criminal damage, driving without reasonable consideration and being drunk in charge of a vehicle. Most of these activities, he insists today, were undertaken in the course of helping the poor of London fight the system.

According to police records, Wally Heaton was born in June 1931 and attended Primrose Hill council school in Stanley, Yorkshire, until he was fourteen, when he started working as a motor mechanic at L. H. Saunders in Leeds. It was the final year of the Second World War and there was plenty of employment for boys on the home front. While still a teenager, Wally also worked as a projectionist at the Palace Cinema in Pudsey. His father was an alcoholic and was physically abusive to Wally and his mother. In 1916, while he was fighting in the First World War, a shell had exploded near him, leaving him badly injured, missing for days and presumed dead. He was eventually found in a crater, eating a grain of rice. 'He didn't come out of hospital until 1921,' recalls Wally. 'There were no roads in the countryside where we were living, there was dead silence all around us, but he would jump up and go berserk, hearing some noise . . . I hated him when I was a child, I was terrified of him. It wasn't his fault; he was shell-shocked to hell.'

At sixteen, Wally escaped by joining the British army, serving in the Coldstream Guards in British Malaya. The fighting there was brutal and intense and he witnessed war crimes such as villagers being shot, their heads severed for souvenir photos. He was discharged in 1953 and came home angry and confused.

Witnessing British internment camps and the oppression of ethnic Chinese brought Wally closer to communism. His police file shows that he bounced from one job to another for eight years after his discharge and began to drink heavily. In 1961 he got a job with W. T. Noble Ltd, in Hornsey in north London, as a lorry driver, and later at Alloys Ltd on Orsman Road as a die-caster. He left that job in 1965 and drifted around until he ended up at the bottling plant.

While on the picket line, he heard about the rich woman who was giving away lots of money. All you had to do was turn up and plead your case. That week, he went to the claimants union seeking help for the strikers. Rose sat him down and listened to his story. She gave him some emergency money for the picketers and vowed to help as much as she could.

Wally came back again and again. He told her about the war crimes in Malaya and how the British army were doing this all over the world – and as close to home as Northern Ireland, which had been racked by violence since 1969. It was all very well paying fuel bills for old ladies, but would that overthrow the system that sent the English poor off to fight in foreign wars? Of course it wouldn't. 'You need to go deeper,' he told her.

They started dating and Wally would stay with Rose for days at a time.

Rose says it was her first sexual relationship with a man. Wally's drinking was so heavy then that he would fall into bed drunk. 'I was no good to her at night,' he recalls. 'Then I'd wake up in the morning and go for her. She called me her morning predator.'

Wally joined Rose in the running of the claimants union and the two became increasingly well-known figures in London's radical left. They had contrasting styles; Rose ostentatiously scruffy, Wally often dressing in sharp suits that Rose paid for.

Despite Wally's urgings to 'armed revolution', Rose was committed to non-violent means, at least initially. In his memoir *I Couldn't Paint Golden Angels*, Albert Meltzer, a British anarchist who had been instrumental in reactivating the Black Cross anarchist aid organization in fascist Spain, would describe Rose at this time as 'a sincere young woman' who was not sure 'what it was she believed in. I thought to interest her in the Anarchist Black Cross since she claimed to be a "non-violent anarchist", and nothing could be more non-violent than helping anarchist prisoners . . . When she heard of the Spanish Resistance (for the first time, incidentally) she closed up like a clam. It was too violent for her, she explained, and I was politely shown the door.'

More and more volunteers came to work at the claimants union. 'It was very regimented,' says Wally. 'They were all middle-class university types coming in to help. They were nice people, their heart was in the right place, but they didn't know the lives of working-class people, they didn't know what suffering really meant.'

Among the volunteers were Nettie Pollard and her girlfriend Gaby Charing. Gaby had been active in a group called Anarchist Student, and in the situationist movement, which sought absurd confrontations with authority. Both she and Nettie were involved in the Gay Liberation Front, a new hard-left group, which led them to the Tottenham Claimants Union.

To Nettie, Rose was 'the most extraordinary person I ever

met in my life. It was all about the movement with Rose; there was no room for laughs, which there was with Wally, who was rather larger than life.'

On Sunday, 30 January 1972, Rose and Nettie set out to visit a family nearby. Rose had already given them money, but now they were broke and trying to survive a bitter winter.

'We went to their house and found the family burning furniture to keep warm,' Nettie recalls. 'I didn't know this kind of thing still happened.' After the group dispersed for the day, news came through of an atrocity in Northern Ireland. A civil rights march by Irish nationalists in Derry had been blocked by an army barricade from reaching its intended destination, Derry's Guildhall. The march was redirected down Rossville Street, where some youths at the back threw stones at paratroopers. The soldiers opened fire on the crowd: round after round after round. Fourteen were shot dead, dozens more were injured.

Bloody Sunday, as it became known, was Northern Ireland's point of no return. On both sides of the border, young people rushed forward to join the IRA. Rose and Wally watched the news in Rose's flat. Wally was pacing up and down, shouting at the TV. 'It's war now!' he said.

From that day onward, he urged Rose to throw herself at Northern Ireland. Revolution wasn't giving cat food to old ladies, it was getting the British working class to unite with the Irish republicans to overthrow the whole bloody system. To fight in Ireland against the British military was to strike a blow for the poor of Tottenham. It was all interlinked.

By now, Rose had learned two important facts about Wally: he was married with two children and he had 'a very bad drinking problem'. Wally recalls: 'Yes, I had a problem, I did. But I was serious about politics. The reason I was banned from one bar, the Ship in Tottenham, was because the National Front attacked me in there, tried to put a screwdriver in my neck. They were always trying to get me, but I had a bit of a drink problem, yeah. I was so damn angry – all the lies, all the right-wing newspapers, people getting awards for lying and murdering people. I was angry, very angry at the time, about injustice. Not imagined injustice, like some of them, but real injustice on the street every day.'

Nettie recalls that when Rose 'encountered people begging in the street, not only did she give them money and other help, but she would stop and talk, discussing how they got into the situation and talking about capitalism but not in a condescending way. In the spirit of Mao, whom she read, she believed that revolutionaries should learn from the working class and peasants.'

More and more, the various groups around Rose were mixing together. 'Gaby and I wore Gay Liberation Front badges all the time in Tottenham,' Nettie recalls. 'It was surprising, perhaps, that we encountered no outright hostility. I imagine that many did not understand the badge, but we also had some interesting discussions. One mother of five said to us, "I was like you when I was your age but then I had to get married."'

By this time, Rose had changed her MG coupé for a Lotus which had headlamps that could be moved up and down from inside the car. In June 1972, with Rose in the passenger seat, Wally drove the Lotus at full speed to the Northern Ireland ferry. For two minds attracted to melodrama, tragedy and revolution, Northern Ireland offered bounteous riches.

They stopped first in Belfast and then went on to Derry. They couldn't fully absorb the sheer scale of the destruction in the city – hundreds of homes burnt out, twisted metal curling through barricaded street corners, black smoke rising from burning tyres that were flung at the police.

Michael Donnelly, a member of the Provisional IRA in Derry at the time, remembers the uprising as a daily exercise in chaotic improvisation. The IRA in Belfast, he says, 'went through the motions of being army men', whereas 'Derry tended to be a citizens' revolution. There was a different approach.' At the start of the Troubles, the first three Derry members of the Provisional IRA blew themselves up with their own bomb, leaving Donnelly as the sole surviving member. 'I didn't know what to do. I got some advice in the South. One of the IRA leaders told me: just build the army and the opportunities will present themselves.'

That year was the worst of the Troubles: over five hundred people were murdered. Every night there were sniper battles between the IRA and the army. In Derry, Rose and Wally watched the emergence of autonomous IRA-supporting enclaves. The system of blocking off streets with barricades was to have a profound influence on them. Wally remembers Derry nationalists digging a vast hole in the ground. 'And then they put this big bus in the crater and filled all around it with concrete so that half the bus was in the hole and half was above it. They had the whole street blocked off to the army and there were riots every single day.'

To Wally, who had a pathological hatred of the British army after his experiences in Malaya, Northern Ireland was an opportunity for revenge – or redemption. The IRA was trying to destroy the British military, and so was he. To Rose, attracted to radical disorder, Northern Ireland was a sudden answer to a much wider longing for social upheaval. Together, they confected an apocalyptic worldview in which the poor of Tottenham would soon join with the IRA in overthrowing the establishment.

They met with IRA figures in Derry and offered both weapons and money for the cause. On 15 June, in Rose's Lotus with the operations officer of Derry's Provisional IRA 2nd Battalion, they were arrested at the Buncrana Road checkpoint and taken to Limavady RUC station.

'We were separated,' Wally recalls, 'and they were asking us all these questions: What were we doing in Northern Ireland? Who were we mixing with? How did we know the fella in the car? I told them I was an ex-soldier who served in Malaya and I knew colonialism when I saw it. Apart from that, I told them nothing and Rose told them nothing. We were out in a few hours.'

By the end of the trip, Rose agreed that Wally had been right: giving fuel vouchers to pensioners wasn't going to solve anything. They needed to take up arms, to convince the London working class to join them in overthrowing British rule in Northern Ireland and rip apart the whole British class system.

Shortly after they returned to London, they set up a Northern Ireland-style 'people's roadblock' at the back of Pentonville Prison in solidarity with dockers who had been jailed for contempt of court for refusing to lift a strike. Declassified police documents show that on Tuesday, 25 July 1972, 'a few hundred people blocked the Caledonian Road and damaged public service vehicles and a lorry in an effort to barricade the street'. Wally addressed a group of radicals and dockers, urging them to support the IRA.

'He spoke in a loud voice and could be clearly heard by people on the opposite side of the road,' Police Inspector George Boyall would recall in a statement prepared for Rose and Wally's trial. Many of the dockers were 'jeering and waving their fists at him. He shouted: "You're all tools of the capitalists. The system has got to be overthrown. The boys in Belfast and Derry are laying down their lives for the cause and the government there is being eroded – it can happen here. Brothers – unite against the system!"'

Inspector Boyall noted that when Wally shouted about a woman who had been shot in her own home by a British army rubber bullet in Northern Ireland, 'an extremely angry docker shouted back: "And the IRA shoot our men in the back. My brother's out there." Dockers were screaming and some of the more angry ones began closing in on Heaton. I went up to him and said: "You've been warned –" Heaton interrupted: "This is free speech, I can say what I like" . . . I arrested him for using insulting words where a breach of the peace was likely to have been occasioned.'

As Inspector Boyall was grabbing Wally by the right arm, Rose grabbed hold of the policeman's arm, just above the elbow. According to Boyall's report, 'She said: "Just a minute. You've got no right to arrest him. Let him go!"'

PC Peter Butcher ordered Rose to let Boyall go and, when she refused, he arrested her for obstructing a police officer. When their case came to court, Rose and Wally asked for an adjournment to call witnesses and both were remanded on bail until February 1973, seven months hence. But when the case came to court again, they had no witnesses. The magistrate found them both guilty of breach of the peace and obstruction. Wally was fined £30 and ordered to pay £20 in costs. Rose wasn't fined, but they each had to put up £50 to be bound over to keep the peace.

The debacle had indicated that the British working class,

who were largely loyal to their country and their Queen, had no intention of joining Rose and Wally's revolution.

On 22 August 1972, four weeks after the Pentonville demonstration, Rose received close to £42,000 from the sale of shares. At Wally's urging, she also gave written notice that she no longer wanted to be a Lloyd's underwriter.

She decided that she should live among the poor, so she withdrew £5,000 from the Matson Trust and bought a flat in an alley off Tottenham High Road. Nettie recalls that Rose met a middle-aged homeless couple, Jim and Gladys, who slept in a cemetery, and invited them to stay at her flat while Rose and Wally slept in squats. Eventually, Rose signed the flat over to them.

Rose and Wally argued, they made up, they gave away money. Wally fought on the streets with public officials and skinheads. He had an untrammelled energy that both fascinated and intimidated Rose – it seemed he was up for any mayhem. Their stunts grew more and more confrontational. They would barge into Islington council meetings, Wally holding the hand of an immigrant child and demanding justice, or invade the offices of council officials, insisting they be given blankets for a family they had housed in a disused flat.

For a period, Rose and Wally had the use of the basement flat in Peter Ady's house in Ponsonby Terrace in Chelsea. Over time, however, the relationship between Peter and her lodgers became strained, and eventually Peter asked them to leave. Rose brought Nettie along to collect her bed. 'I remember there was quite a bit of tension between them, nothing said directly, but you could feel it,' Nettie recalls. 'We collected the rather fine bed, tied it to the top of the car, and off we went.'

After a day at the claimants union, Nettie, Gaby, Rose and Wally would all go to the local pub. Rose would discreetly give Wally the money to buy the drinks so he wouldn't lose face in front of the group. 'Back then it was very important for a man to be seen to be the one buying the drinks for a woman, not the other way around,' says Nettie.

Occasionally, Wally would bring Rose back to his home on Sydney Road in north London, where his wife, Audrey, would stare at Rose and say little. One day, Audrey flung coffee at Wally and Rose after finding them in bed together. Wally says it didn't upset him because Audrey threw coffee at him 'all the time'. 'It never bothered me,' he says. 'People starving on the streets bothered me.'

Rose and Wally returned repeatedly to Northern Ireland to meet IRA members in Belfast and Derry. In January 1973 they were photographed in the *Derry Journal* waving an illegal Irish tricolour at a rally marking the first anniversary of Bloody Sunday. According to Wally, on that trip they drove from Derry to Long Kesh prison in Belfast, hoping to meet the deputy head of the Derry IRA. Perhaps because they were both well dressed, and because Rose spoke with an upper-class English accent and drove a sports car, they were let straight into the prison car park.

'They thought we were government officials,' Wally says, 'and when we said we wanted to see the number two of the Derry IRA they were furious. They were effing and blinding us and telling us not to fucking try that again.'

Back home, Rose and Wally continued trying to organize Northern Ireland-style resistance among the poor of London.

Nettie Pollard recalls a barricade they built to stop the police from breaking into a squat occupied by a Scottish couple, John and Florence McGowan, and their children.

'Wally suggested we bring attention to the housing situation by barricading a street as they did in Derry. We built a barricade in a street off Stroud Green Road. We used rubble from a nearby demolished house as a test. We then went for a drink in the Earl of Essex pub, where Wally sang Irish rebel songs. Then, a few days later, we built a barricade in Lesley Street. The media got interested. The BBC came and did an interview with Wally and with Florence McGowan. One evening, about 9 p.m., dozens of police officers appeared in Lesley Street and dismantled the barricades. Sometime later, an inspector came to the squat and arrested Johnny McGowan for alleged non-payment of rates. The sociologist Mary McIntosh, a friend of mine from the Gay Liberation Front, lived nearby. I explained what had happened and she went with Wally and somehow obtained the money from her bank. We all went round to the police station and paid the money and went back with Johnny. Rose later paid Mary back.'

The McGowans were of particular interest to Rose. When they were about to lose their children because they lived in a squat, Rose convinced Nettie to dress up in a suit and impersonate a social worker to represent them in court. Nettie went to court and won the case for the family.

Rose and Wally were eager to stockpile weapons for the coming revolution. Rose drove around the country in her sports car, looking for weapons. 'I remember the Lotus,' says Jenny Grove, who had remained friends with Rose. 'How much of a Communist could you be in a sports car? A socialist, maybe, but not a Communist.'

Wally was related by marriage to a part-time crook named

Ginger Mann and thought Mann might be able to get them weapons. Rose bought Mann a car and travelled with him to buy weapons from hoodlums in Manchester. She also encouraged him to steal explosives. A criminal and car dealer named Thomas Card would later tell police that Rose and Wally visited Mann's home in Manchester in March 1973. Rose produced a rucksack, he said, along with a tent and maps, and suggested that Card and Mann visit North Wales and reconnoitre quarries to locate explosives. She said to pay particular attention to a large mine near Snowdon. They wouldn't have to steal the explosives, just identify their whereabouts, and others would steal them. The 'boys from Ireland' would then take possession of the explosives, Card said.

Rose and Wally started making trips on the ferry from Stranraer to Larne, bringing the weapons they'd sourced to Belfast for distribution to the IRA. Unknown to them, their trips were being monitored by the Special Branch.

By this point, Rose's relationship with her family had all but completely broken down. In a later statement to police, her father dated the sundering to 'about January 1972' – the month of Bloody Sunday, coincidentally or not. Eric Dugdale recalled that he invited Rose to dinner 'once a week', but that she would turn up late or not at all. 'Eventually, my wife said: "What stops you from seeing us? Who is the boss?" Finally, the boss, Mr Walter Heaton, was brought to dinner.'

This first encounter between Wally and the Dugdale family was a disaster. Wally refused to sit down unless the servants also ate with them. 'I said: "No, no, no! I don't want to be served,"' Wally recalls. 'So we went down to the servants and we ate with them.'

Wally later turned up at Eric Dugdale's office at Lloyd's of London and began haranguing him and his colleagues. 'I went right into his office,' Wally recalls. 'I said: "You are stealing off the poor people. You're supposed to be a gentleman, you are nothing of it. You are a rogue and a scoundrel like everyone else in this building." He had security throw me out. They have no sense of humour, these people.'

At Wally's urging, Rose paid £25,000 (equivalent to more than £300,000 today) into an account that was held by his wife, Audrey – but required Wally's countersignature for withdrawals. She also gave £10,000 to Wally, with which he bought a Mercedes and several suits.

They made contact with the Angry Brigade, a far-left group that had launched a series of bomb attacks on state and establishment properties and become public hate figures. One of them, Hilary Creek, was moved from a Category-A prison to a mental institution in 1973 after developing anorexia and a nervous condition. According to J. D. Taylor's *Waiting for the Revolution*, a study of the British far left at the time, news of Creek's transfer broke as a scoop in the *Daily Mail*, leading to an outcry among conservatives that she was being treated too leniently.

MPs demanded an immediate inquiry into the transfer, but the Home Secretary, Robert Carr, whose house had been bombed by the Angry Brigade, refused to bow to pressure and allowed Creek to continue her treatment in the hospital. Like Rose, Creek came from a well-off background, had a father who worked in finance and had specialized in economics in college. Rose liked her more than most of the other Angry Brigade members. 'I was concerned about her because she was very frail and, I believe, was going to go on hunger strike,' Rose recalls.

One night, amid the national outcry, Rose and Wally visited Creek at Friern Hospital in London, to plan her escape. 'We were going to take her up to Sweden: that's where all the American Vietnam draft dodgers were going, so we thought it would be a good place for her,' Wally recalls. 'We went to her ward and told her the plan and she started screaming. She didn't want anything more to do with it . . . She was screaming and the alarm went off, so myself and Rose legged it back to the car.'

Overall, their relationship with the Angry Brigade was fraught. Wally's view is that he and Rose were 'too radical'. 'We suggested many things but it was never accepted, like blowing up police stations. Rose was fearless, absolutely fearless, but it was too much for them.'

Rose and Wally, in the end, were too angry even for the Angry Brigade.

Rose continued to burn through her fortune. In May 1973, she disposed of her shareholding in Dugdale [J.F.C.] Proprietary Ltd, netting close to £43,000.

Around this time, her father wrote her a letter.

During my life I have lived through two wars and I know that the condition of life of everybody in this country has improved beyond all measure and it is still improving. It surprises me that someone of your acute intelligence does not notice this [. . .] it is completely illogical to brand a whole class of people as being either honourable or dishonourable. I believe that our family have made some contribution to the improvement of life in England. [. . .] our families have provided employment at a fair wage and under decent conditions of service, and I do not think either branch of your family have anything of which to be ashamed. I wrote you a letter some weeks ago and I told

you I would never slam the door. Although you have had all the money
that I have to give, you will always find a welcome if you return.

Five weeks later, Rose replied, seeking to separate the
father she loved from the reactionary imperialist she hated.
Cruelly, it hinted at both her IRA connections and Wally's
spendthrift ways.

Dear Daddy,

I hope that you won't shelter under such sanctimony as accusations
that I have cut all love between us away. As one of the boys across
the water said to me the other day, I will die fighting the oppressor but
I will give my life for the poor people. So let's not have any more about
the self-sacrifices of our ancestors who died while ordering the men out
over the trenches to death for nothing but the wellbeing of a handful
of rich men who own the world: there will always be a place for you
amongst the brave men who are prepared to shoot in the back those
commanders. The jolliest time for Lloyds was the last war, was it not?
When Guardsman Heaton takes your money it is his for the taking.
You can't take your accumulated theft with you of course, though you
can be a man who refuses to dishonour himself and his family whilst
mothers with children are thrown on to the streets which their
ancestors built.

Love . . . ROSE

Wally reminded Rose that her family had lots of paintings
and heirlooms. Why not steal those to fund the IRA?

During the first weekend of June 1973, Rose travelled to
the Dugdale estate in Devon with three career criminals supplied by Ginger Mann: Thomas Card, Michael Cronin and
Ronald Sanders. She knew that her parents would be away at

the Races in Epsom. As her father would later remark in court, the dogs didn't bark because they recognized Rose and let her pass with her friends. Rose knew the security system and which window to lift to get in. She directed the others to the items that were worth taking and put Card in charge of taking eight of her father's oil paintings and some rare Meissen figurines. In all, they stole silver, art and antiques worth £80,000 (roughly £1 million today) and quickly fled. Eric Dugdale would later tell police that he got a call from the Yarty housekeeper, Rosemary Hicks, on 7 June, informing him that there had been a burglary.

Initially, the loot was stored at Ginger Mann's home in Manchester, but Wally was uncomfortable with this arrangement and he and Rose soon collected it.

There were any number of radical leftist squats and Irish republican safe houses in London where Rose could have taken the goods. Instead, she drove to Peter Ady's house in Oxford and put eight suitcases in the basement while Peter was out. She later told Peter about the suitcases, and Peter phoned the Dugdales, who phoned the police. Eventually, having received the assistance of Ginger Mann and the three associates who had taken part in the burglary, police arrested Rose and Wally in a pub in Tottenham.

The family silver was lined up on a table at Exeter Crown Court for a trial that ran through the summer of 1973. Representing herself, for the defence, was Dr Rose Dugdale. She and Wally were on trial for the burglary. Rose was determined to turn it into a trial of the establishment.

Her initial tactic was to claim that she wouldn't have stolen her parents' haut bourgeois trappings because she had rejected such materialism a long time ago. Speaking directly to the jurors, she said she had developed a distaste for her father's wealth. 'Quite genuinely, my parents believe I must be deranged,' she told them. 'I will try to put across to you why I could never have committed a burglary at my parents' home. I would never have had a motive.'

She said that 'some kind of awareness of the limitations of the way my parents lived came in on me. The round of parties at massive expense, immense amounts of money being spent on clothes, food and wine, seemed utterly aimless.' The differences with her parents grew wider when she went to Oxford, she said. 'I grew into a most dislikeable kind of intellectual.'

In the witness stand was her father, Colonel Eric Dugdale: the chief prosecution witness. The two of them examined the court exhibits: family heirlooms from the Yarty estate. In front of a long line of reporters, Colonel Dugdale told his daughter that he still loved her and that, when this all ended, she could always come home. She had once been his 'special friend', he said.

She was equally effusive in her declarations of love for her father, but also resigned to conflict. 'There is a massive battle between us which nothing will remove but the disappearance of one of us,' she said. 'I love you, Daddy, and if there were any danger threatening you, I would stand between you and that danger. But I hate everything you stand for.' The press loved it.

Rose was remanded on bail for psychiatric reports and judged to be sane.

On 22 October 1973, Rose was found guilty of burglary; Wally was found guilty of the lesser charge of handling stolen goods.

Before she was sentenced, Rose told the judge: 'I am certainly not going to ask you for mercy because I don't think it's a quality that you and your ilk know anything of. You will sentence me to the longest sentence you can give me without becoming the laughing stock history will make you. You will [sentence me] from fear of the united strength of people of no property, brave men and true, and you are afraid of this because one day these men – and I believe it will be very shortly – will brush you and other yeomen aside and deprive you of the power and privilege you abrogate and abuse. In returning a verdict of guilty, you have turned me from an intellectual recalcitrant into a freedom fighter. I don't know of a finer or better title.' She ended with a rallying cry: 'Power to the people. History will absolve us!'

Showing early signs of the revolutionary Christianity that was later to dominate his life, Wally told the court that not since Christ had authorities committed such an injustice. He struck a mystical note: 'You cannot imprison Rose and me because we don't exist. But we are everywhere – invincible, incorruptible and indestructible.'

Judge Parker handed down a two-year suspended sentence, telling Rose: 'I think the risks that you will ever again commit burglary or any dishonesty are extremely remote.'

Wally Heaton, though convicted on a lesser charge, was the real culprit, in the judge's eyes. He had 'exploited' Rose in order to provide himself, his wife and his children with a better life. Noting that Wally had a long line of previous convictions, Judge Parker sentenced him to six years in prison.

Rose was outraged that Wally had got a much heavier sentence than she had. 'Class justice, if I may say so!' she told reporters waiting outside. 'A poor man goes away for six years on a lesser charge; a rich girl gets two years suspended.'

*

In November 1973, less than a month after receiving a suspended sentence for burgling her own family, Rose was placed on trial for an earlier charge of refusing a blood-alcohol test. According to a court report in the *Guardian*, she had been seen driving on a footpath and hitting a pedestrian before she refused the test. In court, she claimed that the pedestrian had been Wally and that she had been trying to prevent him from re-entering a pub. She was able to call Wally as a witness for the trial. He remembers being brought from prison to the courtroom under tight security to back up her story.

Judge T. K. Edie rejected Rose's revolutionary proclamations to the court, in which she alleged the police were trying to silence her. 'If you wanted to make a stand for liberty, you should have chosen better ground ... There is nothing to suggest you had an undue amount to drink. If you had taken the test it may well have cleared you, but you insisted on this confrontation. Now I have to punish somebody I have no desire to punish.' He fined her £25 and suspended her driver's licence for a year.

'It was worth it to see Wally again,' Rose told reporters afterwards.

She visited him frequently in prison and held demonstrations outside. 'Rose led all these "Free Wally Heaton" protests, but I could never see them,' says Wally. 'They had me buried down in the basement of the prison, where I could never see out. I would write to Rose, but it was so heavily censored, it would just say: "Dear Rose, I hope you are well. Black line, black line, black line, Love, Wally."'

He was being held with IRA prisoners, two of whom were on hunger strike, and with an Angry Brigade member, Jimmy Greenfield, who was serving ten years. Wally's support for the IRA set him out as a traitor to some of the prison officers, who beat him, he says.

Wally sensed that Rose became less enthusiastic about her visits to him as the months passed. He remembers her last visit. 'When the prison officers weren't looking, she leaned in and she said: "I will get revenge for you, Wally."'

It was the last time they would speak for over forty years.

5. The Spark

Rose might have ended up like the others. Like her friend Gaby, who went on to join the Labour Party, train as a solicitor and join middle-class liberal society. Or like Vanessa Stilwell, a Jewish radical in the London squatter scene who, decades later, would receive a tumultuous standing ovation at the Labour Party conference for backing party leader Jeremy Corbyn during the party's anti-Semitism scandal. Or like Corbyn himself, who rose to the Labour leadership despite his early support for hard-line Irish republicanism.

Instead, she stayed on the militant path. At some point in 1973 she developed a close friendship with an IRA member from Donegal named Eddie Gallagher, who was in England to make money and look for bombing targets.

Eddie Gallagher, a professional tunneller by trade, had a fast, active brain and an intense stare that unnerved those who crossed him. He could be both charming and dangerous, depending on his mood. 'Wiry' is a word almost universally used to describe him. He had dark hair and a broad moustache.

At the start of the Troubles, Eddie had little interest in the IRA, which he believed to be sectarian and regressive. He was a socialist and a trade unionist, fighting for better working conditions for men tunnelling the Victoria Line of the London Underground.

On weekends, Eddie went to Speakers' Corner in Hyde Park with his tunnelling team, many of whom were from the IRA heartland of South Armagh. He remembers one speaker who 'was given the mission to be the official spokesperson for Sinn Féin/IRA in London'. The man was tall and wore a grey trench coat and a beret. 'He was up on a soapbox giving it everything – the IRA this and that. This guy was an out-and-out fucking nut, to put it in a nutshell, and the guy with him had been the spokesman for Oswald Mosley at one point. He stood there in a pinstripe suit and a bowler hat and a brolly. That was the beginnings of the Provisional IRA in London. Such an outfit!'

One Sunday, the man in the beret appealed for volunteers to go to Belfast. 'He was a really good speaker, he could really give the talk. He said: "And I have an IRA volunteer I will be able to present next week." So we are all waiting the next week to see the volunteer. The next week he is giving his big speech and he goes: "And now we have an IRA volunteer who will be on the streets of Belfast tomorrow night in the thick of the strife." He took the "volunteer" to the front of the stage to introduce him. Who was it only Tommy, a wee man from a pub in Finsbury Park who used to be collecting the glasses. The shape of tiny little Tommy, the poor creature.'

Eddie Gallagher ended up in Northern Ireland for a completely different reason: to work on major water-tunnelling projects in Belfast in Comber, Co. Down. On 7 August 1971, on the Falls Road in Belfast, he and his workmates heard several gunshots. One of their drivers, Harry Thornton, crashed into a lamppost. He was dead, shot twice by a British soldier who had run out from a barracks on the Springfield Road after hearing Harry's van backfire.

Several Royal Ulster Constabulary police officers came

running out of the barracks and pulled the passenger, Arthur Murphy, out of the van. 'I remember two Land Rovers came screaming down the road with open backs and paras holding on to the rails,' Eddie Gallagher recalls. 'One jumped out and in a London accent shouted: "One down and one to go." I remember him putting the gun up to Arthur's head.' Among the members of the work crew, Gallagher says, 'There was a lot of talk of getting even.'

Decades later, at the end of an inquest into the death of Harry Thornton, Senior Coroner Brian Sherrard would rule that a soldier falsely claimed he saw a gun in the van and that Thornton was shot without provocation.

Eddie Gallagher went back to Donegal the day after the incident, and 'Two days later I joined the Provos. Maybe it was the wrong reason for joining. It was an emotional reaction, it was about getting even, but I joined them anyway.' The swearing-in ceremony, he says, 'was like joining the Hells Angels'.

Eddie was immediately trained up as a bomber for the IRA's campaign in Donegal.

'At that time bombs were pretty basic, it was clocks you were using,' he says. 'So one of the older IRA members, he had a shop in Donegal. I was buying a dozen clocks for bombs from him. I remember his wife coming to me and saying: "He is giving it to you at wholesale prices!"'

His unit was sometimes based in the village of Pettigo, which sits right on the border; on the Co. Fermanagh side it is known as Tullyhommon. Eddie was set on killing a part-time Ulster Defence Regiment soldier named Mervyn Johnston, a mechanic who specialized in fixing Minis. Johnston's garage was just on the Tullyhommon side of the border, with a British customs post outside his door.

On one occasion, the IRA pushed Mervyn Johnston

towards the customs post and shot at him. The bullet missed him but hit his apprentice. Johnston rushed into his garage, grabbed his revolver and fired several shots back. Over several months, Eddie and the others in his unit exploded a number of incendiary bombs at the garage, but Johnston survived without injury and continued to walk across the border to go to the pub. There are few people in Northern Ireland who survived as many assassination attempts as Mervyn Johnston.

Eddie was getting irritated. The Provisional IRA and the British army held a ceasefire from 26 June to 9 July 1972, and there was talk of another. Eddie wanted to strike before orders from Belfast came to stop all operations.

'We tried a few times to get him and he tried dirty tricks on a few of the men involved, so we reckoned that if this bloody ceasefire is to come, we would never get an opportunity to get him again. We couldn't figure out his routine – he was pretty good. We decided if we couldn't get him, we could at least destroy his garage.'

On 21 July 1972, Eddie struck, along with two other IRA members from Offaly: 26-year-old Joe Coughlan of Tullamore and 22-year-old Thomas Dignam of Clara.

'We decided to put a car bomb in his garage and destroy his business, so we went up early one morning. It was the first thing that Martin McGuinness was involved in with us: he gave us the car for the car bomb. We put it in there [the garage], with an hour's timer as usual, and we headed off back to Donegal. There's a wee narrow road to Donegal town. We got stuck behind about ten pilgrimage buses leaving Lough Derg. I was driving. I got past most of them but this one hoor was out in the middle of the road. I couldn't pass them for a long fucking time.'

Eddie rushed to the phone box on the main square in

Donegal town to call in the bomb warning to the garda station in Pettigo, but 'Before I could get through to the station, a garda car pulled up and a garda pulled me out of the phone box.'

The three IRA men were arrested. A state barrister, A. J. Hederman, would later tell the anti-terrorist Special Criminal Court in Dublin that Thomas Dignam had given a false name and that a document found on one of the three men contained a list of materials that included an alarm clock, bell wire, batteries, plastic tape, clothes pegs and micro switches.

As A. J. Hederman would tell the Special Criminal Court, Joe Coughlan took one of the garda sergeants aside and asked him to clear Main Street in Pettigo: on both sides of the street and both sides of the border. 'The sergeant wanted to know did he leave a bomb there,' Eddie recalls. 'Joe said: "You've been told. It's on your conscience, now clear the street."'

The sergeant made a call from Donegal town to the station in Pettigo, where a garda, John McCarthy, rushed to have the street cleared and told the Royal Ulster Constabulary on the Northern side of the village to do the same.

Shortly thereafter, the bomb detonated, destroying Mervyn Johnston's garage. Because the bombers had been caught in the Republic of Ireland and there was no cross-border extradition at the time, they were charged in the Republic, and only for acts committed in the Republic: handling explosives and criminal damage to a shop on the Donegal side. The explosion itself, which took place on the Northern side, and the destruction of Johnston's garage, were beyond the scope of the prosecution. In August, a three-judge panel of the Special Criminal Court sentenced all three bombers to four months' imprisonment in the Curragh military prison.

Eddie was relieved at the light sentence, which he

attributes in part to the relatively minor charges that could be brought in the Republic, and in part to the IRA men's efforts to get the village cleared after they'd been arrested. 'I think the judge knew that we didn't have to tell them that there was a bomb there – we could have kept our mouths shut.'

IRA members in the Curragh asked him to put his tunnelling skills to use. With Joe O'Connell – who would later become notorious as a bomber in England – and the other two members of the team that had bombed Mervyn Johnston's garage, Eddie started 'sinking a shaft in an Official IRA man's cell'.

On 29 October, the tunnel was ready, and seven prisoners escaped through it. Five of them were Provisional IRA men, Eddie says, 'and within three months, two or three of those five escapees were dead'.

Eddie served three months of his four-month sentence. He was broke when he got out, and resentful that the IRA provided little financial backing for its prisoners. If he was to re-dedicate himself to the IRA, he wanted to be able to earn a living meanwhile, tunnelling in England. This is how he came to meet Rose Dugdale – for whom financial stability was an ideological burden she was eager to remove.

'The IRA told me to come back into Donegal again for gun training,' Eddie recalls, 'and I said: "No, keep your guns because I have a [work] contract in England and I'm heading off again."'

The tunnelling job was in Tunbridge Wells, the Kent spa town, and Eddie 'used to be up and down to London'. He joined anti-Vietnam War protests and, through contacts in the student-led anti-colonialist left, he heard about Rose Dugdale and what they were now calling the Civil Rights Union in Tottenham. He decided to meet her and to volunteer.

Eddie quickly established himself as a close collaborator with Rose. To Wally's annoyance, Eddie and Rose went around together to identify empty houses and put squatters in them. While doing so, Eddie learned things about poverty and cynicism. 'We put a homeless Scottish family in this empty house we found. It was nice. They were so glad to have a roof over their heads and a new place to live. There were two flats in that house. We came back a week later to put in another homeless family in the other flat and the Scottish family wouldn't let them in. They said it was their place. That was a good lesson in human nature. They said: "We have people coming down from Scotland. This is *our* home." They were so grateful to get off the streets just a week earlier. It shows you a lot about people.'

He was impressed by Rose's determination and idealism: 'She was genuinely trying to help people. Also, she had extremely good information, stuff that I wouldn't be able to get my hands on otherwise. She had good contacts: she knew the ropes in a part of British society that I had never dipped my toe into. She was able to explain how the system worked better than anyone I knew: who pulls the strings, which clubs the decisions were made in, what were the important old-boy networks. She was able to fill in the gaps in a lot of things that I wouldn't have known about before.'

Some in the IRA felt that Rose must be a plant and told Eddie to stay clear of her. The difficulty wasn't just that Rose was English and upper class. It was also that she was a Marxist. The Provisional IRA had grown out of a bitter split with Marxists in the Official IRA, and the Provisional chief of staff, Seamus Twomey, had a particular suspicion of Rose.

'The problem wasn't with Dáithí Ó Conaill and the southern leadership,' says Eddie. 'I never heard anything negative about her at all from Dáithí. It was more Seamus Twomey and Joe Cahill in Belfast. Whatever political outlook they had . . . it would have been at total odds with her thinking, what she stood for, what she professed. Twomey in particular was saying: "This is another Brit coming in, she must be a spy." That kind of thing.'

Rose joined Eddie in Pettigo at some point in 1973, though it is not clear when. She was taken to a small training camp, which was little more than a caravan in a field, where the IRA would assemble and disassemble weapons. To raise money for the unit, Eddie would poach salmon by dropping gelignite into rivers to stun the fish, which would then float into nets downstream. One night when he and Rose were poaching on a bridge over the River Finn, he recalls, they could hear two bailiffs on another bridge, two or three hundred yards away. 'The moon was out and it was a still night. We could hear the two men on the bridge talking, we could hear every word . . . We were waiting ages and ages and they were talking. I said to Rose: "Throw the fucking thing, it will be alight." She lit it and threw it and it landed on this big rock in the middle of the river. It went off like an atomic bomb in the stillness of the night, it was such a big explosion. And all of a sudden, no talk from the bailiffs on the other bridge. Silence. And they left very quickly.'

Eddie had big plans and was assembling a team. At the time, the British army frequently invited the media along for helicopter rides to show their dominance of the airspace over South Armagh and West Tyrone, where IRA attacks had been ferocious.

Eddie confided to Rose that he would give anything to be able to counter the British army in the skies.

*

I am sitting with Rose at her nursing home in Dublin. Sister Sarah, a retired member of the Poor Servants of the Mother of God, passes by on her Zimmer frame. 'How are you, Rose? Good afternoon.'

Rose is sitting up in bed. I have brought Jaffa Cakes. Rose raises one weakly to acknowledge Sister Sarah.

I have a list of questions. 'How many are left?' Rose asks.

I feel she is getting tired, so I try a cheerful question.

'What was the happiest day of your life?'

Rose pauses twenty seconds, while biting on a Jaffa Cake. 'Oh, I think the happiest day of my life was the bombing in Strabane. Yes. It was the first time I felt like I was really at the centre of things, that I was really doing as I said I would do. It was what you might call an electric feeling.'

On 9 January 1974 Captain John Hobday, retired from the Royal Air Force, was sitting in the bar of McFadden's Hotel in Gortahork, Co. Donegal, when he was approached by 'a blonde young woman with a distinguished British accent'. The woman introduced herself as Stephanie Grant. Captain Hobday, who was staying at the hotel, was employed by a company called Irish Helicopters to take people and supplies to and from lighthouses in both the Republic and Northern Ireland.

He was relieved to find a fellow Brit in the wilds of Donegal. Stephanie Grant told him that her father also had military experience. She was a freelance journalist who had been commissioned by the *Guardian* to write an article about Tory Island, one of the Donegal islands on Captain Hobday's regular route. She said she had a photographer and two local guides with her and they were hoping to go to see Tory Island in the next few days.

Captain Hobday told Stephanie that he would be delighted to take her and her companions but she must first clear it with Irish Helicopters head office in Dublin.

Stephanie – who was in fact Rose Dugdale – arranged this with some phone calls, and after a few days she arrived back at McFadden's, along with the other members of her entourage: Eddie Gallagher and two very young men: Patrick Anthony Treacy, twenty, and Eamon McNulty, eighteen, of Strabane, Co. Tyrone. Strabane was known as the most bombed town in Northern Ireland – there was barely a street in its centre that hadn't been gutted, as a film crew for *60 Minutes* would show the following year. It was a majority-nationalist town with a major British army and police intelligence centre that was a frequent target for the IRA. The town hall had been bombed or burned down five times in five years. In all, there had been three hundred bombings in six years, by both nationalists and loyalists.

The plan was to stay a night in the hotel and then go out with Captain Hobday the following morning. However, there was a problem in Gortahork: the hotel was doing repairs and there were no available rooms. Rose explained at the desk that they were journalists over from England to show off the beauty of the area to an international audience and said the *Guardian* had booked rooms for them months in advance.

A worried receptionist, who would later make a statement to police, hastily apologized and found them two rooms: one for Eddie and Tracey, and one for Rose and McNulty, who were registered as being married. (This made no sense in terms of Rose's cover story, but in that time and place it was easier for everyone to pretend or assume that a cohabiting woman and man were married.)

When the four met Captain Hobday the next morning, the helicopter needed some repairs, and they waited around the helipad until Hobday said it was safe to fly. Finally, at about 11 a.m., they set off. Rose sat in the front with Captain Hobday, who told her of his RAF experience, while the three men sat silently in the back.

The helicopter rose to 150 metres and a speed of 185kph, Hobday would later recall in court. Just as they were passing over the island of Inishbofin, Eddie struck an automatic pistol hard into Captain Hobday's side. In the din of the chopper, Stephanie handed the captain a note: 'Go to Ards Abbey' – a Capuchin monastery, properly known as Ards Friary, on the coast a short distance to the east.

Captain Hobday looked at Stephanie. Her fashionable green military parka, beloved of 1970s journalists and students, now took on a different meaning. She leaned across and pointed at a small stone jetty beside the abbey and told him to land there.

As soon as they were on the ground, Rose and the three men loaded the helicopter with five milk churns from a nearby shed. The team had spent weeks preparing the bombs, with external help from a Provisional IRA bomb-maker, but they had no sanction from the IRA leadership.

'It was the only way you could survive in that type of situation,' says Eddie. 'You tell the least amount of people. That's how we always operated. If you don't trust us, well, too bad; and if you do, you can read about it in the newspaper afterwards.'

The bombs, Eddie says, 'were made up of creamery urns that had been tightly shut with wire to condense the blast. There was a core of gelignite and surrounding that there was the wider core of fertilizer explosive that we were able to mix ourselves. Each one would have weighed about a hundred pounds.'

With Eddie's gun still pressing into his side, Captain Hobday helped the group remove the back seats and cargo compartments to make room for the bombs. But there was a problem: with the milk churns crammed inside, the cargo doors could not be closed properly and had to be secured with baling twine.

Captain Hobday told Eddie that he couldn't take off with such a heavy payload: that the helicopter would crash. The bombers took this seriously enough that they returned one of the milk churns to the shed.

Meanwhile, Father Simeon, guardian of the Capuchin monastery, came outside with Brother Richard to investigate the helicopter landing. A man emerged from behind a wall and held the two Capuchins at gunpoint, and Father Simeon could see a number of people lifting or handling a milk churn. He would later recall that the man with the gun told them: 'No telephoning now for half an hour,' then got into the helicopter.

The bombers got back into the helicopter and Captain Hobday took off. The helicopter was swaying badly – though it is not clear whether this was because of the excess weight on board or by the design of Captain Hobday. Eddie believed it was the former and was afraid the chopper would crash, so they dropped two of the bombs into the sea.

Treacy was holding on to the cargo doors as tightly as he could, but the pressure was enormous and the baling twine was about to break. If the doors blew open, the remaining bombs would fall out. The helicopter landed in a field nearby, and Rose managed to shut the doors properly before they took off again. Now Eddie jumped into the front of the helicopter and crouched down in front of her with his gun pressed to Captain Hobday's stomach. Captain Hobday was ordered to head for Strabane police and army barracks, some 30 miles to the south-east. He used a map and, as the helicopter drew nearer, Treacy and McNulty, the two Strabane men, shouted instructions. He was to aim for a white building between the Catholic and Protestant churches.

Townspeople looked up to see a helicopter flying in fast towards the heavily fortified barracks. It had withstood car bombs, grenades and a mortar. The army had not expected what a BBC journalist would later call 'the IRA airforce'.

Captain Hobday was now told they were on a bombing mission. McNulty lit one of the fuses on the urns. They had only seconds before it would explode. At this point, Hobday stopped following instructions.

'He was told to hover over the barracks, which was the intelligence centre for the North at the time,' Eddie recalls. 'The idea was to throw the bombs into the base and destroy it, but he went in there like he was on a bombing run. When it was time to throw the bombs, he was [past] the base and there were houses all around the base. The bombs would have killed civilians.'

Now the bombers were in fear of their own lives. 'I thought we were all going to die,' says Rose. They decided to try to dump the bomb whose fuse had been lit into the River Mourne, which runs through the town, before it exploded.

By now, crowds were looking up from the bridge. While Eddie kept the gun pressed on Hobday, McNulty pushed the lit bomb out of the helicopter. The bomb plunged into the river. The wire around the top kept it airtight. It exploded on the riverbed.

Eddie recalls that he ordered Hobday to fly back to the barracks and to hover over it this time. Captain Hobday replied: 'You can shoot me if you want, but I'm not hovering. They'll shoot us all.'

Eddie shouted back: 'All right, all right, just go back in.'

Captain Hobday had a major advantage: none of the others could fly a helicopter. If they shot him, they would likely die with him. He would recall in court that he did a second circuit of the town, back towards the army barracks. One of the male bombers shouted that soldiers were firing up at them from the barracks.

As they approached, McNulty lit a second bomb. When the helicopter was over the barracks, he pushed the milk churn out and it fell on the buildings below. 'It fell down off the roof into the yard and exploded,' Eddie recalls. 'It shattered a concrete post, but only the inner core of the bomb went off; the outer core didn't.'

Captain Hobday got the helicopter away from the barracks unscathed, and asked: 'Where do you want to go?' He would recall in court that one of them replied: 'The Free State.' That was the extent of their plan: simply to cross the border and escape. The helicopter flew the few hundred metres across the border and landed in Cloughfin, Co. Donegal. There, the bombers hijacked a car from a man named John Patterson, who was driving home. McNulty and Treacy jumped in, leaving Captain Hobday to find his way back to the hotel.

The bombers were elated. They hadn't done any real damage, but they had shown that they could launch a direct attack on one of the most heavily fortified barracks in Europe. They drove quickly and dumped the car at a shopping centre in Letterkenny. Treacy and McNulty stayed at a safe house in the county. Rose and Eddie headed down to Dublin.

It did not take long for the police on both sides of the border to work out that 'Stephanie Grant', the supposed

English journalist, was Rose Dugdale, and that Eddie Gallagher had also been involved. The fingerprints of all four hijackers were found in rooms in McFadden's and in the helicopter. The note passed to Captain Hobday bore Rose's prints, and Hobday had given police a detailed description of Stephanie that was a strong match for Rose.

The RUC quickly issued wanted posters that were pinned up in police stations and distributed to every soldier serving in Northern Ireland. The wanted poster shows a laughing Rose:

Have You Seen This Woman? Bridget Rose Dugdale.
Required for Interview by the Police.
AGE: 32 YEARS. HEIGHT: 5FT 6INS – PROPORTIONATE BUILD – MASCULINE APPEARANCE

FEATURES: HAIR: LONG, FAIR AND STRAIGHT
COMPLEXION: SALLOW EYES: BLUE/GREY
DRESS: USUALLY WEARS SLACKS AND SUEDE
JACKETS OF DIRTY AND UNTIDY APPEARANCE
SPEECH: EDUCATED ACCENT OR SOMETIMES
ADOPTS AN IRISH ACCENT
ALIAS: KNOWN TO HAVE A DRIVING LICENCE
IN THE NAME OF MARGARET LINDA CROWTHER

IF RECOGNIZED SHE SHOULD BE DETAINED
You should telephone any information to Lisburn Military.

A copy of the poster was brought down to Eddie and Rose in the south Dublin suburb of Rathmines, where an IRA supporter had offered them an apartment.

'The poster didn't scare me at all,' Rose says. 'It was expected work.'

Major Richard Earle, 1st Battalion Royal Fusiliers, had watched the helicopter attack from the ground and was dismissive of it, at least officially, to a journalist from BBC1's *Midweek* programme. 'I think the effect generally was good for morale, because it's always satisfactory to see one's enemy making a fool of himself. There was some useful discussion in barracks on this new military weapon – the AGMIC – the air-to-ground milk-churn, and some unfavourable comparison between this attack and others which we've been subjected to the in the past, such as Dunkirk and Tobruk,' he said.

Rose and Eddie started sleeping together after the Strabane attack. I ask Eddie about how their romance developed.

'There was no romance in the relationship between me and Rose Dugdale,' he says. 'You know the way when you are thrown together and there is a shower of hounds chasing you to try and put you in prison and you end up in the one bed. So what are you going to do, like? You can only talk for so long. It's not very romantic, is it?'

On 24 February 1974, more than a month after the helicopter raid, an arrest warrant was issued for Rose by Manchester police, who charged her with conspiring to smuggle arms into Northern Ireland and with arms possession. The charges related to her activities with Wally Heaton before her relocation to Ireland. The front page of the *Irish Times* two days later carried an article headed 'Gardaí Deny Knowledge of Dr Dugdale', with a photograph of the smiling suspect and the caption 'Dr Bridget Rose Dugdale, aged 32, for whom British police have issued a warrant concerning arms charges.'

The paper noted that 'Her description, it is also alleged, may fit that of the girl who assisted three men on the Strabane helicopter raid. That girl, a blonde, told the pilot before the hijacking that her name was Stephanie Grant. She was said to have spoken with an educated English accent and to have given a Leeds address.' The article cited British police as saying that 'Dr Dugdale, educated at Oxford University and a doctor of philosophy, may be living somewhere in Ireland disguised and under an assumed name.'

The article quoted a police spokesman in Exeter: 'She normally wears her brown hair long and straight but she may have purchased a wig or altered the style. She normally speaks with a cultured voice, but she may now be using an Irish accent. She normally wears jumpers and jeans, but she could now be wearing skirts and high heels.'

Rose and Eddie were staying in the flat in Rathmines. Rose cut her hair short and washed out the blonde. She began to wear dresses and blouses again, to blend in with middle-class south Dublin.

Soon afterwards, they began to plot their next mission.

6. The Heist

In January 1974, while Rose and Eddie were launching their raid on Strabane, two sisters were refusing food in Brixton Prison.

Every day, the prison wardens would grab 19-year-old Marian Price and her 22-year-old sister, Dolours, prise open their clenched teeth, put a wedge in their mouths to stop them biting down, then a tube, and pour liquid nutrients through a funnel and into the tube. The Price sisters were the only two female prisoners in the maximum-security prison and they were prepared to die for their demand to be treated as political prisoners.

The previous March, the pair had been part of an IRA team that planted four car bombs in London. Two of the bombs exploded: one in Whitehall and one outside the Old Bailey court building. The latter explosion injured 250 people, and one person died of a heart attack caused by the bombing. Two other members of the IRA bombing team, Hugh Feeney and Gerry Kelly, joined the Price sisters on their hunger strike. By January, according to a lobby group for Irish republican prisoners in the UK, Dolours and Marian Price had each lost two and a half stone.

The Price sisters' father, Albert, was a long-time IRA member who boasted to his daughters of joining the bombing campaign in England in the 1930s. During one of his prison terms, his wife, Chrissie, gave birth to a baby daughter who died before Albert could ever see her. Chrissie, too, came from a deeply committed republican family.

For the newspapers, the Price sisters were great copy – two beautiful young IRA women on hunger strike. For Rose and her fellow feminist republicans, they were a cause célèbre, a vanguard of brave young women taking up a cause that had been dominated by middle-aged Catholic men for far too long. The Prices and the other hunger strikers were a major priority for the IRA leadership, too, but Rose and Eddie remember themselves as having been especially committed to the cause.

Rose recalls: 'I didn't like some of the IRA leadership – the old guard like Dáithí Ó Conaill. I liked the Price sisters very much: they were young and idealistic and they could see the bigger picture about feminism and all these things, so I wanted to help them in any way I could.'

Eddie remembers meeting their father, Albert Price, at an IRA safe house in Dublin in early 1974. 'He just happened to come in the same time that I was there. He was looking for help for his daughters, who were being force-fed for a couple of months by that point. So basically, after that meeting, I decided to start putting pressure on [southern IRA leader] Ruairí Ó Brádaigh to do more than just organize fundraising dances and meetings for the Prices.'

Soon afterwards, a series of curious events began in London.

Late on 23 February 1974, someone used a sledgehammer to smash through a shuttered and barred window at Kenwood House in Hampstead to steal a painting called *The Guitar Player* by the Dutch master Johannes Vermeer, which was then valued at about £2 million. The Greater London

Council, which owned the painting, offered a reward of £10,000 for information on its return.

On the 25th, the painting's frame and fragments of glass were found in a bush about a mile away. A few days after that, a man with an Irish accent phoned Illtyd Harrington, deputy leader of the Greater London Council, offering to return the painting if the four Old Bailey bombers who were on hunger strike were returned to Ireland. Hoping to convince Harrington that he had the painting, the caller mentioned certain features of it that would not have been generally known.

On 6 March, *The Times* received a letter mentioning five details about the painting and the theft that would not have been known to the public, and saying the painting would be burned if the Price sisters were not returned to Ireland. A small piece of the canvas of *The Guitar Player* was attached; the letter described this as a 'piece of picture removed from side of stretcher.' The stretcher, across which the canvas is stretched so that it remains taut, is not visible to the public – it was a way of saying that the sample removed from the painting was marginal and the public would not notice the damage if the painting was returned.

Asked for a response to this development, Albert Price told reporters that Dolours was an art student and would never approve of the destruction of great cultural works. He asked the thieves to return the painting.

On the 17th, the deadline for the destruction of the painting passed without comment from the thieves. The Old Bailey bombers remained in Brixton Prison, where they continued to be force-fed. The following day, as reporters descended on the Price home in West Belfast, Albert Price repeated his plea for the return of the painting. 'My daughters do not want it destroyed or damaged. They are very anxious that it should be returned. They appreciate the effort that is being made on their behalf but do not want anything to happen to the painting.'

Given the timing of his conversation with Albert Price, and in light of subsequent events, it is natural to wonder if Eddie Gallagher had anything to do with the theft of *The Guitar Player*. He denies any hand in the theft or any knowledge of who did it. 'There were all sorts of people helping the republican cause in England at the time,' he says. 'The Price sisters were fading away and emotions were running high.'

When I asked Rose if she had any hand in stealing *The Guitar Player*, she said no. 'And I expect your next question will be who did? I don't know. Did the taking of that painting put Russborough in our minds? Probably.'

Regardless of who was responsible, one obvious conclusion to draw from *The Guitar Player* affair was that stealing valuable art and holding it to ransom was not an effective way of compelling the UK authorities to repatriate the Old Bailey bombers – and even less so if the art was not even in a UK collection. This was not the conclusion that Rose Dugdale and Eddie Gallagher drew, however. Perhaps they felt that the sole flaw in the Kenwood House heist was that only a single painting had been stolen.

In any event, Eddie took a trip alone to the National Gallery of Ireland. As usual, he had a pistol in his backpack. At the museum, there were Vermeers and Murillos and Goyas. He noticed that many of the greatest paintings belonged to one collector: Sir Alfred Beit, who lent them out for months at a time to the museum.

Eddie went home and told Rose about the Beit collection. She had heard of the Beit family. The Ironsides, whom she knew from school, were good friends of the Beits, as was her mother's close friend Eddy Sackville-West.

Eddie and Rose started doing research. For a trip to the National Library, two of the most wanted people in the country wore uncharacteristically formal clothes: Rose was in a dress, Eddie in a shirt and tie. At the library, they consulted books and newspapers and Thom's Directory. *Who's Who* was, as Eddie put it, full of details about people who 'spew out information about themselves'. Rose filled notebooks with information about the Beit family and their art collection. She and Eddie copied photographs of their Irish mansion – a Palladian pile on the Russborough estate in Co. Wicklow. It was regarded as the longest house in Ireland: essentially three grey, hulking mansions with two long colonnades connecting them. At a time when many people in rural Ireland still didn't have a phone, the Beits had an internal phone system so that servants in one wing of the house could call those in the other.

Sir Alfred Beit's father, Otto Beit, was the son of a Jewish family, originally from Hamburg. In 1875, the first Alfred Beit, Sir Alfred's uncle, was sent by a Dutch jewellery company to South Africa to buy diamonds after a strike in the Kimberley mine. Alfred and his partner, Julius Wernher, set up Wernher, Beit & Co., a mining finance company that helped establish a cartel to exploit some of the world's richest diamond and gold deposits. The firm lent money to Cecil Rhodes, founder of De Beers, which dominated the diamond industry, and to Ernest Oppenheimer, who went on to head De Beers after Rhodes's death.

The first Alfred Beit became a close business associate of

Cecil Rhodes, later the prime minister of the Cape Colony in South Africa. Wernher, Beit & Co. lobbied successfully for the passage of punitive laws aimed at the black majority, including a 'hut tax', which taxed any dwelling inhabited by an adult male, forcing men to work in the mines and send money home. The work was dangerous and badly paid.

The Randlords, as the white oligarchs of South Africa were known, also perfected a labour camp system in which miners had to live in company accommodation and were forbidden to change employers. Anyone suspected of stealing diamonds or gold by swallowing them was given a dose of laxatives and their faeces were checked for treasure.

Soon vast fortunes were made for the Beits, the Oppenheimers and other families in the mining industry. They craved European sophistication and competed with each other to buy Old Master paintings, pushing up prices internationally. By the time he died in 1906, the first Alfred Beit was one of the richest men in the world. He passed his fortune, and his art collection, to his brother Otto, who passed it on to his son, Alfred Lane Beit. The younger Alfred was elected a Conservative MP for St Pancras South East at the 1931 general election and was re-elected in 1935. During the Second World War he served in the Royal Air Force Bomber Command, before losing his seat in the Labour landslide of 1945.

Alfred Lane Beit and his wife moved to Ireland in the 1950s to buy the vast Russborough estate. For servants in Russborough House, life revolved around the every need of Sir Alfred and Lady Beit.

'I can only describe it as a very, very luxurious hotel for two people,' says Gerry Pollard, whose father, John Noel, and uncle, Tom, were butlers in the house. The entire Pollard family lived in an apartment in Russborough but were never allowed to mix with the Beits. 'I remember being in the table tennis room, which was directly beneath the music room. Sir Alfred started to play the piano above me. It was extraordinary – the first time I ever really felt humanity in him, a connection with us.'

After dinner, the Pollards would come in to clean up. 'It was the richest smell I have experienced in my life. Imagine Cuban cigars and Brazilian mahogany and Chanel perfume all mixing in the air with French wine,' says Gerry. 'There was just this aroma of wealth that we didn't share in the servants' quarters.'

The staff and their children had fun among themselves and could relax when the Beits went to South Africa for the winter. But even then, it was like living in one of the world's great art museums.

Gerry recalls a visit to the Prado in Madrid years later, where he 'saw their collection of Murillo paintings. They had these three sketches on the wall of *The Return of the Prodigal Son*. Well, the actual painting itself was hanging in the dining room of Russborough House, along with [Beit's] other Murillos.'

The Beits became increasingly vocal critics of South Africa's apartheid system but wintered there in comfort and continued to profit from the labour of poorly treated black workers. As British establishment figures living in a great mansion in Ireland, they were an attractive target for Irish republicans. For Rose, with her background in international economics, the Beits were also exploiters of black Africans.

Rose and Eddie were forming a plan: break into Russborough House, steal paintings that were worth the equivalent of over €100 million today and threaten to destroy them unless four IRA bombers who had been captured in London – Gerry Kelly, Hugh Feeney and the sisters Dolours and Marian Price – were transferred from England to a prison in Northern Ireland. They would also ask for political status for the four, who had been on hunger strike demanding they be treated as prisoners of war. The Price sisters were being force-fed, which was leading to fights and scuffles with prison staff. And, if they were to take the Beit paintings, it would have to be soon: before the hunger strike and force-feeding left the Prices with permanent health damage.

Eddie did not disclose his plans to Albert Price. But he believed that an art heist could bring about the release of the prisoners 'if there was the threat of those paintings being burnt. We could see that Sir Alfred Beit was a very influential man in many ways. He had ties going back into the very top echelons of British society and of the Tory Party.'

Every winter, when the Beits were in South Africa, their paintings were lent to the Irish National Gallery. And when the Beits returned to Russborough House, the collection would be returned to the house as well. With the Beits still in South Africa in the early months of 1974, Eddie sent word to IRA friends that he needed two young recruits to help with a major operation to help the Price sisters. As with the Strabane operation, Eddie felt no need to consult the IRA leadership: they could read about it in the newspapers.

He received two recruits, whom I'll call Padraig and Pius. Padraig was from Clare, and at the time he was preparing to move to England to join the London bombing campaign. Pius was an IRA man from west Waterford. The group drove to Wicklow several times to check out the security at Russborough House and concluded that there was not very much.

Rose continued to keep an eye on the National Gallery. When the Beit exhibition closed for the season, she knew the

Beits were back in Wicklow and they would soon be reunited with their paintings.

Shortly after 9.15 p.m. on 26 April 1974, a stolen grey Ford Cortina station wagon pulled up under a line of beech trees on the Russborough estate. Rose Dugdale, masquerading as a French tourist, got out of the car, walked to the servants' entrance and knocked on the door.

The three men got out of the car behind her. Padraig and Pius were armed with AK-47 assault rifles; Eddie carried a handgun. They were also equipped with women's nylons, electrical tape, knives and screwdrivers.

Alfred and Lady Beit were listening to classical records on a gramophone in the library upstairs. Downstairs, servant James Horrigan went to answer the door. Beside him was Gerry Pollard's 14-year-old brother, Patrick.

When Horrigan opened the door, he saw a woman in jeans and a green military jumper. The woman spoke French, saying that her *voiture* was *en panne*. As she spoke, she pointed to the station wagon. Pollard looked out of the door at the car. Three masked men rushed in and grabbed both James and Patrick. Horrigan could feel an assault rifle being pushed into his face.

'Lead us to them!' Eddie shouted.

'To who?' asked Horrigan.

'The Beits!'

Rose pulled a handgun from her jeans. The masked men pushed the two servants upstairs. In the library, Alfred could hear a commotion and stood up. 'I was playing the gramophone when the door burst open and there were four people brandishing weapons and one male voice shouted: "Get down, get down,"' he later told reporters. 'They made us lie down with our faces looking to the floor. When I looked up at one of them, I got a knock on the head with the butt of a gun.'

Rose denies being the one who hit Sir Alfred but confirms 'he did get a clattering' and insists: 'They deserved it, every bit of it.'

The group moved quickly to rip out the panic alarm on the wall that was linked to the local garda station. They believed, wrongly, that the paintings were alarmed, and searched for a security system to shut off.

Rose shouted, 'Capitalist pigs!' at Sir Alfred and Lady Beit, who lay on the ground under the first painting to be stolen – Goya's *Portrait of Doña Antonia Zárate*.

While Eddie kept the Beits in the library, Rose and the two other IRA men ordered Patrick Pollard to take them to the servants' quarters: the plan was to prevent the servants from raising the alarm. There they found Patrick's 16-year-old sister, Anne, and their father, John Noel. A 17-year-old maid, Mary Flood, from nearby Dunlavin, was having a bath. Patrick told her to come out: there was a man with a gun.

Gerry Pollard recalls: 'She thought he was joking. There was quite a bit of joking among staff and their families. So she didn't get out of the bath.'

One of the two men kicked at the door and told her to get dressed quickly or she'd be shot. She put on a bathrobe and opened the door. She was led at gunpoint to the library.

Gerry Pollard recalls that his father was one of the last to be led into the library and 'came in and saw James Horrigan lying on the ground. The painting above him was missing and my father thought that the painting must have fallen on James's head and knocked him out.' Then he saw that everyone was lying on the ground, including his family members.

One of the men grabbed Lady Beit and took her out of the room and down the stairs. He showed her a knife and said that her husband would be killed unless she cooperated. She later recalled turning around to look back at Sir Alfred, thinking it would be the last time she would see him alive.

Downstairs, she was told to show the raiders where they kept their money. She said they had no money in the house. The raiders tied her hands and feet with nylons and left her there.

When Sir Alfred asked Eddie if they were members of a particular political group, Eddie told him to shut up.

Rose began selecting paintings for the men to take off the wall of the library. She was still using her fake French accent. '*Oui, oui*, we take zis one,' she said. Padraig and Pius used screwdrivers to prise open the frames and, where needed, knives to free the paintings. From the floor, Sir Alfred could see that the woman had a good eye for art. 'She clearly knew what she was about,' he said later.

One of the men grabbed Patrick Pollard and led him to Rose so that he could show her where the paintings were hanging throughout the house.

Patrick took her through the long hallways, Rose walking beside him, directing Padraig and Pius in her faux French accent. 'Zis one, and zis one. *Non!* Not zat one.' They went from room to room. The men took some of the smaller paintings, known as caprices, with their frames intact.

Rose took a total of nineteen paintings. She knew eleven of them from their wintertime loan to the National Gallery and she had read about the other eight. They included *Portrait of a Woman in a Black Dress* by Goya; *Kitchen Maid with the Supper at Emmaus* by Velázquez; and, the most famous and valuable of them all, *Lady Writing a Letter with Her Maid* by

Vermeer. There was also *A Lady with a Lace Collar* by the Dutch artist Paulus Moreelse; two paintings by the Dutch painter Gabriel Metsu, one of a man writing a letter and one of a woman reading it; *The Lute Player* by Frans Hals; and three works by Rubens.

In addition, there were also two Gainsborough paintings – a portrait of an Italian ballerina, Madame Baccelli, and a small landscape – and four paintings by the Venetian artist Francesco Guardi: two views of St Mark's Square in Venice and two very small caprices, of just five by six inches, which were taken in their frames. The raiders also took *The Calm Sea with Boats* by Willem van de Velde; a small picture by the English Victorian artist Edwin Landseer of a swan in a pond; and a Jacob van Ruisdael, *The Cornfield*.

None of the valuable Murillos were taken – Rose felt they were too large and difficult to manage.

In the hallway, the raiders gathered the paintings together in groups and stuck them together with tape at the edges. Once the gang had the stolen canvases organized, they brought all the people in the library to different rooms, tied them up with tights and told them not to struggle.

They grabbed a pair of field glasses and some clocks, and kept James Horrigan's spectacles, in order to hinder him in case he broke free and ran from the house to raise the alarm.

They made a final check that Sir Alfred was tied tightly and then fled the house.

After a few minutes, when he was sure the thieves had gone, Sir Alfred called out to the other rooms. He could hear some of the staff shouting back. Everyone struggled to get free. After half an hour, James Horrigan managed to pull himself out of his binds and freed Sir Alfred before going from room to room to untie everyone else.

For a while there was a fear that the gang had kidnapped Lady Beit, but she was eventually located downstairs, tied up and lying on the ground.

It was past 10 p.m. before Sir Alfred called the gardaí. By then, the raiders were long out of Wicklow and heading west.

Eddie was driving. He knew not to go too fast: he didn't want to attract attention. Beside him was Rose, looking out for checkpoints, and in the back, Padraig and Pious, holding their assault rifles, delighted that it had gone so well. Behind them, in the spacious back of the station wagon, were nineteen canvases carefully selected from one of the world's great private art collections.

They spent the night in a safe house. On Saturday, in the Tipperary countryside not far from Cashel, they drove the Cortina station wagon into a field hidden from the road by a hedge. They took the paintings out of the boot and fled in another stolen car, this time heading for Glandore in West Cork, where Rose had booked a cottage under the name Ms Merrimée. She gave an address on a non-existent London street when making the booking with a local farmer, Con Hayes. The cottage was 40 yards back from sea cliffs, where gulls and petrels whirled in the breeze.

By this time, the theft had attracted enormous international attention. Gardaí all over Ireland were instructed to look out for a French woman in her thirties, the leader of a gang of international art thieves. Chief Superintendent James Murphy, who led the investigation, was asked by journalists if he thought the woman was Rose Dugdale. He firmly said he did not believe it was.

The *Irish Times* reported: 'A theory that the civil rights leader, Dr Bridget Rose Dugdale, wanted for questioning by the RUC in connection with the attempted helicopter bombing of a Strabane police station, was involved, was discounted yesterday when gardaí showed pictures of Dr Dugdale to the staff at Russborough House, who had seen the mystery woman, who spoke with a French accent.

They said positively that the female gang leader, who pointed out the pictures which were to be taken, was not Dr Dugdale.'

Although her disguise had worked on the staff at Russborough, Rose's decision to retain her French persona for the booking in West Cork was, she concedes in retrospect, a 'mistake'.

In Tipperary, a farmer named John Ryan saw the Cortina in his field. When gardaí arrived, they found shards of painting frames on the floor of the car. They also found a driver's licence for a Vanessa Kelly of Martello Est., Portmarnock, Dublin; and when they traced the original application for the licence, Rose Dugdale's fingerprints were on it. Later, John Ryan's family discovered sheet music belonging to Sir Alfred Beit in the field.

When the gang arrived at the cottage in West Cork, they carried some of the canvases into the house, leaving some in the car. Rose and Eddie stayed in the cottage, while Padraig and Pious stole another car and drove to a safe house in Mayo.

The next morning, Rose and Eddie checked the radio: their heist was the first item on the news. It was also the lead story in the *Irish Times*, which had held back its first edition to cover the theft.

At Russborough, Sir Alfred and the gardaí were arranging a press conference. Dozens of journalists showed up. For some, the trip to Russborough was an exciting day out of newsrooms in Dublin and London. A reporter noted:

'Television crews and pressmen gathered by the score in front of the house, admiring the splendid views of the lakes and mountains . . .'

At 11.30 a.m., the journalists rang the doorbell. Sir Alfred, the *Irish Times* noted, inspected press cards as reporters came into his house. The only visible sign of the attack was a small plaster on the back of his head, where he had been hit with the revolver butt.

The press conference was held in the main reception area, just inside the door.

Sir Alfred began with a prepared statement.

He referred to the 'fairly fancy valuations' of the stolen paintings that had been published in the press but declined to offer his own valuations. He said that he had not seen the face of the female raider, as he was facing down when she came into the library.

'The woman – who, I must say, was the leader of the whole operation and who knew what she was about – pointed to the pictures in the different rooms which they were to grab,' he said. 'I am sure the woman is associated with an international art gang and the men were purely hired thugs.'

Asked about the possibility that the gang were from a paramilitary group, he replied: 'I haven't the faintest idea who these men were, and whether they represented any organization, or what. I asked them and they didn't answer. All I can tell you is that they made violent and insulting anti-capitalist remarks.' As an example, he said his family had been called 'exploiters of the workers of the world'.

Asked what they looked like, he said that he would only recognize two. One he described as 'short and stubby, dark and with a little moustache and sideburns': this was Eddie Gallagher. The other was 'even shorter and was blond'.

Sir Alfred then introduced 14-year-old Patrick Pollard, who told the journalists that one of the robbers 'had a gun and he grabbed me by the scruff of the neck', and went on to describe how he was forced to bring the French woman around the house while she picked out paintings.

The journalists went off to write their stories, some of them phoned in from pubs in nearby villages. The heist made the front page of all the newspapers in Ireland and the UK the next day, and it was picked up as a major news story around the world.

The *Irish Times* felt it was probable the thieves were left-wing revolutionaries, and observed: 'It is more likely that the horrible happening will have a happy ending if the thieves are ordinary criminals than if a group with pretentions to some selective higher purpose wish to use them as counters in some sociological or political game or are impelled by ideological motives such as caused puritans to wreak artistic havoc in Cromwell's England.'

Having consulted with scholars and art dealers, the *Irish Times* declared on 29 April, three days after the robbery, that the art theft was 'the largest on record in the world'.

At the cottage in West Cork, things became tense between Rose and Eddie as the days passed. There was no real plan. They only had a slow, stolen car for escape.

They had lined up the paintings in the kitchen and put three upstairs. Rose was particularly careful with the Vermeer, her favourite.

On 3 May, a week after the heist, Rose wrote out a note demanding the transfer of the four IRA bombers from England to a prison 'in Ireland'. Once that was done, five of the paintings would be returned. The remaining fourteen would be returned upon receipt of £500,000. If the demand was not met by 14 May, the paintings would be burned.

In Russborough House, Rose had ripped pages from Sir Alfred Beit's appointments diary. Now she put the ransom demand in an envelope with a page from the diary, as proof that the letter was authentic, and gave it to Eddie. Leaving the cottage to arrange for the transfer of the paintings to somewhere more secure, he sent the ransom note to an IRA courier in Belfast, who then posted it to James White, director of the National Gallery in Dublin.

Eddie says that Rose was adamant about burning the paintings if their demands weren't met, but that he was against it. A woman who went to finishing school in Paris, who was taken to the Louvre and the Rodin Museum to appreciate the great European artists, who had marvelled at Margot Fonteyn as a child, was now in an isolated cottage in Cork, prepared to pour petrol over some of the world's great artworks and watch them burn.

Asked about whether she really would have destroyed the paintings, Rose speaks not of the role they might have played in achieving the IRA's aims but of 'the beatings in South Africa, men forced out of their villages to go and work for the Beits in the dangerous mines. Is a painting worth their lives?' She says she isn't sure what she'd have done if the situation had arisen, but that she would not have burned 'the whole lot'.

Albert Price spoke to the newspapers and begged the thieves not to destroy the paintings. While he appreciated the effort they had made on his daughters' behalf, it would be a 'sin' to destroy something so beautiful. He asked them to return the paintings, so that the public could enjoy them every summer when the Beits were in South Africa.

After Eddie left, Rose was alone in the cottage with nineteen paintings that could, along with the charges she was already facing, get her put away for life.

Eddie phoned her to report that he had arranged to transport the paintings by sea. Rose's task was to bring them to Baltimore harbour. (Where they intended to send the paintings, neither Eddie nor Rose is willing to say.)

Rose, not wanting to risk having the ailing getaway car break down completely with stolen paintings on board, brought it to a local garage to be fixed. The mechanic was struck by how upset she was – she was still speaking in a French accent – when told it would take several days to make the repairs.

Having already borrowed a Morris Minor belonging to Con Hayes, the farmer from whom she had rented the cottage, she now borrowed it again for the purpose of bringing the paintings to Baltimore harbour.

The gardaí believed that the thieves were likely still in Ireland, and officers searched every guest house and bed and breakfast in the countryside. Sergeant Pat O'Leary and Garda Willie Creedon had been asking around the Glandore area, and Con Hayes told them about the French woman renting his cottage. On Saturday, 4 May 1974. Sergeant O'Leary knocked on the cottage door. Rose opened it, speaking French and broken English. (Years later, she would tell the TG4 documentary that she answered the door wearing 'my little wig, and I tried to speak French to let on that I was a foreign tourist. But ... apparently it didn't convince them.') The gardaí tried to look in the cottage, but Rose stepped outside and kept the door tight against her as she spoke.

Sergeant O'Leary told her they were just making routine

inquiries and asked if she had been renting for long. 'She wasn't surprised to see me,' O'Leary later told the American author Matthew Hart. 'I just asked her if she'd rented the house long. She answered in very broken English, saying no, she'd just taken it for a holiday. I remember standing in the yard and looking at her and thinking it might be her. Your sixth sense will tell you that.'

Sergeant O'Leary thanked her and went back to the garda station and told his superior that a French woman had rented a cottage two days before the Russborough heist and arrived there shortly after it. She was on edge and had been sure to close the door behind her as she spoke. He hadn't been convinced by her French accent either.

Sergeant O'Leary kept watch on the house for hours in an unmarked car, with additional officers in cars further down the road, ready to set up a roadblock.

At some point, Eddie phoned Rose, telling her to bring the paintings to Baltimore harbour. She should keep a few behind, in case those she transferred were captured. She loaded up sixteen of the paintings into the Morris Minor and hid the other three in the cottage. She drove out the driveway, right past the gardaí, who kept their heads down as she went by. They called in support from a public phone box. Soon gardaí were scrambling from Skibbereen, Bandon and Clonakilty.

Rose waited by Baltimore harbour. Gardaí could see her smoking a cigarette and looking out to sea. She waited an hour. No boat or car arrived. With today's equivalent of more than €100 million worth of artwork in the back of a beat-up old car, she drove back to the cottage.

The gardaí, having observed her peculiar trip to the harbour, were now convinced that she was the person they were looking for. With Con Hayes's permission, they entered the cottage and found pages from Sir Alfred Beit's diary. They also found three of the Beits' brass clocks.

Just before six o'clock, Rose returned to the cottage. As she did so, waiting gardaí ran from the side of the house. Two garda cars raced up the driveway and blocked her from escaping. One garda ran at the Morris Minor, pulled back a cover in the back seat and found the paintings.

Rose recalls that she did not put up any resistance. 'I didn't see the point. It was clear that it was over at that point.'

They led her into the house and searched it while she sat at the kitchen table. They found the other three paintings upstairs, and Rose was arrested.

They also found her ID. 'Are you Bridget Rose Dugdale?' asked Sergeant O'Leary. She refused to answer.

'Hello, Rose,' said one of the gardaí. Again, she refused to answer.

Further searching of the cottage turned up a carriage clock and binoculars from Russborough House. And, in the fireplace, they found the burnt remains of a pair of spectacles. The idea of burning them had been to melt the metal and destroy the serial number, but enough remained to identify them as James Horrigan's glasses.

The gardaí took Rose to the local station. As she waited in a cell, the paintings were unveiled to press photographers. Superintendent Tom Barrett, Sergeant Patrick O'Leary, Detective Garda Jerry O'Sullivan and Garda William Creedon lined up with *The Lute Player* by Frans Hals and Goya's *Portrait of Doña Antonia Zárate*, under which Sir Alfred had proposed to his wife.

Rose was kept in the cell for the night. 'It was a rather grim little place, if I recall,' says Rose. 'There was a tiny little bed, and I was told that I wouldn't have to wait long until they would take me to prison.'

The next morning, she was transferred under heavy escort to Dublin for questioning. Her arrest was now the main news story in Ireland, and the debutante revolutionary was on front pages in the US, Australia, the UK and in many other countries in Europe.

Dáithí Ó Conaill was quick to distance the movement from her and from the heist. 'Well, Dr Dugdale was not a member of the republican movement,' he told the BBC's *Midweek* programme. 'She was known to personnel in the movement . . . From what one knows she was a very dedicated person, one with deep convictions.' Asked where Rose fitted within the republican movement, he replied: 'Well, she was on the fringe.'

According to a member of Rose's family, her parents were 'inconsolable' that their daughter was under arrest and seemingly had been conspiring with the IRA. Between this and outstanding weapons charges in Britain, she would get a long sentence.

On 6 May 1974, two days after Rose was caught, and a day after news of her arrest appeared in newspapers in the UK, *The Guitar Player* was found in the graveyard of St Bartholomew's Church in London, following an anonymous tip-off to the police. It was wrapped in that day's copy of the *Evening News*, secured around the painting with string.

A police spokesperson said that there was nothing to indicate any connection with the Beit robbery.

7. The Most Guarded Woman
in Europe

On Monday, 6 May 1974, Rose was taken to the Special Criminal Court for arraignment. By then, hundreds of IRA members had appeared before the anti-terrorist court, but few made more than a paragraph in the newspapers. Dr Dugdale was the only one who made the front page of all the Irish newspapers, and the spectacular eccentricity of her case brought a cascade of headlines around the world.

Rose was determined – as the Baader–Meinhof group in Germany and the Chicago Seven in the US had been, and she herself in Exeter the previous October – to put the establishment on trial. Under Irish law, TV and radio stations were banned from broadcasting quotes from members of the IRA or its political wing, Sinn Féin. But court reporting was exempt from the restrictions – an exemption that Rose was determined to use to get publicity for the IRA around the world.

When she arrived at the Special Criminal Court on Dublin's Green Street, there were soldiers on the roof and on the street, a sight not typical for the court. There was a police motorcycle escort, two police vans and an army jeep containing troops holding Gustav sub-machine guns. Journalists were asked to leave the court while the army and police did a security sweep, something they hadn't seen before.

Rose was brought in, dressed in an open-necked blouse, mauve cardigan and wine-coloured slacks under a green brass-buttoned duffel coat. She was flanked by two gardaí and two prison guards. The court clerk asked her if she was Bridget Rose Dugdale. She put her head down and didn't reply.

Asked by Judge Conroy if she was applying for bail, she gave no answer.

The arraignment was over. As she was about to be led from the court, she saw her chance. 'There are still four hunger strikers in prison in England. The British still are in occupation of a small part of Ireland, but not for very long!'

The media loved it: 'The British'. If she had been from West Belfast, this would be as expected. From a Chelsea debutante, it inspired all kinds of pop psychology. Dozens of people wrote to the Dugdale family offering advice and support.

One letter was from a man named Thomas Khaw, who wrote to Rose's father from Kepala Batas, Malaysia, two days after Rose's court appearance. It was headed: 'Programme to Help Your Daughter'.

Dear Sir,

Your agony is my suffering. I pray that all will end well. I wish to lend a helping hand if you will co-operate. I feel strongly that your daughter needs something more than parental love and money. Perhaps I am not presumptuous if I suggest that you permit me to marry your daughter. This is because she requires a poor, handsome, loving, strong, diligent and intelligent husband, besides I do not smoke, drink, gamble or womanise. I am a pious Buddhist who believes in good deeds.

Referring to Wally Heaton, who had been mentioned in international reports about the revolutionary debutante, Mr Khaw wrote:

If she stays in Britain, she will be influenced by crooks and thieves.
Further, by living with a convict and sharing with outlaws, she will
end up in disaster, both for herself and her family. Though I am a
virgin and very much younger than her, I shall make the sacrifice if
you think I can save her from her present, tragic life. I am prepared
to forget her past and her seniority of over seven years my age.

On 20 May *Newsweek* magazine featured a lengthy article about Rose, headlined 'The Reluctant Debutante', which included several photos: Rose's Mount Holyoke cowgirl picture, her wanted poster and a photo of her with Wally Heaton. Like many articles of the time, it included speculative claims about her yearly allowance:

> She was one of those upper-class British girls who seemed to have all the advantages – indulgent parents, the best schools and a handsome $200,000 annual allowance of her own. But like so many other young people who came of age in the 1960s, Bridget Rose Dugdale said good-bye to all that. Never really pretty to begin with, she affected rough clothes and rougher language and sought her own identity in radical causes.

For the moment, she was held in Mountjoy jail in Dublin, but the government wanted her in a cell, by herself, in Limerick prison – one of the most dilapidated in the country. Its accommodation block for female officers, a two-storey house, was at that time unused. It could be converted into a one-woman female prison for Rose.

According to Philip Bray, one of the prison officers in Limerick at the time, the house 'had bedrooms upstairs and a small recreation room, and there was a tennis court put in solely for Rose'. Over the next several weeks, the army and police built turrets all around the prison yard so that armed soldiers could keep an eye on her. Bray, a large, looming man with a wide moustache, recalls that the prison also erected wires 'to stop helicopters' and that the guards had a machine gun 'to take down light aircraft'.

Before her transfer to Limerick, Rose had another appearance at the Special Criminal Court on Friday, 17 May.

'I came prepared,' she recalls. 'I knew that this would be the only way to get around the law and get my message out.' Wearing a long coat and jeans, she told Justice Finlay that she stood in 'absolute condemnation' of the Irish government, which clung to its territorial claim on Northern Ireland but refused to join the fight. The Irish government was, she said, 'trading on the victories of our armies in the North'.

Justice Finlay turned to her and dryly said that the court was sitting only to fix a trial date.

But Rose continued: she spoke about the IRA hunger strikers whose transfer to Northern Ireland she had hoped to secure via the stolen paintings. 'I propose to go on a hunger strike until the demands of these people are met, and I will be in a pretty weak state when the trial comes up,' she shouted. She left the dock with the cry: 'Up the Provos, the people's army.'

As she left in a prison van under police and army escort, she gave a big smile and a clenched-fist salute to waiting photographers. It became one of the defining images of her.

She was taken at speed to her cell in Mountjoy prison. Shortly before lunchtime, an army helicopter landed at the prison and took off with her and her prison officer and army escorts. Just over an hour later, the helicopter landed at Sarsfield army barracks in Limerick. Rose was transferred to a black garda van and taken across the city to the prison on

Musgrave Street. Behind the van was a military jeep with six soldiers inside and a garda car following. The whole operation was so secretive that most soldiers and gardaí in the city weren't aware it was going on, and an *Irish Times* reporter noted a puzzled traffic garda watching the procession go by.

Upon arrival at the prison, Rose was taken to her newly fitted-out compound. She unpacked her clothes and her books and looked out of her small, barred window at the high, grey wall and the turreted army posts outside. Later that day, she was taken for her first walk around the mesh-covered exercise yard, soldiers watching on all four sides – and so began what she describes as 'a pretty ghastly existence'.

Philip Bray, assigned to Rose's yard, would stand there, watching her walking during her exercise breaks. 'We were out there in hail, rain and snow and no sentry box, and that's how it worked, pissing rain or sun, watching Rose go around and around. It could be ferociously hot in the summer. It was very uncomfortable to stand there in uniform, but we didn't mind. We were getting two men's wages, three sometimes.'

Prison officers quickly discovered that working the Rose Dugdale compound was an easy ticket to good pay: there was extra money on terrorist wings and they had only one prisoner to guard.

'Three of them bought sites beside each other in the east Limerick village of Cappamore,' says Philip Bray. 'A local postman jokingly called it Dugdale Avenue because the three prison officers had the money to buy them one after the other. God forgive me, but crime pays. It certainly paid for me.'

Rose spent her time reading books and writing to her family and to Peter Ady: chipper letters in which she reassured them that she was fine, and that she was doing what she wanted to do.

She read revolutionary books from Cuba and South America, and reread *War and Peace*, underlining passage after passage, particularly those in which Tolstoy muses on the nature of humanity.

Philip Bray says that 'occasionally they brought down female prisoners from Dublin, ones that were well behaved and hadn't got long to serve in their sentence'. Some of these prisoners, mostly petty criminals, were thrilled to discover their new home had a tennis court. 'Occasionally, the wilder Dublin women would come out and hit the ball around three or four times, but they had never done it before so they didn't keep it up for long.'

At the end of May, newspapers reported that Rose had taken only tea, coffee and water for two weeks and was refusing meals. That was only partly true. She did skip meals, she says, but 'Some meals I ate and told them I had flushed it down the toilet.'

A proper hunger strike was no longer feasible, for a reason nobody could know about. Rose phoned her solicitor, Myles Shevlin, and said she urgently needed to see him. Shevlin was a republican who had a young family with his wife, Nora, in Chapelizod, a pretty village on the River Liffey, just west of Dublin city centre. He drove down from Dublin a few days later.

In the privacy of a solicitor's consultation room, Rose handed him a urine sample. She hadn't had a period for months and suspected she was pregnant.

Shevlin was startled. Was she sure? No. Reduced food and the stress of capture and prison might explain the absence of periods.

Shevlin put the sample in his briefcase. A week later he wrote to her. Knowing that prison officers read all mail, he framed the news very carefully. 'The answer to your question is yes,' he wrote.

Rose Dugdale was pregnant. Shevlin smuggled out a tiny, crumpled message from Rose and delivered it to Eddie, who recalls that he was 'very surprised' at the news. 'I wrote back to Rose to tell her that she must not tell anyone. If I couldn't get her sprung out of prison by the time she was ready to deliver, then we would get her and the baby out of Limerick hospital after she gave birth. As far as I was concerned, they were coming out and that was that.'

Following the death of Michael Gaughan, an IRA hunger striker being held in a prison on the Isle of Wight, on 3 June, the UK Home Secretary announced that Dolours and Marian Price, Hugh Feeney and Gerry Kelly, all of whom were in a dire condition themselves, would be transferred to prisons in Northern Ireland, as they had long demanded. Rose now formally called off her own 'hunger strike'.

Security in Rose's compound continued to be strengthened as the weeks passed. Armour-plated glass pillboxes were set up around the perimeter of the prison with telephone lines to Garda headquarters in Dublin. A new security box for army and gardaí was also set up at the prison's front entrance. On 7 June, Irish aviation authorities sent out a teleprint to airlines all over the world announcing that the minimum height that aircraft could fly within a 2-mile radius of Limerick city had increased from 1,000 to 2,000 feet.

'Although no official explanation was given, it is generally accepted among airline people that this is a safety precaution to prevent private aircraft coming in low over Limerick prison, where Dr Rose Dugdale [is being held],' the *Irish Times* reported. It is understood that there is provision for any aircraft breaking the regulation, including firing warning shots.'

Given the prison's aerial defences, Eddie says, 'It was obvious that a helicopter wouldn't work – it would have to be underground.' He went down to Limerick to speak to local IRA members about a prison break for Rose. In a few days they came back with startling news: there was already a tunnel that had been used to spring IRA prisoners from the prison in the 1940s.

Eddie: 'Local IRA knowledge told me about this tunnel that went back to the 1930s or 1940s. It was built from within the prison and the information was reliable.' Eddie began to devise a plan to reopen the tunnel, get Rose out and bring her to a safe house where she could spend the rest of her pregnancy and where a young child could be safely raised.

At the time, he was staying at the home of Betty and John O'Neill in Navan, Co. Meath, a busy IRA safe house. Betty, a soft-spoken seamstress, came from a strongly republican family. Her grandfather Jack Mulligan had fled to America with two of his brothers while volunteering for the IRA in the 1920s. He had since come back and was now living with her. He carried with him republican stories of daring and honour.

In the 1970s, as the Troubles worsened, the O'Neill house was frequently raided by gardaí looking for IRA members. Jack Mulligan would try to delay the gardaí by shouting at them. 'He would give them hell,' Betty O'Neill recalls. 'He would shout: "Let me at them bowsies! I am an American citizen and you are invading the home of an American citizen! Get out of my granddaughter's house!"'

Her home had become a makeshift hospital for injured IRA members. She learned how to treat burns, explosives injuries and bullet wounds. During garda raids, IRA members were spirited out through her parents' house on the other side of the garden.

Betty's network of watchers included a nurse named Mrs Doyle, who lived down the street and was a sister of Frank Stagg, who died on hunger strike in England in 1976. 'Mrs Doyle would call me and say: "The gardaí are on the prowl, I don't know if they will come to me first, but be ready." '

Eddie's scheme to spring Rose from Limerick prison was thwarted, he says, after an IRA informant in Limerick called to the Henry Street garda station. He had been in a bar, and one of his comrades had revealed that Rose Dugdale would not be long in prison: they were working on a tunnel that had been lying idle for decades.

The gardaí were incredulous, as was the prison governor. They checked, and found the old tunnel. Within twenty-four hours, they had filled it in. (Philip Bray, for his part, knew about that tunnel because his own uncle had 'escaped through it in the 1940s'.)

Eddie blames himself for the failure of the tunnel operation. 'I shouldn't have just trusted the Limerick IRA with it. Some fella blabbing his mouth off in a pub and it was discovered just when we were getting the men in to do the digging and reopen it. That was probably the only prospect of a tunnel we had, given the security at the prison.'

For Rose's court appearance on 19 June, two army jeeps followed the garda van that carried the prisoner. Further charges on the Strabane helicopter bombing were added, including unlawfully seizing control of an aircraft and armed hijacking of the getaway car.

*

Rose's trial for the Russborough heist began on 24 June. She was brought up to Mountjoy prison the night before under military escort.

In court, she was wearing a blue suede jacket over a white blouse. She was in a good mood and, she recalls, 'eager to get a few words in again'. When asked to answer the charges, she pulled out a piece of paper and addressed the three judges. 'We have the right to take up arms in reclaiming the wealth of Ireland to her own. For where was the right of the court to deprive them of their freedom to fight for Ireland? The Republic owed its very existence to the fact that others had fought and died for this principle.'

With a wave at the public gallery, she was taken away by the police and army and back to her holding cell in Dublin's Mountjoy prison. The print media were free to report her comments and a dozen reporters wrote articles about her first day on trial.

The state broadcaster, RTÉ, was under pressure from the government not to allow Rose Dugdale to turn the trial into a propaganda coup. At RTÉ headquarters, there was a stand-up shouting match between the security correspondent, Tom McCaughren, and the news editor, Rory O'Connor.

McCaughren insisted that Rose's comments were court speech and therefore exempt from Section 29 of the Broadcasting Act, which banned the broadcast of interviews or spoken statements by IRA members and their supporters. McCaughren and other reporters called in the National Union of Journalists, and they threatened a mass boycott and walkout unless RTÉ changed its policy. That evening, the union tried another, novel form of protest: journalists completely refused to mention the trial on RTÉ TV or radio. They intended to continue this approach unless RTÉ allowed

Rose's comments to be broadcast. An emergency meeting between RTÉ and the NUJ failed to resolve the impasse. The NUJ said that it had instructed RTÉ journalists to stop all court reporting completely and not to handle any document or report about any court case anywhere in the country until the Dugdale crisis was resolved.

The next day, the court was due to hear the first full day of evidence, in the absence of reporters from the national broadcaster. That morning in court, Rose told her solicitor, Myles Shevlin, that she was going to change her plea to guilty on a charge of possession of the Russborough paintings.

'I am proudly and incorruptibly guilty,' she told the court, to claps from her republican supporters in the public gallery. She was, she said, 'the perpetrator of a calm political act to change the corporate conscience of a Cabinet.

'There will be, and there could be, no trial today. There is no court of justice that I can see, and there is no crime that I can apprehend, for where is the right of this court, your right to put us on trial, to intern us and deprive us of the freedom of the Irish people? You have no such right!' she shouted.

On Russborough and the Beits, she charged: 'I hold that the whole people of Ireland have and are solely entitled to the wealth of this land which they laboured to produce. The wealth of this land may not be appropriated from them. It neither belongs to the Englishman or his Orangeman Carsonite lackey, nor his Green Tory lapdog in Dublin.'

She asked to address the court on her reasons for pleading guilty. Justice O'Keeffe told her that she would have an opportunity at a later date. When the prosecuting barrister, Noel MacDonald, started to outline how a group of men and one woman had broken into Russborough House and stolen the paintings, Rose repeatedly interrupted him, asking over and over for the chance to explain why she was pleading guilty.

Garda Chief Superintendent Anthony MacMahon told the court that Rose Dugdale was born on 25 March 1941 at Axminster in Devon, 'one of five children of a very wealthy family'. Rose interrupted, asking what right he had to use evidence obtained outside the court's jurisdiction. 'Anything that occurs to an English person in England has no relevance to the proceedings of this so-called court in the Republic of Ireland,' she shouted. This, too, prompted claps and cheers from her supporters. She seemed to be enjoying herself.

The three judges adjourned to consider their verdict. Rose and her supporters remained seated when they returned.

Justice O'Keeffe, speaking for the court, moved quickly through an outline of the evidence before jailing Rose for nine years.

Rose gave a grin and a clenched-fist salute as she was taken away with an army escort. That evening she was flown by helicopter back to Limerick.

While Rose had been awaiting sentencing, her former Oxford lecturer, Iris Murdoch, had visited the Beits at Russborough. It would later emerge that Murdoch was examining the possibility of writing a book about Rose, and she might have been conducting research. At the time of her visit, the stolen paintings were being restored at the National Gallery in Dublin. Andrew O'Connor, the museum's head of conservation, worked on the Vermeer in an attic, accompanied by a young garda armed with an Uzi machine pistol.

On 20 July, after returning to Oxford, Iris Murdoch wrote to Lady Beit.

Thank you so much for sending the Russborough booklet and for your kind letter. I so greatly enjoyed talking to you at the luncheon party. What a beautiful, magical house – I feel extremely sad and distressed to think of your dreadful experience with those thugs, and the loss of those great *pictures. [. . .]*

As for Rose, who was such an intelligent and nice and handsome pupil – how can she have ruined her life and the lives of others this way?

The IRA is horribly and incomprehensibly wicked – and I fear not too unpopular with many people in the south.

It is amazing that Rose is still involved in the IRA and its activities. I suppose once one has worked for them one cannot escape, but I fear in this case there is no change of heart.

Every day, in Limerick prison, Rose would look at her growing belly in the tiny mirror in her cell. She still hoped that Eddie would launch an escape plan.

At exercise time, she would wear her heavy duffel coat and walk around the yard under the watchful eye of Philip Bray. 'I remember she never, ever had that duffel coat off her, even indoors,' he says.

Myles Shevlin passed on advice to Rose from his wife, Nora, on foods she should eat for a pregnancy.

Eddie, meanwhile, was busy working on a tunnel to free the republicans in Mountjoy. He and his men had a cabin to work in across the road from the prison. The tunnel was more than three-quarters complete when a soldier became suspicious. Eddie wasn't on site at the time, and when he found out the scheme had been discovered, he left Dublin and went back to Betty O'Neill's house in Navan.

He then turned his attention to a mass escape plan for IRA republican prisoners in Portlaoise prison. After a month, during which he and his team managed to smuggle gelignite to the prisoners, their plan was complete. Eddie was waiting for a signal from the prisoners that they were about to escape, so that he could have a line of getaway cars waiting. But the signal did not come. 'There was half a dozen cars organized to take people away, and for some reason they didn't break out. We were expecting them out for two or three days, but we had heard nothing.'

While he was in Portlaoise, waiting, he got word that a London friend of Rose's had good contacts with revolutionary leftist groups in Mozambique and Angola. He wanted to introduce this woman, whom I'll call Marie Claire, to Irish republicans.

At Treacy's Bar in Portlaoise on 15 August 1975, Eddie met Marie Claire and Richard Behal, who was in 'foreign relations' for the IRA. Behal had been jailed for firing at a British naval ship in Waterford in 1965, causing thousands of pounds' worth of damage. He had escaped from Limerick prison in 1966 by hacksawing the window bars and covering himself in butter to slide out of the window and had then climbed down using bed sheets. He was known to set up roadblocks even while on the run and had joined the Provisional IRA when it was formed in 1969. Later, he and Eddie had been prisoners together in the Curragh.

Eddie recalls: 'The meeting started and I have never met a woman before or after who could talk as much as [Marie Claire]. I sat and I listened for about half an hour or so. I was in a bad mood anyway with the escape not happening in the jail.'

Eddie asked Mrs Tracey, the bar manager, to get him a bottle of whiskey to relieve the tension. 'I went into the back room and by the time the meeting was over I was drunk.

Behal had his little wee Mini car with him. I got into the back and she was in the front. Three or four hundred yards further down the heath, a Special Branch car pulled us in. One of them came around to the side of the car with a pistol and took the woman out and then looked in the back at me and said: "Who do we have here?"'

When he got out of the car, Eddie tried to make a run for it, and pulled a gun when Detective Garda Joseph Gleeson grabbed him. Eddie recalls that Detective Gleeson 'knocked my pistol and he was looking for it on the ground, in the darkness. When he came up I hit him as hard as I could, kicked him in the shins and took off as fast as I could. He went after me and he was fitter than I was and I was drunk. I was halfway across the heath in Portlaoise when he rugby-tackled me to the ground and pushed his gun under my chin.'

Eddie was carrying a penknife in his pocket, 'and with my free hand I put it up to his jugular. He still had his gun to my chin and he said: "If you stick that in me, I will pull the trigger." He was very cool.'

Eddie and Richard Behal were taken to Portlaoise garda station and charged with possession of a revolver and assault before being put in a cell together.

'Richard had been up to Portlaoise the week before and had been giving shit to the gardaí and prison officers outside the prison. They recognized him and now they're giving it back to him through the spy hole. They're saying: "Oh, it's Richard the Freedom Fighter, down looking for British soldiers in the heath." They keep up the taunting for hours. He is a good singer and I said: "Sing us a song." I knew he could make a really good job of "The Rose of Mooncoin". He started singing and, for some reason, that stopped the taunting, maybe because we couldn't hear them.'

Eddie was held on remand at the republican wing in Portlaoise – which, in one sense, was exactly where he wanted to be. As soon as he got inside, he demanded to know why all his men had been waiting in safe houses for days, with getaway cars, and nothing was happening with his escape plan.

The IRA prisoners told him they were waiting for the right time, and he offered to take over. Among those ready to escape were Kevin Mallon, an IRA friend of Eddie's from Coalisland, and two brothers who had been convicted of murdering an Irish senator, Billy Fox.

At 12.30 p.m. on Sunday, 18 August 1974, a group of nineteen IRA prisoners overpowered guards on the main cell block, stole their uniforms and used their keys to get on to an adjoining flat roof before climbing down to ground level and running to the walls of the governor's house. By now, some of the prisoners were wearing the prison officers' uniforms. A prison officer sounded the alarm and soldiers on the turrets were about to shoot when they spotted the uniforms and held fire, fearing that the prisoners had taken hostages. The IRA men then used explosive charges to blow up a gate leading to the governor's residence, and then blew another hole in the perimeter wall, through which they escaped. It was the largest mass escape in Irish prison history. The men jumped into stolen cars and disappeared into safe houses across the country.

Eddie Gallagher was out of Ireland's most secure prison less than twenty-four hours after he had been put in there. It was a huge embarrassment for the government. The opposition called for the Justice Minister's resignation.

In late August, there was big news – Limerick was about to get a second female republican prisoner. Twenty-four-year-old Angela Duffin, a barwoman from a family of nine in

West Belfast, was a member of a 'fundraising' cell of the Official IRA, the left-wing rival of the larger Provisional IRA. She and her team had moved south to steal cash from businesses to fund the conflict in the North. On 24 June 1974 she burst into the Hotel Blarney in Cork with a loaded revolver and demanded money from the manager while an accomplice stood guard.

Angela Duffin recalls: 'He was holding his dog at the time. He said: "Do what you have to do, but please, don't hurt my dog." I was struck by how brave he was. Two gardaí who were in the hotel at the time had this big *Starsky and Hutch* story about how they intervened, but that man with the dog was the brave one. I admired him standing up for his dog.' She stole £4,400 in cash and £300 in cheques before fleeing the building.

On 15 August, the day that Eddie was arrested in Portlaoise, Angela Duffin's team struck again in Galway while many of the city's residents were at Mass for the Feast of the Assumption. Jerome O'Connor, a wages clerk with the Sisk construction company, had just withdrawn that week's wages from Allied Irish Bank when he was confronted by 17-year-old Vincent Daly and 24-year-old John Duffy. He resisted and grabbed Duffy's sawn-off shotgun. The gun went off, blasting O'Connor in the chest and killing him instantly.

Another Sisk employee chased the raiders. Duffy abandoned his shotgun and parka in a nearby church grounds, while Daly fled with the money, hiding in a church during Mass before running back to his apartment. Gardaí found a set of keys in Duffy's parka that led them to another apartment that the Official IRA was using as a base. Hundreds of gardaí were involved in follow-up searches in what the *Connacht Tribune* said at the time was the most intense police investigation in Galway history. All roads out of the city were shut down and gardaí combed hotels and guest houses.

In these searches, and amid a huge public outcry, they arrested seven men, and Angela Duffin, who was charged with handling the stolen money. Not long after she was arrested and photographed, she became prime suspect in the robbery of the Hotel Blarney.

She was taken under armed escort to the female section of Limerick prison, whose inmate population was made up of Rose Dugdale and a growing group of prostitutes, shoplifters and petty criminals.

Before Angela even met Rose, she disliked her.

'All these other women, these young kids really, were saying: "We get our cigarettes from Rosie. Do you want cigarettes? Rosie will get your cigarettes. Rosie will sort out this, Rosie will sort out that." I felt angry about that because she was controlling the thing and I thought: who is she to be controlling it?

'I got to meet her anyway. I thought she would be arrogant, but she wasn't at all. She was unbelievable. She would help me out whenever I needed it and give me cigarettes. She was a really lovely, warm person. At that time, I was up and back, up and back to the Special Criminal Court for the Galway case and then the Cork case. Rose was really concerned about it and she would ask me about it and she told me all about why she was in prison. Soon, we were best friends.'

Angela sometimes teased Rose. 'She was always telling stories and could take a joke. I would joke with her about her being in the royal family and she would laugh back.'

She recalls that Rose would tell her and the other female prisoners about growing up in a townhouse in Chelsea, a world that a young woman from West Belfast knew nothing about. 'She used to tell us stories about when she was in one townhouse and her mummy was in the other house next door.'

As winter approached, the furnace in the women's section was barely working. When the furnace had to be stoked, Philip Bray would take a male prisoner with him and a female prison officer would lock them in the furnace room while the male prisoner shoved coal into the burner. 'The smoke was so strong that you couldn't catch your breath,' Bray recalls. 'It was a disgrace, and it never heated anything. Nothing was ever warm up there in the women's section.'

In late October, Rose had her first visit from her parents. Lieutenant Colonel Dugdale looked for their Limerick hotel reservation under his own name but was told that they were booked in under 'Mr and Mrs Smith', in the hope of escaping the attention of reporters.

Eric and Carol went shopping for an hour, then asked hotel staff how to get to Limerick prison. The press, who had got wind of the visit, gathered outside the prison and photographed them going in and out. Eric and Carol sat across the visiting table from Rose and made stilted conversation. Eric offered some suggestions for how she might stay warm. He advised Rose that, upon release, she should apply for a support role in the IRA and leave the fighting to others.

Outside the prison, he told waiting reporters. 'The whole beastly thing is very painful for us.' Asked if all the writing and reading his daughter was doing was for a university thesis, he said: "I hope so – it will keep her mind occupied – but already she has so many academic degrees."'

Colonel Dugdale seemed to be trying to strike a friendly note with the reporters and mentioned he had visited Ireland many times, mainly in connection with the horse industry.

That same week, in a note smuggled into Limerick prison by Myles Shevlin, Eddie told Rose that when she went into labour, he could spring her from the maternity hospital.

'There was someone in the hospital who was a republican,' Eddie recalls. 'We were confident that when Rose was taken there, that would be the moment. Security was much lower in the hospital and as soon as she was in labour they would have no choice but to take her to hospital.'

In November, Rose was tried and convicted, along with Eamon McNulty and Patrick Treacy, for their parts in the Strabane bombing. Rose was sentenced to nine years in prison, to run concurrently with her sentence for the Russborough heist. Nobody seemed to notice that she was heavily pregnant.

Rose got bigger and bigger; the kicks became more and more pronounced. One day in mid-December, as the country was preparing for Christmas, her waters broke.

8. Born in Captivity

Angela Duffin could hear Rose moaning in the cell next door. 'Our mummy had nine children, I had seen this before, and I realized she was in labour.' She shouted to the prison officers for help.

'They went in to Rose and locked the door and they rang the alarm bell. The matron [senior prison officer] came up and said: "What's going on?" I said: "She's in labour! She's in labour!"'

One of the prison officers went running down the corridor. 'Rose Dugdale is having a baby! Rose Dugdale is having a baby!' The female warden called the governor.

Philip Bray remembers the panic as prison officers tried to work out if the most-guarded prisoner in the country could have become pregnant on their watch. 'There were two prison officers. I remember one of them was counting back the months on his finger. 'Five months, four months, three months.' Eventually they worked out that she must have been at least two months pregnant when she went in. They wouldn't lose their jobs.

The governor tried to call the Justice Minister but couldn't reach him. Bray recalls 'a general feeling that something was up' – that Rose's secrecy about her pregnancy must have been part of an escape strategy. 'There was a big debate between prison officers and Paddy Gallagher, the prison doctor. There was this big confrontation about whether she was going to have the child in prison or in the regional hospital.'

Prison officials determined that there wasn't time to get the army and gardaí deployed at the maternity hospital, or have the hospital staff screened. And so it was decided that Rose Dugdale should have her baby in her prison cell.

The senior obstetrician at Limerick Regional Hospital, Dr Ivan Holloway, got a call requesting that a midwife be dispatched to the prison. Two senior midwives, Margaret Dalton and Maureen O'Carroll, arrived shortly before 9 p.m. They were told only that a female prisoner was having a baby and needed their attention.

At just after 10.30 p.m. on 12 December 1974, Rose gave birth to an 8lb fair-haired boy. The midwife placed him in Rose's arms. 'Oh, he is lovely,' she said. Thoughts of Eddie and the escape plan drifted away.

Rose was moved the next day to an improvised nursery at the end of the corridor on the first floor of the women's prison. A member of the visiting committee was allowed to see her the following morning. 'I stayed for just a short time and found Dr Dugdale and her baby were in very comfortable surroundings and receiving great attention,' she told the reporters gathering outside.

Later that day, prison officers let Angela Duffin in to see her. At one point in the conversation, Angela referred to the baby boy as 'it'. 'Rose snapped at me: "It's not 'it'! It's a boy." It wasn't nasty, but she was letting me know.'

Rose's baby was front-page news across the country. Now republicans had to manage the public relations. Maureen McGuire of the IRA-supporting Irish Political Hostages Campaign told reporters that Rose and her unnamed 'husband', a republican, had been married since 1972. The Press Association quoted McGuire as saying that Rose had met her husband in England; that she came with him to Ireland, where they subsequently married; and that he was currently in Port-laoise prison. This was an odd mixture of truth and falsehood, which might have been intended at least in part to reassure Catholic Ireland as to Rose's morals. Myles Shevlin was put out in front of the media with the message that Rose and her unnamed husband were planning their future together.

Over the coming days, Rose seemed serene and happy. One prison official told reporters that motherhood had calmed Rose. She was no longer the 'angry young woman agitating for everything and being completely anti-establishment'.

Jenny Grove, her Oxford friend, read about the drama in the newspapers. 'I bought a very nice teddy bear in Harrods and sent it to her, but I don't think it ever arrived,' she recalls.

By law, Rose had three months before she had to register the baby's birth. She wouldn't have to name the baby's father until then.

The newspapers reported that Rose had told a visiting friend that the young baby would grow up to be a 'guerrilla fighter' like his mother. But she strongly denies ever saying this, and a family member insists that Rose told her half-brothers, Simon and Tim, that the comment was a media invention.

In any case, the child's future would have to be decided. Under Irish prison rules, a child could stay with a mother only until breastfeeding ended, but it was clear that Rose wanted him to have a life outside the prison long before then.

'Her baby wasn't with her long,' says Philip Bray. 'Probably for his own sake.' He speculates that she didn't want to bond with the baby and then have him taken away from her.

Eddie Gallagher, who was moving between safe houses, called in to Betty O'Neill unannounced one night. As usual, she put on a late dinner. Betty had two adopted children, Sean and Andrea, who had come to her within eight months of each other and were now toddlers.

'You usually had to wait two years for a second child,' Betty recalls. 'Sean was only seven months old when Andrea came up for adoption and the nuns called me and asked me would I take her. So I had my own two and there was my grandfather to look after and the IRA injury cases coming in and out the whole time.'

Betty remembers Eddie 'studying' the two adopted toddlers. She thinks he 'may have been trying to suss us out before getting his baby to us'.

Rose, meanwhile, was breastfeeding her young son and getting cards from all over the world, some with congratulations, some with sharp admonishment that no child should be born into a prison. In Limerick City Council meetings, too, the birth of Rose Dugdale's baby caused divisions. Sean Doherty of Fianna Fáil told a council meeting that it was terrible that Rose Dugdale had been deprived of the right to go to hospital to deliver her baby.

The chairman of the council, Paddy Concannon, of Fine Gael, ruled Doherty out of order. When Doherty wouldn't stop talking about Rose Dugdale, Concannon adjourned the meeting for five minutes, but most of the councillors stayed in the room to hear Doherty demand an explanation for why Rose had to give birth in prison. The leader of the Labour Party on the council, Stephen Coughlan, was far less sympathetic: he called on the Minister for Health and Social Welfare to block Rose Dugdale from getting children's allowance for her son while in prison. 'As it will cost more than a million pounds to keep this lady in prison over the next nine years, I see no reason why the Irish taxpayer should have to pay still further,' he said. Similarly, the trade unionist and councillor Frank Prendergast objected to what he called specialized top-class maternity services, including two midwives, being provided to Dr Dugdale, when they would not be available to the ordinary rate-paying public.

After a few weeks, Myles Shevlin convinced Rose that, as she would soon have to give up her son, he should be christened. Shevlin also offered that he and his wife could take care of the boy. Rose accepted this offer; and, after thinking about the child's name for a few days, decided on Ruairi. 'I didn't care for religion, and it wasn't a saint's name,' she says of the decision.

Rose's nursery was overflowing with female prisoners coming in to see the new baby. She had Christmas dinner with them while some of the remand prisoners looked after Ruairi. She seemed upbeat, enjoying her baby and the new life he brought.

Early in the new year, Ruairi started running a temperature and was looking unwell. When a doctor didn't come quickly enough, Angela Duffin became angry and demanded to see the visitor committee. She then organized the other prisoners to join her in a protest: they would refuse to come back to their cells after exercise until a doctor visited Ruairi.

Angela recalls: 'There must have been an informer because when it was time for exercise, I could see a lot of screws, including male screws, coming from different corners into the exercise yard, and they never did that before. Then they swooped in. They grabbed all the others first, and that left me. And then they came for me and they dragged me back inside. I complained on Rose's behalf to the visitor committee. One of the prisoners backed me up and when she was finished speaking, the matron says: "Oh, so you're a revolutionary too!" The poor girl was transferred to Mount-joy soon afterwards, but, luckily, Ruairi was all right.'

Philip Bray confirms that the officers were running informers among the non-republican prisoners. 'Well, there is always a "rat", for want of a better word; prisons couldn't run without them. If you are a task officer, you have to have a top cat. It could be a prisoner brought down from Dublin who would have something knocked off their sentence for telling the task officer what was going on.'

In February 1975, Eddie and some republicans in Limer-ick managed to get a small hacksaw to Rose via another prisoner. Richard Behal had used a hacksaw to escape from Limerick prison and they were hoping she could do the same, while holding Ruairi in her arms.

She used the saw to cut through a bar in one of her win-dows, while Ruairi, two months old, slept beside her.

On a prison cell inspection that month, the guards found that one of the bars was loose, and then discovered the hack-saw. They searched the entire female wing and discovered that one of the bars in the first-floor women's toilets had also been loosened. Rose was denied phone calls and radio for a month while the prison carried out an investigation into how the most guarded female prisoner in the country had man-aged to get a hacksaw.

By this point, escape seemed impossible. Rose decided to give Ruairi over to Myles Shevlin and his wife, Nora.

'It was terribly, terribly upsetting,' Rose recalls. 'But I knew that he would have a better life with them than he would in the prison. There was no crèche or anything like that and no place for education.'

Angela recalls: 'Rose was talking to me about him and said she had friends who were going to take him, and I remember thinking she is going to be very upset. But once she handed him over, she was out back, playing tennis. That's when I knew that she realized she had to get on with it. She had to just hand over the baby and get on with it.'

Ruairi settled in well with the Shevlins at their home in Chapelizod, on the bank of the River Liffey, just upstream from Dublin city centre. But Eddie was adamant that Ruairi should go to the O'Neill safe house in Navan, where he could get a proper republican upbringing, far from the niceties of a middle-class solicitor's home.

Eddie returned to Betty's house unannounced. Betty remembers his words: 'I'm hoping you might be able to take in someone for us.'

'I thought he was talking about an IRA person. I didn't like one or two of them, I just had a bad feeling about them, or they weren't polite, so I said: "You have to tell me who it is," and he says: "It's the young fella."'

Betty's eyes widen as she tells the story. '"You mean your young fella, the little baby?"'

'"Yeah. Could you take him in?"'

'"I don't know. For how long?" Oh god, every child should have a home. Eddie was determined that Ruairi should come to us, but Myles Shevlin didn't want to give him up.'

Eddie, still wanted for the Portlaoise breakout, drove to Chapelizod and convinced Myles Shevlin to hand over the baby immediately. And, at some point, Peter Ady travelled to Navan from Oxford with her new partner, a journalist and former Oxford student named Georgina Moore, to assess the suitability of the O'Neill home for Ruairi.

Betty had never met a college professor before, certainly not one from Oxford. She took out the best china. Today, she recalls 'Professor Ady' with great reverence: 'She was a very beautiful woman and she had such good manners. She sat down and had tea and heard about my family.' Peter and Georgina reported favourably to Rose.

Betty recalls: 'There was a job to get Ruairi off Shevlin . . . Shevlin had Ruairi a few months at that point. He wasn't giving him back, so Eddie and another republican had to go and actually take Ruairi.'

Eddie drove back to Navan with Ruairi and handed him over to Betty. With two small children already in the house and a retinue of on-the-run IRA members coming for medical treatment, Betty was always busy. Rock Ruairi in his crib; get her own children their breakfast; change a dressing on an IRA man's wound; cook dinner for her husband, John, and escaped prisoners; give her son Sean a bottle to feed Ruairi.

The IRA sent word to Betty: it was time for Ruairi to be baptized. And because those who wished to attend were on the run, it would have to be organized immediately.

'It was a Thursday night when they called to me,' Betty recalls. 'They wanted a baptism on Saturday morning – and normally there is a wait of weeks for a baptism.'

She remembers her conversation with the parish priest.

'I need to get a baby baptized as soon as possible.'

'Why? Is it your baby?'

'No.'

'Where's the mother?'

'She's indisposed.'

'What do you mean, she's indisposed?'

'She's in prison.'

The priest knew of Betty's IRA link and had seen the blanket coverage of Rose Dugdale and her prison baby in the newspapers.

'Oh,' he said. 'It's not who I think it is, is it?'

'It probably is. And she wants him raised Catholic. If he's not – her family are Protestants and he'll be raised as a Protestant.'

The priest smiled. He could see what Betty was doing.

'Well, we'll have to do something for him,' he said.

On the day, Martin McGuinness, a member of the IRA army council who had supplied a bomb car to Eddie's IRA unit in Donegal and who would have been acquainted with Betty as well, arrived to take the role as Ruairí's godfather.

Marion Coyle, on the run from authorities north and south of the border, was nominated as godmother. Tall, with fine features and jet-black hair, she came from a staunchly republican family and had been part of Eddie's group in the Donegal/Derry area. In 1970, her favourite uncle, Joe Coyle, had been killed when a bomb he was preparing exploded prematurely. She was in a relationship with Kevin Mallon, who had been among the IRA escapees from Portlaoise with Eddie Gallagher but had subsequently been captured and returned to prison.

Marion had crashed a car while driving Eddie and a Tyrone IRA man, Sean Hughes, to another Meath safe house. The car rolled three or four times, down an embankment. Marion, badly injured, was rushed to Betty.

'That was the first time I saw Marion,' Betty recalls. 'She was going in and out of it, in and out of consciousness, lying on the settee. She had bruises on her forehead. Grandad was sitting on the armchair. He would say to me: "That girl is not right! Get help for that girl!"'

Betty knew of two doctors who could be relied upon to make discreet house calls. When one of the doctors arrived, he could see that Marion was badly injured and agreed to treat her for several days on Betty's couch.

Willie Lynskey, a neighbour of the O'Neills, was a Sinn Féin volunteer and a frequent visitor to the house. After Marion recovered from her injuries, he and Betty would sometimes drive her to plan IRA operations. 'Marion was one cool customer,' Lynskey remembers. 'One night, we were in Aughnacloy on the border and we were going back into Monaghan town. We went into the Four Seasons Hotel and in a few minutes she came out to the car dressed as an old lady. She would never tell you what was happening. She would just say: "I want to go to such and such a place." She was very, very secretive but very nice.'

Martin McGuinness and Marion Coyle feared arrest for IRA membership, so the baptism had to be quick. Eddie, for his part, decided that he couldn't risk attending as a prison escapee.

Betty held Ruairi in her arms as the priest poured the water on his forehead. The godparents wished Betty the best and left within minutes.

Eddie was working on a major new project to free dozens more prisoners from Portlaoise, despite a tightening of security at the prison following the big escape. He and his helpers welded armoured plates on to a truck and christened it 'The Bridget Rose'. 'At that point, I don't think Rose was being taken seriously by the IRA,' he recalls. 'I wanted to say: this is a woman who should be honoured.'

The Bridget Rose crashed through the outer perimeter fence of Portlaoise prison on St Patrick's Day 1975: the idea was that the IRA escapees could have St Patrick's Day celebration drinks in freedom that night. The truck rammed through barbed-wire entanglements and steel gates into the exercise yard. The impact smashed the truck's cooling system and the engine began to seize. At the back of the truck was a large bulletproof steel box that the escaping prisoners could climb into.

An IRA man named Tom Smith was one of the men who had been told in advance of the escape. He and his companions used smuggled explosives to blow open a door leading from the prison workshop to the exercise yard. The escaping prisoners rushed through the door and towards the gate while under fire from the soldiers above them on the wall. The reluctance of soldiers to shoot the previous year had allowed the escape of nineteen IRA prisoners. Now, there was no hesitation. Tom Smith was shot dead, and three others were wounded. The rest surrendered when they saw the Bridget Rose couldn't move.

A few days later, Eddie dropped in to Betty's to see Ruairi. Other IRA members came streaming down in the middle of the night after a gun battle with the British army in the North. Betty was told that one of them had a 'minor injury'. In reality, she recalls, 'You could see in one side of his ankle and out the other.'

The injured man sat in the living room for weeks, putting his injured foot up by the fire. When Betty asked that he rearrange himself so that his elevated leg did not block the children from coming into and out of the room, he refused. He never said 'please' or 'thank you'. 'I suppose they assumed that I was being paid by Sinn Féin or the IRA, but I never was,' said Betty. 'So some of them just expected you to wait on them and you never heard one word of thanks from them afterwards.'

Betty was naturally very maternal and good with children, which created its own problems. When Ruairi was old enough to say a few gurgled words, he learned from the other children and started calling Betty 'Mama' and 'Mammy'.

'I'd say to Ruairi: "No, love, no. Mammy is in Limerick. That's Mammy. I'm Betty." And Ruairi would repeat: "Mammy", and I would plead: "No, Ruairi, Mammy is in Limerick. We'll go and visit Mammy."'

Betty would put Ruairi into her car and make the long drive to Limerick to visit Rose every Saturday. They would meet at a table in the visiting room and Rose would take Ruairi in her arms and cuddle him. When prison officers objected, Betty would say: 'She's the child's mother!'

Ruairi loved being in Rose's arms, Betty recalls, but sometimes he would turn to Betty, point and say: 'Mammy!'

'I was embarrassed,' Betty says. 'I was afraid Rose would think that I was trying to take Ruairi as my own. I would say: "No, Ruairi. This is Mammy here. This is Mammy," and Rose would say: "It's OK, it's OK, don't worry."'

Rose felt herself becoming harder – inured to the prison system, and less willing to compromise – and she could see that Betty was 'a very kind woman, a warm woman. It was better if Ruairi was with her.'

In April, Limerick prison took in its third female republican prisoner: 32-year-old mother-of-three Rita O'Hare, who was jailed for smuggling explosives into Portlaoise prison two months earlier.

O'Hare was known as a committed IRA volunteer. In 1971, she had been shot during a gun battle with British soldiers in West Belfast. She was captured, charged with attempted murder of a soldier and fled south when released on bail in the following year.

Outlining the Portlaoise explosives smuggling case, prosecution barrister Seamus Egan SC told the Special Criminal Court that prison officers saw O'Hare pass something to an

IRA man, Peter Lynch, when O'Hare was visiting the prison. When prison officers checked Lynch's jacket, they found gelignite stuffed into three layers of condoms, wrapped in cellophane. The cellophane was analysed and found to contain an enzyme, phosphatase, which is commonly found in vaginal secretions.

As a defence witness for O'Hare, Lynch claimed in court that he had had explosives in his jacket even before O'Hare's visit. When Justice Pringle asked him what condition the explosives were in, he replied: 'As a soldier of the Irish Republican Army, I refuse to answer that question.'

O'Hare was jailed for three years. As she was leaving the dock, she said loudly to her husband: 'Look after the kids.'

From the moment Rita O'Hare went into prison, the relationship between Rose and Angela Duffin changed, according to Angela. 'Rose was spending more and more time with Rita, who was very well in with the Provisional IRA leadership, and I felt Rita was very much excluding me from that,' she says. 'From then on, it wasn't just me and Rose any more and I never did regain that really close relationship.'

For Philip Bray, Rita O'Hare was an unwelcome addition to Limerick prison. 'Everyone knew that she mixed with the IRA big boys and Rita O'Hare was a difficult kettle of fish. Oh, she held the fucking ground! She had that dangerous red hair and I don't think she liked anyone. It just radiated off her.'

Now resigned to the fact that Rose could not be freed by conventional means because of the increased security at Limerick prison, Eddie Gallagher was spending more time in the city, trying to work out a new way to free her.

According to the *Irish Times*, Eddie had seriously fallen out with the Provisional IRA at this point. The newspaper claimed that Gallagher had held on to £200,000 from a bank robbery in Navan that summer, rather than turning it over, and that the IRA feared he was setting up a breakaway leftist group. (Eddie denies any financial wrongdoing.)

While this drama was playing out, an IRA supporter and trade union activist had told Eddie about a strike that was underway in Limerick. A German materials company called Ferenka, which produced wire for car tyres, was the city's largest employer, but there was long-standing tension between a group of hard-left workers and the main Irish trade union, the ITGWU. When the smaller group went on strike in February 1975, because of objections to a productivity plan, the ITGWU workers voted by three to one to continue working, though they had their own disputes with management about pay and conditions.

A new manager, named Tiede Herrema, was brought in from the Netherlands to oversee the labour negotiations and run the plant. He had been a prisoner of the Nazis during the Second World War and he had a doctorate in philosophy. He and his wife lived in the middle-class Castletroy neighbourhood of Limerick.

Eddie began stalking Herrema. He invited Marion Coyle down to Limerick to join him in this surveillance for several days, and then they drove to Navan.

Betty remembers Marion coming into the kitchen with an air of urgency. She did not give Betty any details. 'She just said that something big was about to happen for Rose.'

9. The Kidnappers

On the morning of Friday, 3 October 1975, as Tiede Herrema was driving out of his Castletroy home on his way to the Ferenka factory, he came to a roadblock, where a uniformed police officer directed him to stop. He did, and the garda asked him where he was going. Before he could answer, the garda pulled a revolver and bundled him into a different car.

The 'garda' was Eddie Gallagher.

As with other operations, Eddie had no IRA approval for this one. In the car were Marion Coyle and two men from Tullamore: a Sinn Féin member and former British soldier named Vincent Walsh, and a Provisional IRA member named Brian McGowan, who had been on active service in Ardboe, Co. Tyrone.

Marion was driving, and leaned back to make sure the adhesive tape being used as a blindfold was on properly. Herrema, ever agreeable, helped to adjust the blindfold. The kidnappers then put a jacket over his head, and Marion drove for three quarters of an hour to a farmhouse in Kinnitty, Co. Offaly, where McGowan got out, gave his gun to Marion and went home to Tullamore for the day. The others took Herrema to a thatched farmhouse near the village of Mountmellick, Co. Laois.

The owner of the house, David Dunne, would later tell gardaí that he had agreed to let his home be used only as an IRA safe house – not for a kidnapping – and that he had said the group could have the house 'as long as they didn't make noise'. He arrived at his house after work and a car pulled up behind his.

He recognized Eddie, Vincent Walsh and an IRA supporter named Thomas Dunne (no relation to David Dunne), who bundled a man with a jacket over his head into the house. Marion followed after them. Still blindfolded, Dr Herrema was taken into a bedroom and thrown on to a bed. His legs and hands were bound with adhesive tape. When the blindfold was removed, he could see that the room had a hard concrete floor. The window was blocked with a combination of hardboard, curtain material and newspapers. He was locked in the room, and the light switch was operated from another room. He could hear a radio and a television in another part of the house, with news reports about his disappearance.

The safe-house operation was being run by Thomas Dunne's friend P. J. Bailey, who delivered hot meals to Dr Herrema.

The kidnappers entered Dr Herrema's room with a tape recorder and prepared texts, which they told him to read into the machine. He recorded that his captors were demanding the release of three republican prisoners – Rose Dugdale, Kevin Mallon and James Hyland – in exchange for Herrema's freedom. Eddie handed the tape to P. J. Bailey, along with a pair of gloves, and instructed him to pass the recording to 'any priest in South Dublin'. Bailey drove up to Dublin and gave the tape to a priest, who arranged for a Capuchin monk, the Revd Donal O'Mahony, to act as mediator.

That evening, Eddie Gallagher told David Dunne that he wanted to see the TV news. They sat together and watched an update about the kidnapping of Dr Herrema – the first time Dunne knew what was going on. He could see that Eddie had a gun tucked into his trousers.

The kidnapping brought about a rare unity in Ireland. Eddie had imagined that kidnapping a factory boss would be popular with the working class, but the IRA understood that it was very unpopular with workers, who feared that foreign employers would pull out of Ireland.

The Provisional IRA phoned a statement into all the newsrooms in Dublin that evening, strongly rejecting claims that it was involved in the kidnapping. 'Furthermore, it is not the policy of the Republican movement nor any of its members to differentiate between Republican prisoners in seeking their release,' it said.

Marion drove from the Laois safe house to Betty O'Neill's house in Navan. 'We have to go now,' she told Betty. News was just starting to break that a Dutch businessman had been kidnapped in Limerick, but Betty still knew nothing about the operation. Marion simply told her that she and the kids had to go to Derry for a while. Betty's friend Willie Lynskey got into the driver's seat, with Marion beside him and Betty holding nine-month-old Ruairi in the back with her own two children, Sean and Andrea, beside her.

Lynskey observed that Marion was 'as cool as always – nothing bothered her, she was very focused'. He drove north-west, crossing the border into what remained, despite Marion's best efforts, the United Kingdom, and on to the Coyle family home on Duncreggan Road, Derry. Betty was given a room for herself and the three children.

In Limerick prison, the female inmates gathered around the television. Rose – who denies having had any foreknowledge of the kidnapping – said nothing.

In the safe house in Laois, Eddie made tea and asked Tiede Herrema if he wanted them to contact the German embassy.

'He told me that he wasn't German, he was Dutch,' Eddie

recalls. 'I didn't know he was Dutch; I had it in my head he was German.'

Eddie says that he 'had a few good talks with him and he said that he was in a prisoner camp during the Second World War. I asked him how he managed the Germans who were running the camp. He said it was extremely difficult, that they were shooting prisoners.'

The gang sent word to the media and to the Dutch embassy that night: Tiede Herrema would be executed in forty-eight hours unless the three prisoners were released.

The next day, the Saturday, five thousand people joined one thousand Ferenka workers and the Mayor of Limerick, Thady Coughlan, on a protest march though the city, demanding the release of Tiede Herrema. Workers held signs that read: 'Herrema is a Co-Worker', 'Stop this Outrage Now' and 'Jobs, not Violence'.

While the march was progressing, Marion was getting a lift back down south with Willie Lynskey, who dropped her off at a safe house outside Kilbeggan, Co. Westmeath, where one of Eddie's group picked her up and took her back to the house where the prisoner was being held.

An hour later, Mayor Coughlan showed up at Limerick prison to plead with Rose to denounce the kidnapping. The governor went to ask Rose if she would speak to him.

'She refused to leave her cell to see me,' says Coughlan. 'She basically told me to fuck off. She called me a fucking fascist, or something like that. She was shouting at a prison officer and then the governor came back into his office and said there was no way she would talk to me.'

It was now less than twenty-four hours until the kidnappers' deadline.

From the prison, Mayor Coughlan called Rose's parents in

London to beg them to persuade her to denounce the kidnapping and prevent the killing of Herrema.

'They were very apologetic and made it clear that they did not support the kidnapping,' Coughlan recalls. 'They both told me they would do everything they could and that they were sorry. Her mother was very upset on the phone. I felt sorry for them because they were decent, good people being thrown into this terrible situation.'

Later, at home, he got a call from Eric Dugdale, who 'said he was terribly sorry, he had spoken to her but she wasn't going to budge'.

Rose, for her part, says, 'I didn't think it was my place to tell them to stop the kidnapping. I didn't know about it and anything I said wasn't going to stop them. There was any amount of people coming in to me every single day asking me to call it off, but it wasn't in my ability to stop it.'

The fact that the kidnappers were demanding the release of Rose Dugdale and Kevin Mallon was a fairly obvious clue as to their identity. On that Saturday, the gardaí revealed that the chief suspects were Eddie Gallagher (whose history with Rose was well known) and Marion Coyle (who had been involved with Kevin Mallon).

The government declared that it would not release any prisoners in exchange for Dr Herrema. The Justice Minister, Patrick Cooney, angrily denounced the kidnapping as a 'stunt' being pulled by a republican group and said that the government could not allow three criminals back on the streets.

The hunt for Dr Herrema unfolded on a vast scale. More than half the police force was tasked with searching every single house in the country and setting up roadblocks on major and minor roads. Border crossings were shut down and every army helicopter was made available. The navy put its ships to sea in case the kidnappers tried to slip Herrema to Britain or France.

On Sunday evening, the deadline for Dr Herrema's execution came and went: it was the first of what would be many bluffs from the kidnappers.

On Tuesday, 7 October, the *Irish Times* reported that the IRA was looking for 'the leader of the group suspected of kidnapping Dutch industrialist Tiede Herrema'. On legal advice, the paper didn't name Eddie Gallagher, but said the friction between him and the IRA 'allegedly reached a head weeks before the kidnapping. The leader of the group is now reported to be "on the run" from both the Provisional IRA and the gardaí in the Republic.'

In Derry, Betty O'Neill was finding it hard to get along with Mrs Coyle. She found her domineering and uninterested in the sacrifices being made by any republican other than her daughter.

'It was all Marion, Marion, Marion,' Betty recalls. 'I was nervous in Derry, to be honest with you, because Mrs Coyle couldn't keep her mouth closed. "Marion is a great girl, Marion will sort all this out, Marion is running the whole thing." I heard her talking to people and then she'd say who I was and why I was there. Ruairi was a baby and I had my own two children, who were very small, and we were up there for safety and you didn't know who these people were that she was talking to. You didn't know who that information could go out to.'

Betty thought the kidnapping was inhumane and pointless. 'It was a really foolish thing to do. Dr Herrema never did anything on them. It was terrible. Then I had to leave my home because they were saying someone would kidnap me or the children because of what Marion had done.

'My husband, John, came to see us one Saturday and I

said: "I'm going home!" I felt safer at home . . . I just packed up and left with the kids.'

For the IRA leadership, the kidnapping was a major crisis. It led to dozens of arrests of members all over the country. Until now, the IRA had benefited from a certain ambiguity in the hearts of the southern public. IRA members weren't extradited to Northern Ireland, and sentencing for terrorist offences was still very lenient. Now the Provos faced a southern crackdown. 'Let's face it, Eddie got a lot of people arrested because of the kidnapping,' says Betty.

The IRA was determined to force Eddie to end the kidnapping. On the way home from a visit to Limerick with Ruairi to see Rose, Betty and her brother-in-law, an IRA member named Seamus 'Beaver' Byrne, stopped at a restaurant in Portlaoise. A car pulled up beside them and a group of men got out. One of them opened the back door of the car and demanded Betty hand over the baby.

Betty, who didn't know the men personally but recognized their faces, recalls: 'I was in shock, but I wouldn't hand him over. I said, "If you want the baby, I'll go with him as well." They said: "No, we don't want you, we want the child."

'I said: "You won't be getting the child. I am republican, all my family are republican." One of them stood back and said: "What do you mean?" I said: "I was raised a republican. If you come after me because of a baby that can't do you any harm, you should go after someone bigger. A child can't fight but my uncles can." They looked at me. I don't know what they said next, but I said: "One of my uncles lives in Armagh and he done his time and the other one lives in Navan and he done his time."'

Her brother-in-law, Seamus Byrne, who had recently been released from prison in Belfast, also stood up to the men.

'With Seamus, they were messing with the wrong fella. He was after doing his time. He says to them: "I know youse boys. I'll be in Dublin tonight and I don't care who is in bed, they'll be out of bed and I'll be dealing with yez." They banged our car door shut and left.'

10. All the World is Watching

Tiede Herrema was lying on his bed in the thatched cottage, blindfolded with tape, his legs and arms bound and his ears stuffed with cotton wool to prevent from him hearing the news, or the kidnappers. He was struggling against disorientation.

If he was to survive, he simply could not allow himself to accept he was there in that room. He had used visualization in a Nazi prison camp in the Netherlands, and now he would use it again.

He needed sensation and movement to stay sane. Every day, he would live through a work day in his head. He would imagine waking up, and take the usual time to wash, to shave, to have breakfast, have a conversation with his wife, practise chess before work, say goodbye to his family and walk to his car; imagine the journey to work, the arguments with staff, the production quotas, the planning meetings, the phone calls to his bosses. He would act out the whole day for hours and then imagine the entire drive home, and meeting his family when he got there. The only time he cried, he would later tell the *Irish Times*, was when he imagined talking to his youngest son.

Thousands of gardaí were involved in searches for him, and Justice Minister Cooney called on 'every person in the country' to report any unusual movements in their neighbourhood.

The group decided to move Dr Herrema to another safe house, six miles away, which had already been searched. The council house, at 1410 St Evin's Park, Monasterevin, Co. Kildare, was the home of 23-year-old Michael Hall, a fitter at the Irish Ropes plant in Newbridge and the brother-in-law of gang member P. J. Bailey. Hall would later tell gardaí that Bailey asked him to take in 'a priest and a girl', and he agreed as a favour to his brother-in-law.

Hall drove to the safe house near Mountmellick, where he found a tall man in a dark cloak, a man dressed as a priest and a woman. He took the three to his home in Monasterevin in the early hours of 12 October – just over a week after the kidnapping. P. J. Bailey told him that the man in the cloak was Tiede Herrema; the others were Eddie Gallagher and Marion Coyle. Bailey's wife, Brigid, who was Hall's sister, told him he should keep his mouth shut because Eddie Gallagher was 'the most dangerous man in Ireland'.

Hall later told gardaí that he and his wife, Catherine, were terrified. They had never agreed to get involved in a kidnapping.

Herrema was placed in a tiny box bedroom upstairs, while Marion and Eddie slept together in the main bedroom. The Halls were relegated to the floor downstairs. Eddie told Michael Hall he would blow his head off if he told anyone what was going on.

On the morning of 14 October, two days after the transfer, the gardaí again came to search all the houses in the estate. Seeing them coming, Eddie and Marion, armed with handguns, rushed Dr Herrema into the attic.

A garda knocked on the door and Mrs Hall let him in. He walked quickly through the house, went upstairs and pressed a broom against the attic door. Eddie recalls that the door was little more than a lightweight lid that lifted into the space above. The searchers did not go up, and within minutes they were gone. Streets and streets of houses lay ahead of them.

Herrema would later recall hearing Marion and Eddie discussing whether to keep him in the attic, but they decided to take him back down to the box bedroom.

With a new confidence that the gardaí would not be back for some time, Eddie was more relaxed with Dr Herrema. The prisoner was allowed out of his room to exercise and eat, and the two of them chatted from time to time. They talked about the industrial dispute at the factory.

Eddie recalls: 'He told me that the plant was running at a loss, so I said: "Why are you operating it then?" and he said that it would be several years before the company introduced the same updated technology as its competitor for making tyres and so Ireland, with its government grants, was the cheapest place to operate a loss-making plant. I thought that was interesting.'

Herrema, for his part, felt a warming towards Eddie.

'It's hard to believe, but he was a nice person,' he later told an RTÉ radio documentary, recalling that Eddie assured him that he would not be hurt and that 'as a soldier, he was not allowed to kill innocent civilians'.

Nineteen-year-old Marion, on the other hand, refused to speak to him and was always cold and remote. 'I couldn't reach her,' Herrema said.

The gardaí were meanwhile building up a picture of the movements of Marion Coyle, Eddie Gallagher and their republican associates, the cars they had used, and the places where they had stayed. They were getting closer.

On Saturday, 18 October, they arrested Brian McGowan, one of the four participants in the abduction, in Tullamore, after he was spotted in a car registered to Eddie Gallagher.

Eddie recalls that at the time of the arrest he had been intending to transfer Herrema to South Armagh, and had asked McGowan and another conspirator to organize the car.

According to Eddie, gardaí 'beat the shit out of' McGowan until he told them where Herrema was being held. Conor Cruise O'Brien, a government minister at the time, would use the same phrase when recounting how the gardaí had learned of the hostage's whereabouts. The gardaí, for their part, claimed that they arrested McGowan, questioned him, and released him without charge, and that when they were giving him a lift home he announced that he wished to make a confession.

1410 St Evin's Park was placed under surveillance. At five o'clock the next morning – by which time Tiede Herrema had been in captivity for nineteen days – armed officers began smashing in the front door of the house.

Eddie and Marion, who were in the main bedroom upstairs, rushed across the landing to the box bedroom. From the window, Eddie fired three shots at the gardaí below. The shots missed, but the gardaí pulled back from the house.

The kidnappers' arsenal consisted of a Smith and Wesson long-barrelled revolver and two semi-automatic pistols. They had no food, no change of clothes. It was just them and their prisoner in one tiny room, aware that snipers were likely already in place if they tried to move around the house.

Armoured cars rolled into the street. Helicopters flew overhead. The house was at the end of the terrace, and armed gardaí took over the house next door. They wore white armbands to help them identify each other. Using a loudspeaker, they ordered the kidnappers to surrender. Eddie shouted back his demands: that the three prisoners be released, and that he and Marion be given a plane bound for the Netherlands with Dr Herrema. (Eddie says that the idea was to drop Herrema off in his home country and then fly on to a Middle Eastern or communist country from which he and Marion could not be extradited.)

Two mediators – the Capuchin monk the Revd Donal O'Mahony and the republican-leaning union organizer Phil Flynn – arrived to negotiate. The pair of them, one in a monk's habit, the other in suit and tie, became an enduring and incongruous image of the siege.

Captain Pearse McCorley of the Irish army was in charge of the sniper team.

'I did a reconnaissance and went to the house directly to the rear of the siege house,' he recalls. 'I asked the family if we could use their house because it looked straight into the kidnap house. They allowed us and I went up to the toilet and I placed two snipers there. From the toilet window, you could see into the bathroom of the siege house. The bathroom door was open in there, so we had a direct line of sight to the box bedroom door.'

If anyone opened it, the army snipers would have a clear shot.

'I moved four or five snipers to the house next door to the siege house. All the snipers were in one room. We could hear all of the negotiations from there. We were there to shoot Gallagher and Coyle dead if we could, but [we] would have to kill them both at the same time, in case the other shot Dr Herrema. The only chance to do that might be if they were moving him out of the house to the airport, but we would have to be told by a chief superintendent to shoot, we couldn't do it off the top of our heads.'

Both of Captain McCorley's parents were from Northern Ireland and he spent his summers in his mother's home town of Dunloy, Co. Antrim, where he watched the Orange Order parade through Catholic areas. His mother had moved south and was the president of the southern fundraising wing of the SDLP, the largest nationalist party in Northern Ireland.

'I knew what the issues were in Northern Ireland. People tend to look at people like Gallagher as gangsters, but he clearly had serious republican ideals behind it and he obviously had leadership skills and was a clever man. I felt it was a mistake to underestimate him and I was going to operate accordingly.'

The siege quickly became the biggest story in Europe. The *Irish Times* estimated that between two hundred and five hundred reporters descended on Monasterevin from around the world. All guest houses and hotels within a 10-mile radius were quickly booked up. Reporters had to share beds and sleep on floors and in hotel lobbies. They knocked on doors in the area, offering cash in return for accommodation. Huge TV lights lit up the police barrier, and TV reporters made a roster of who could stand there, with the house in the background, as they recorded their reports. The *Irish Times* reported seeing bleary-eyed reporters sleeping in their cars while the siege continued.

Captain McCorley caught an RTÉ cameraman trying to get stew from the army food van that came down from the Curragh barracks every day. 'I said: "What do you think you are doing?" He says: "I am ex-[military], I am ex! I was in the Air Corps!" We had journalists trying to get free stew every day.'

The various media organizations set up caravans on the GAA pitch beside the estate, so that journalists could write up their stories. 'It was like a wee village, with all the caravans, with phone lines installed in each one,' recalls Deric Henderson, who was reporting for the *Belfast Telegraph*. 'We shared a phone line with the *Irish Times* and, while there was competition between the newspapers for a scoop, we knew we were in for a long haul so we tried to help each other out.'

The gardaí called in two eavesdropping specialists from the London Metropolitan Police, who arrived in Dublin by RAF plane and set up equipment at St Evin's Park that they could use to listen in from 500 yards away. They also brought a small video camera and fibre-optic cable, unheard of in Ireland at the time, which could allow gardaí a view into the room next to the box bedroom. Captain McCorley recalls that the gardaí had a handyman who drilled a hole into the wall to install the camera, 'but Eddie heard it and started shouting so they had to stop. We were thinking what to do. Then one of our army guys had this bag and out fell a mouth organ [harmonica].

'I said: "What the fuck did you bring a mouth organ here for?" and he said: "One of my kids must have thrown it in the bag. I didn't know it was there." I said: "Well, fuck . . . what if we played the mouth organ when they are boring the hole? Maybe Gallagher won't hear the drill." And that's what we did and it worked. A garda put the fibre-optic cable in there and we could see that there was nothing in the big bedroom except a case on the bed. But we learned a lot – they weren't using the big bedroom, they were staying in the little room with Dr Herrema.'

Garda Chief Superintendent Lawrence Wren was in Monasterevin to manage the crisis. Originally from Abbeyfeale in rural Limerick, he mixed police formality with folksiness. Before Wren got involved, other gardaí established ground rules with the kidnappers. They guaranteed that they would not enter the siege house as long as Dr Herrema wasn't harmed.

Wren approached the house. 'Marion, Marion! Eddie!' he shouted at the upstairs window. 'Dr Herrema! Dr Herrema, can you hear me? Hello?'

There was a long pause before a woman's voice answered the call for Marion. 'Yeah, I'm here,' she said.

The gardaí made recordings of their negotiations with Eddie and Marion. The transcripts of these conversations, which haven't been published until now, reveal the way Wren used his ability to control the kidnappers' nourishment as a negotiating chip. The 'basket' to which Wren repeatedly refers in the recordings was a shopping basket rigged to a pulley system that allowed the gardaí to send food and water up the outside wall and in through the window.

> Chief Superintendent Wren: This is a recording made at about midday on the 23rd of October, 1975, at Evin's Park, Monasterevin, of the kidnappers of Dr Herrema. Marion, it's the chief superintendent back again. Marion, do you hear me?
>
> Marion: Yeah.
>
> Wren: You asked me for some chocolate when I was here last.
>
> Marion: Yeah.
>
> Wren: I have got some for you. I have got some [chocolate] bars for you. I will put them into the basket. Now pull up this basket, will you, please? I also asked for the ambassador. We'll have to deal with that when we get it. Will you pull up this basket?
>
> Marion: Will you send up the salt there as well, please?
>
> Wren: Oh, sorry. Where is the salt here? There is salt in the house. You can test it when you get it. You were

probably using it yourself anyway [before the siege].

OK. Go . . . pull away.

Marion asks for a bottle of cider.

Wren: Cider? Oh my goodness, you'll get drunk! Cider is
not the best thing on an empty stomach. That would just
sicken you! Cider would sicken you!

Marion: Just some cider.

Wren: I'll try to get it, but if you get sick, 'tis you that's looking for
it, not me. I'll get you the bread and butter for a start anyway.

In his rural Limerick accent, the word 'start' is pronounced
'schtart'.

At times, Wren complains that Marion wants too much –
bread, butter and a bottle of gin: 'Wait a while now, take it
easy, we'll take it step by step, Marion. I'd want to be on
roller-skates to keep it all going.'

The kidnappers' demands for food and alcohol were irri-
tating the army snipers, who were listening to the negotiations
from next door and who were living on basic army stew.
When Marion asked for a pineapple, Captain McCorley light-
heartedly complained about it to a Special Branch officer
outside the house next door.

'I said to one of the Special Branch officers – they are
looking for pineapple and we are getting army stew and the
sandwiches we bring here ourselves,' McCorley recalls. 'An
hour and a half later there was a knock on the door downstairs and it was Wren. He said to me: "You are after repeating
something that you overheard!" I said: "What do you mean?
The only thing I repeated was to the Special Branch man
outside the door here." He says: "Well, someone is leaking
information to the press and they know what is happening!"
I said: "I can guarantee it wasn't me and I don't think it was

any of my lads. My wife doesn't even know I am here. She may suspect it, but she doesn't know."'

It later emerged that a journalist had gained access to a house in the estate that was close enough for him to overhear the negotiations and report the details.

In one of the negotiation tapes, Wren refers to the kidnappers' demands, sent in a letter to the Dutch embassy before the siege, that Rose and the two other prisoners be released and that the kidnappers be given a plane to the Netherlands. 'There is nothing I can do about that,' he tells them, adding that it will require government approval, and that their demands for a plane cannot be met unless they can guarantee that it will not be hijacked.

Wren: There are a number of questions that will be asked, I have no doubt about that, by the government and the minister. The first one is this: What guarantee has the government here that if you were given this concession – which, frankly, I doubt, but I'm not making the decision – but anyway, what guarantee have they that Dr Herrema will be safely landed in Holland and that you or anybody wouldn't have a gun to the pilot's head and land in, say, Paris, Rome, Libya or anywhere else? I'm going to ask that question and try and get an answer so I'm not delaying time on the thing.

Dr Herrema intervenes, at Eddie's urging.

Herrema: Do you hear me? OK, I agree with Marion, I don't see any other way out.

Wren: Just a minute now, Doctor, please. My question is to Marion and Eddie at the moment. It is *they* who will be giving the answer. What guarantee is there? Can you hear me, Marion?

Marion: Yes, we won't harm the doctor.

Wren: Unfortunately, that is not a guarantee. The government will want some guarantee.

All three in the box room were using a bucket for their waste. The gardaí agreed to send up a portable toilet attached to the shopping basket. The portable toilet soon became full. Chief Superintendent Wren offered reassurance, over and over, that the kidnappers could safely come downstairs and use the bathroom.

After Wren promised that he would step back from the front door of the house, Marion started walking down the stairs. On the audio tape, she sounds like a frightened deer being slowly coaxed. Her footsteps can be heard. She tells Wren she is carrying a gun and her handbag. She says she wants to check that the back door is properly locked. Wren tells her there is no question of that happening and that she should return upstairs immediately after using the bathroom.

Dr Herrema can be heard on the tapes expressing fear that Eddie will shoot him unless their demands are met. (Eddie claims that it was his idea for Herrema to 'pretend I'm some madman that could kill everyone, that he was really scared of me'.)

Wren's exchanges with Eddie got testier as time went on. On one occasion, Wren shouted to Dr Herrema that the kidnappers would not shoot him, that there was nothing to be gained from that.

Eddie: You said that last fucking time.

Wren: Don't shout at me! I don't shout at you! [*Pause*] You can shout as long as you want, I don't intend shouting back at you.

Wren decided to make conditions for the kidnappers even more difficult. On 31 October, he ordered an officer to remove the window from the bathroom upstairs, to create a draught and also to allow a possible entry point for an army raid, which was being rehearsed in a barracks.

A Special Branch officer climbed a ladder but struggled to get the window out.

Captain McCorley recalls: 'The Garda top brass were getting pissed off because it was taking too long. Wren ordered that a Sergeant Egan go up the ladder to help the other garda. There was all this bulletproof material that came over from England and we were ordered to dress Egan in it and he climbed the ladder.'

The box bedroom had a skylight window. Eddie looked down and could see the two men on the ladder, trying to remove the glass from the bathroom window.

Eddie pulled open the skylight and fired a shot at Egan. He recalls: 'He was trying to get the putty out of the glass. I think he was acting up for the benefit of the media, the TV cameras, being photographed doing something. You could see his hand going up and down. I wasn't aiming for the finger but I shot the top of it off him.'

Egan came down the ladder immediately, with blood streaming from the hand with the top of his finger blown off. He was rushed by ambulance to hospital.

By now, Captain McCorley had developed a system of secret communication between the gardaí and Dr Herrema.

'Dr Herrema was doing most of the negotiation at the window,' he recalls. 'They were standing behind him, telling him what to say, of course. I suggested to the gardaí that we get a blackboard and write out questions with yes or no answers with instructions to lift his fingers in response – if he lifted one finger, it was yes, two fingers it was no.'

Numerical answers could also be given by this method. When a garda asked Herrema, 'How many guns do they have?' the captive held three fingers close to his body, while continuing to demand a plane to the Netherlands.

Captain McCorley could see that Dr Herrema was leaning further out the window as the days went by. 'His head was sticking out the window until eventually he was bending out. Soon, nearly all of his body to waist level was out the window.' The army and gardaí saw it as an opportunity.

In the first week of November, gardaí wrote on the blackboard: 'Are you willing to jump? One finger: yes; two fingers: no.' Dr Herrema held up one finger.

They consulted Captain McCorley, who brought in thick pole-vaulting mats from the Curragh gym to cushion Dr Herrema's fall.

However, journalists spotted the mats piled outside the house and the news was broadcast on the radio. Eddie had a small transistor radio, and was able to follow coverage of the siege. Captain McCorley sensed that, after hearing the report about the mats on the radio, Eddie began to suspect that Dr Herrema was deceiving him. 'From then on, they only let him go as far as the window and didn't let him lean out at all.'

As the siege continued into November, gardaí restricted food and water supplies. Dr Herrema advised Eddie to suck his finger to stimulate saliva in his dry mouth. Eddie tried drinking his own urine.

Dr Herrema would later tell RTÉ radio that he did everything he could to relieve the tension, even giving Eddie shoulder massages. All three were emotionally exhausted and physically weak. Eddie had abdominal cramps and head-aches. Dr Herrema felt Eddie was looking for a way out. He encouraged this by suggesting that Eddie might have meningitis.

Eddie had by now abandoned any hope of getting Rose and the others out of jail, or of getting a plane out of Ire-land. He began negotiating a reduced sentence.

Captain McCorley recalls: 'A number of senior counsel came down, acting for the state. They were under the win-dows and they were talking up to Eddie. They were saying he would have to do five years in prison. He was saying: "No, three years!" and he mentioned a number of other unsolved crimes that he wished to be covered by the sentence. Eddie eventually said: "You know what you can do? You can fuck off." They decided they would leave and Gallagher took the disposable toilet and threw its contents down on top of them.'

On 7 November, Marion told Chief Superintendent Wren that they were ready to come down. She was about to surren-der but hesitated and said she had to go back up for a minute.

Wren shouted: 'No, no, come down, Marion, come down.' He assured her again and again that she would not be harmed.

She and Eddie threw two guns out of the window. The gardaí shouted back that they knew there was a third gun and, after a pause, the third gun flew out the window.

Marion lifted her blouse to show she was not armed. She walked down the stairs slowly and surrendered.

Eddie gave Dr Herrema a souvenir bullet, and then they came down too. They were given water, which they gulped down quickly, then tea. Eddie and Marion were arrested and a medic checked them over before they were taken under heavy army and police escort to Dublin, with dozens of reporters' cars in pursuit. Dr Herrema had been a captive for thirty-six days.

On the day after the surrender, Saturday, 8 November 1975, Eddie and Marion were taken to the Special Criminal Court.

Eddie confirmed his name, and then launched into an attack on IRA leader Joe Cahill and his associate Gerry O'Hare, the husband of Rose's prison friend Rita O'Hare.

'I would not be here but for Joe Cahill and Gerry O'Hare. They are two informers, two police informers and so-called members of the Provisional IRA,' he said. This was non-sense: there was, and is, no reason to believe that either Cahill or O'Hare was an informer or had any hand in leading the authorities to the house in Monasterevin. Any chance of a reconciliation between Eddie and the IRA ended in that moment.

Asked by Justice Pringle if he wanted to apply for bail, he said he refused to recognize the court and 'all you three political bastards who sit on the bench'.

Marion was far quieter. She waved at friends and declined to apply for bail. Newspapers reported that she looked on the verge of tears.

Eddie was taken to the republican wing of Portlaoise prison, where he was kept with a mixed group of far-left prisoners, away from the larger block of Provisional IRA inmates.

'I spent more than ten years in Portlaoise [for the kidnapping] and I was never with the Provos,' Eddie says. 'I was basically non-Provo or a non-person to the Provos. I was on a separate landing with the Official IRA and people connected to the kidnapping. Also, the INLA was formed by then, so they were there, and three people from the [Marxist] People's Democracy.'

Marion was sent to Limerick prison, where she joined Angela Duffin, Rita O'Hare and Rose Dugdale, who was now thirty-four years of age, and nearly two years into her nine-year sentence for helicopter hijacking, art theft and handling explosives. 'Marion had proven herself, she was a fantastic volunteer,' says Rose. 'I was looking forward to seeing her, after so many months of just seeing her on the TV.'

11. Barbed-wire Love

As soon as Marion Coyle arrived, there was a change in the internal relationships among the republican women prisoners. Rose now spent lots of time with Marion, and both Angela and Rita felt excluded. It led to tension between Rita and Marion.

'Rita was frozen out a bit,' says Angela Duffin. 'There was maybe a bit of hurt. There were arguments, too, between Marion and Rita and I would have been brought into it.'

Rita criticized Marion for failing to obey Provisional IRA orders with the Herrema kidnapping. 'Rita would have been very Provisional IRA and very well got with Gerry Adams,' says Angela. 'Marion at that time was considered a bit of a renegade and a rogue. They had no authority for the kidnapping and yet she agreed with it.'

Fighting back, Marion would taunt Rita for being from Belfast, while the real urban guerrillas were in her home city of Derry, where they considered themselves to be winning the war.

To Rita's annoyance, Rose and Marion walked around the prison yard every day, laughing and joking. Marion tried to teach Rose table tennis, but failed. They talked for hours about politics.

Despite the tensions, the four republican women practised marching and standing to attention. 'We were doing drill in the kitchen and one day I said: "Right, stand to attention,"' says Angela Duffin. 'Marion took offence at that and said: "WHO are YOU? You are not republican!" There were things like that, but Rose would laugh it off and try to keep the peace.'

Marion and Rose did artwork together for republicans outside. One large piece, signed by both, was later confiscated, and a garda gave it to Tiede Herrema as a gift. It shows an IRA man with a machine gun in front of a map of a barbed-wire-enclosed Ireland and has a quote from Padraig Pearse: 'Let no man be mistaken as to who will be lord in Ireland when Ireland is free. The people will be lord and master.'

Within days of Marion's arrival, another political prisoner, Marie Murray, was transferred from Mountjoy. She was on remand for the murder of a garda in September 1975 while robbing a bank for a revolutionary anarchist group. The off-duty garda had been chasing her through St Anne's Park in Dublin when she turned around and shot him dead. She was to be jointly tried with her husband, Noel, and they were likely to face a mandatory death penalty for capital murder. No woman had ever been executed in the history of the state. Marie Murray was neatly dressed and wore thick glasses, and looked more like a librarian than a revolutionary anarchist.

Angela Duffin remembers Marie Murray as 'a lovely person and highly intelligent. She started talking to Rita, and Rita latched on to her because she couldn't be with Rose with Marion around.'

Every Saturday, Ruairi was put into the back of Betty's car – first to see Eddie in Portlaoise, then on to Limerick to see Rose. Betty would hold him up while Portlaoise prison officers searched his nappy or, when he got older, his pockets.

'In Portlaoise, there was no physical contact allowed at all,' Betty recalls. 'Eddie was sitting behind two wire mesh screens, but the meshes weren't aligned, so you would try to look past one only to see the other, and then you are trying to see Eddie, who was sitting behind that with a prison officer beside him. I used to come out of there with terrible migraines.'

There was an official no-touching policy in Limerick, too, but Betty ignored it, even when admonished by the prison guard. 'I would pretend I didn't hear and hug Rose and hand over Ruairi to her. He loved that.'

Betty learned how to stare down prison officers who searched Ruairi's nappy.

'There was one prison officer and he used to give me an awful bad time. An IRA man who did his time in Long Kesh said to me: "What you do is: you look him up and down as if you were saying: 'OK, I have you in my mind now,' and give him a smile as if to say: 'That's the last smile you'll ever see.'"' The prison officer never searched Ruairi's nappy again – he must have thought that I was going to tell someone on the outside what he was like.'

With five notorious female political prisoners in Limerick prison, all of them considered high escape risks, the authorities were clamping down. Rose Dugdale had bombed a police station from the air; Rita O'Hare had smuggled explosives into a prison in her vagina; Marie Murray had murdered a garda; Marion Coyle had kidnapped a businessman; and Angela Duffin had been involved in a robbery in which a wages clerk was murdered. Rita was refusing prison visits because she was not allowed to touch her children when they came to see her. John O'Neill had gone to the newspapers to complain about it, telling the *Irish Times* that Rita considered it an 'inhumane' restriction.

Whatever the personal tensions among them, the five political prisoners agreed to stay united against the prison system. Their grievance was simple, as Rose recalls it: 'I wanted to hold Ruairi and Rita wanted to hold her children.' On Saturday, 22 November 1975, the five objected to no-touch prison visits and shouted at prison officers and the governor during visiting time.

The governor brought in Garda reinforcements for the rest of the week.

On the following Wednesday, 26 November, the five women boiled kettles in the kitchen, pretending to be making tea. Garda Sergeant Delia McTigue came in at 10.20 a.m. to see 'what they were up to', as she later told a compensation hearing. She noticed that there were multiple kettles all boiling at the same time, and Rose Dugdale was pouring water into a basin. Rose turned around suddenly and flung the boiling water into Sergeant McTigue's face: 'She whipped it up and gave it to me right into the face from about arm's length.' Marion Coyle threw a teapot and a kettle at her while her face was burning. The other prisoners threw boiling water at the other female garda who came into the room behind Sergeant McTigue, and then barricaded themselves inside.

The gardaí, furious, brought in both their own members and prison officers in riot gear. They broke open the door and sprayed them all with a fire hose before dragging them out. In the melee, Rose received an injury to her lip that required four stitches. Sergeant McTigue, for her part, was off work for fourteen weeks, with a burn mark five inches by three inches on her right temple and a five-inch burn mark on her right wrist.

The five were each placed in solitary confinement and denied visits.

'We were put "on the boards" with just a mattress on the

floor,' says Angela. 'Mice were a comfort to me then and I hate mice. You could hear a *click, click, click* sound and the mice would have broken through and were eating something. One of the screws looked in and was screaming. I thought it was hilarious. That was the only time I liked mice, when they frightened the screws.'

Mayor Coughlan released a media statement strongly denouncing the attack on Sergeant McTigue and suggested that the five political prisoners should be given manual labour to occupy their time.

When the five were let out of solitary, relations between them began slowly to improve.

Angela, who knew that Rose was fond of Southern Comfort, got a prison officer to help her procure Southern Comfort-flavoured chocolates as a Christmas present. The five 'toasted' Christmas 'by holding up these liqueur chocolates because there is a wee bit of alcohol in them, which isn't allowed. I tried to order them again for Rose, but the prison officers stopped it.'

Marion and Eddie went before the Special Criminal Court again in January 1976 for a pre-trial hearing. Eddie's defence barristers told him he would get twenty years at least for the Herrema kidnapping.

Eddie recalls: 'I decided to play it up. I knew I was going away for a long time so I might as well show up the court.'

He strongly objected to Portlaoise prison searches for baby Ruairi, he told Justice Pringle. 'Surely, they don't think a one-year-old baby would carry in a revolver,' he told the packed courtroom.

With Fine Gael in power, Eddie also took the opportunity to bring up the party's embarrassing links to the fascist

Blueshirts in the 1930s. 'I consider that when a person is on remand he is entitled to all privileges, but in this Blueshirt state, they are denied,' he said.

Asked if he objected to being tried by Justice Pringle, he replied: 'You are only a hack – a Blueshirt political hack.'

Both he and Marion announced that they would represent themselves in court, with the assistance of state-funded legal counsel.

It took weeks to prepare the security for the trial, which began in February. Twenty vehicles accompanied Eddie Gallagher to court and back again to Portlaoise prison.

On 28 February, while the trial was ongoing, Betty brought Ruairi to see Rose in Limerick – the first time Rose was allowed to see her son since her attack on Sergeant McTigue the previous November. Three days later, Betty brought Ruairi to the Special Criminal Court in Dublin for Eddie's trial. As Eddie was about to resume a cross-examination, he was told that Ruairi was in court. He turned around. Betty stood, lifted Ruairi and encouraged him to wave. Ruairi waved and said loudly: 'Daddy! Daddy!' Eddie smiled broadly and waved back.

Later that week, he and Marion were convicted of falsely imprisoning Tiede Herrema. Eddie was also convicted of causing grievous bodily harm to Detective Sergeant Egan, attempting to obstruct the executive branch of government, and possession of a weapon without a licence. On 11 March, Eddie was jailed for twenty years, Marion for fifteen. On the same day, David Dunne, who ran the safe house in Mountmellick, got a three-year suspended sentence. Kidnappers Vincent Walsh and Brian McGowan were jailed for eight years each, and Thomas Dunne for seven years. Michael Hall and P. J. Bailey were given five years each.

*

Less than two weeks after Eddie and Marion were jailed, Wally Heaton, who was due to be released after serving over half the four-year sentence he had received for the burglary at the Dugdale family estate, was jailed for an additional six years at Liverpool Crown Court for conspiracy with Rose to obtain explosives and firearms for terrorism.

John Hall QC, for the prosecution, had told the court that Wally and Rose had smuggled small arms and ammunition on the ferry from Stranraer to Larne to be used by the IRA. After hearing evidence from a Special Branch officer who had followed them, Justice Caulfield told Wally at sentencing: 'Plainly, the woman with whom you conspired was Rose Dugdale. On my assessment of the facts that have been proved, I think you joined this conspiracy for two reasons, the first being a woman and the second, money.'

Marion Coyle was twenty years old when she was sentenced for her role in the Herrema kidnapping. If she had to serve the full term, she would be thirty-five when she got out. With good behaviour, she might be out in ten, having spent all of her twenties in prison.

She and Rose grew very close. She would curl up in Rose's bed during the day and they would read newspapers together and smoke.

Angela Duffin, who was in and out of court many times for both the Galway and Cork heists, also found Rose an invaluable support. 'She would talk over my case with me and reassure me. I was up and down to the Special Criminal Court every few weeks. She was always there with a few cigarettes and advice for whoever was going to court and she talked it over with me when I told her I wanted to leave the Official IRA.'

They all had words of consolation for Marie Murray, who was sentenced to death on 9 June, along with her husband, Noel, after a trial so disruptive that they both had to be lifted out of the dock and placed in holding cells below.

The Supreme Court overturned the death sentences the following December, finding that it wasn't proven that Marie Murray knew the man she shot was a police officer when she pulled the trigger. Instead the Murrays received a life sentence, of which they would serve seventeen years.

The closer Rose and Marion became, the less Rose wanted anything to do with Eddie Gallagher. But her Limerick solicitor, Gordon Hayes, was advocating she marry him – as a way of avoiding deportation.

Rose was still wanted in the UK for importing weapons into Northern Ireland with Wally Heaton, and for the Strabane helicopter bombing. She and Eddie agreed with Gordon Hayes that it was best for Ruairi if they were married, even if there was little love between them. If they were successful, it would be the first time in Irish history that two prisoners married.

In March 1977, the Justice Minister, Patrick Cooney, turned down their request to get married in either Portlaoise or Limerick prison. As soon as the refusal came in, Hayes applied for Rose and Eddie's right to a 'proxy' wedding, with a nominated replacement making the necessary declarations on behalf of the absent party. Hayes argued that Ruairi was 'entitled to have his position regularized' and said he would bring a High Court challenge if the minister refused.

In July that same year, Iris Murdoch – by then viewed as one of the greatest British novelists and philosophers of the twentieth century – wrote a letter to the Irish embassy in

London pleading for better prison reading material for Rose. She had considered writing a novel about Rose, but news of her research leaked to the *Spectator* and she abandoned the idea. Murdoch had gone from youthful Marxist to middle-aged hard-line unionist and was bitterly opposed to Irish republicanism – even denouncing her own novel about the 1916 Easter Rising because she feared it would be used by the IRA as propaganda. 'The Troubles were the one topic that could move her to tears of anger and distress,' her authorized biographer, Peter J. Conradi, wrote. But despite her hatred of the IRA, she took up the cause of Rose's reading list after a request from Peter Ady.

From her home in Oxford, Murdoch wrote to the newly appointed Irish ambassador to the UK, Paul Keating.

Dear Mr Keating,

I am sorry to trouble you, but I wonder if you could advise me or give some help in a matter related to my former pupil, Rose Dugdale? I am worried because I fear she is not being allowed to receive serious and learned matter (on economics and history), which various people are wanting to send her. She wishes to study but cannot, a terrible extra punishment to an intellectual person.

Needless to say, I detest her actions and views, I have not written to her or seen her, and do not propose to. But I feel this loss of serious reading is a grave matter, not least because any hope of 'a change of heart' lies in the possibility of reflection. If she could write and think, there might be some hope for her in the future. Condemned to reading thrillers, in the company of uneducated IRA ladies, she is most likely to emerge an embittered urban guerrilla.

Can anything be done to alter this aspect of her punishment? Is there anyone in the new government I could usefully write to? Or perhaps you could make some representations in the appropriate quarter if you felt sympathetic? I do apologise for bothering you thus out of the blue – most gratefully and with all my fond wishes,

Yours sincerely,
Iris Murdoch

The embassy in London wrote to the Secretary of the Irish Department of Foreign Affairs:

I attach a typed copy of the letter which the ambassador in London received from the well-known writer Miss Iris Murdoch, concerning access to reading matter for Rose Dugdale.

The ambassador would like to send Miss Murdoch a reply of a reassuring kind as regards Miss Dugdale's access to books she may require. With this in mind, perhaps you could look into the matters raised and let us have material for reply.

The letter was passed on to the Secretary of the Department of Justice, seeking a response to the 'well-known writer, Miss Iris Murdoch'. The Department of Justice contacted the governor of Limerick prison the same day, seeking a list of the books available in the prison library.

While two government departments, the Irish ambassador and the prison governor were formulating a response to Iris Murdoch, Rose and the other prisoners were immersed in far less cerebral cultural enrichment. Elvis Presley died on 16 August, inspiring an impromptu Elvis night among the republican prisoners. 'Rose turned up the radio,' Angela Duffin recalls, 'and we were crying listening to it and singing along.'

In September, Richard Crowe, a senior Department of

Justice official, wrote back to the Minister for Foreign Affairs about Rose's reading list.

For security reasons, persons in custody in closed prisons, including Rose Dugdale, may not receive parcels of food or books. In Limerick Female Prison, the prisoners have access to a library, which is stocked by the City Public Library. Attached is a list currently in the library. These will be changed as necessary for other titles. Rose Dugdale made out a list some time ago of books which she would like to have available in the prison library. Most of these have been supplied and the rest are being obtained.

Apart from books, Rose Dugdale is allowed to buy one newspaper of her choice (including on Sunday); Hibernia *magazine (a fortnightly) and* The New Yorker *and* Scientific American *(both monthlies).*

Mr Crowe enclosed a list of every book available in the prison library, including *Voyages of Discovery* by Captain James Cook; *Red Hand: The Ulster Colony* by C. Fitzgibbon; *Guerrilla Days in Ireland* by the War of Independence leader Tom Barry; and *Memoirs of an Art Thief* by E. Moat. There were just over a hundred books on the list. Many were purchased especially for the female section of Limerick prison on Rose's request, such as *Economics* by S. E. Thomas, the 1975 Trade Statistics from the Central Statistics Office and *Analytical Psychology* by David Cox.

That same month, the solicitor Gordon Hayes appealed to the new Justice Minister, Gerry Collins, to allow Rose and Eddie's wedding to go ahead. 'I wish the minister would make up his mind to what should be a simple transaction, for I hope that the politicians are not playing politics with the emotions of my clients,' he said in a media statement.

In November, after Minister Collins was served with a High Court writ, he appeared on RTÉ radio and said that 'The possibility of a wedding is under consideration for the sake of the child.' And when Hayes announced on the 20th of that month that he would return to the High Court that week to seek a summary judgement against the state, Minister Collins caved in. On 2 December, the Department of Justice told Rose and Eddie in writing that they would be allowed to marry in prison. 'I'm not sure I wanted to marry him,' says Rose. 'But they wanted me for the Strabane bombing, and I wasn't going to hand myself over to them.'

12. Steel-bar Wedding

Extra soldiers and gardaí were brought in to Limerick prison for what was surely to be the most heavily guarded wedding in Irish history.

Philip Bray was not alone in feeling there must be an ulterior motive for the wedding. 'Part of my time as a prison officer was spent in the censorship room, reading prisoner letters. There was nothing romantic about the letters between Eddie Gallagher and Rose Dugdale,' he says. 'You had to wonder if this was an escape attempt or just a ploy to keep Rose in the country.'

Still, 'an air of excitement' was building in Limerick about the wedding, the *Irish Times* reported. 'Miss Dugdale was brought up a member of the Church of England and Mr Gallagher is a Catholic. Arrangements for the mixed marriage were made by the Bishop of Kildare and Leighlin, Dr Lennon, and Dr Newman, the Bishop of Limerick.'

Betty's neighbour Willie Lynskey was tasked with collecting the wedding cake from a baker in Lucan, Co. Dublin. IRA members called him with security instructions.

'I was under strict orders that the cake shouldn't be handed over to the prison officers until the night before the wedding,' Lynskey recalls. 'There was a lot of security. I never even took a photograph of the wedding cake because I was afraid in case the gardaí got a hold of the photo and used it to detain me.'

On the morning of the wedding, 24 January 1978, dozens of reporters gathered at the prison gate, hoping to photograph or interview anyone going in. The newspapers were offering big money for photos of the wedding, and Philip Bray searched the small group of wedding guests, under instruction to seize any cameras. 'I was told that if there were any photos in the newspapers the next day, I was out of a job,' he says.

Betty and 3-year-old Ruairi – smartly dressed in a light blue coat, striped jumper and grey flannel trousers – were greeted by a media scrum outside. The groom was brought from Portlaoise in a prison van early in the morning, with two army trucks, two garda cars, and a car of plainclothes Special Branch officers. Included in the military escort was Captain Pearse McCorley, the army officer who had been in charge of the sniper team at the Monasterevin siege. Once, he had managed a sniper team that might have been asked to kill Eddie Gallagher; now, he was escorting him to his wedding.

When he arrived at the prison, wearing jeans and a blue jersey, Eddie was thoroughly searched, including his shoes and socks. His brother and best man, Patsy Gallagher, gave him a dark striped suit to change into.

In the prison chapel, Rose greeted Eddie with a kiss on the cheek and a 'thank you'. She was wearing a blue velvet jacket and brown corduroy slacks and was carrying a white rose given to her by a fellow prisoner.

Eddie handed her a piece of chewing gum and said it was one of his few earthly possessions to offer. He also gave her a silver crown coin with a picture of Queen Victoria on one side.

They had not seen each other since 1974, when Rose was arrested with the Russborough paintings.

Eddie leaned in and hugged her. Their youth was disappearing. Rose was thirty-six. Eddie, still just twenty-eight, would be in his forties by the time he got out of prison.

The prison officers kept the timing as tight as possible: the wedding had to be over by the close of visiting hours. The Justice Minister, Gerry Collins, had made it clear: this was not an IRA celebrity wedding. Get him in, get him out.

By the time Betty and Ruairi made it through security and into the prison chapel, Rose and Eddie were already at the altar. 'I walked up to Rose with Ruairi in my arms,' Betty recalls. 'The prison officers wouldn't even let me shake hands with Eddie, it all moved so fast.'

The wedding Mass was in Latin, per Rose's request, and included a reading from the Book of Amos about fighting injustice. The priest, Father O'Connell, quickly ran through the ceremony, conscious of the time restraints and the couple's lack of religious fervour. They exchanged plain gold rings, which had been purchased by Betty using money provided by Rose's solicitor. Several times during the ceremony, Ruairi broke free from Betty and ran to Rose, only to be gently brought back again by Betty and a prison officer.

After the ceremony, Betty brought Ruairi up to Rose and Eddie. It was the first time they had seen and held their child together.

Knives were not allowed, so someone used a pen to cut the cake and began to hand out slices on paper plates. A prison officer called time on the hurried reception before Betty even got a slice. Eddie and Rose were led to a room off the dining room for the day's standard prison meal of roast beef and cabbage, watched closely by the prison officers. At 2 p.m., mealtime was over, and they embraced. Eddie was hustled into a prison van and sent back to Portlaoise.

On the road back to Portlaoise, Captain McCorley recalls, 'Ordinary people flashed their headlights and waved from the side of the road to wish Gallagher the best.'

Father O'Connell stopped to tell the media swarm that it was a pity that the bride and groom were not allowed to consummate their marriage. 'It seems against all natural law, or any law I know, that they were not left together for a while,' he said.

In a Limerick pub after the brief ceremony, an Associated Press photographer staged a shot of Ruairi raising a half-pint glass to celebrate his parents' wedding. The *Irish Times* gave front-page coverage to the wedding the next day, with a picture of Eddie in the prison van on the way in as the main image. On the inside pages, there was an extensive report and a picture of Patsy Gallagher carrying Ruairi out of the prison.

Peter Ady came for a visit with her partner, Georgina Moore, soon after the wedding. She and Rose joked about the romance of it all. Peter then travelled to Navan, where Betty tried to ensure that she didn't have to see anything that would embarrass her. The IRA men who occasionally stayed in the house were told to keep away during her visit.

Betty was impressed by Peter – she was always so polite and she always brought presents for all three children. 'Some of Eddie's people would come through and they would have something for Ruairi but not the other two. But Ms Ady always had something for all three. It was always something educational, always some book for the children to learn something, and she always had such lovely manners. We were all very fond of Miss Ady. She and Miss Moore, they were lovely to talk to and down to earth. They couldn't understand how Rose went this way. I think it upset them, going in to see her. I was going to offer them to stay and I thought: "Do I put them in the one room or two?"' But Peter and Georgina stayed at the Russell Arms in Navan.

Another visitor to Ruairi in the safe house from time to time was Rose's half-brother Tim Mosley, who stayed loyal to Rose even as her sister, Caroline, shunned her. Betty remembers him as lively and friendly.

In early 1978, a new prisoner arrived in the women's section of Limerick prison; I will call her Ashling. She had severe mental health problems and had been smashing windows in her home town, including at a garda station.

She was notorious locally. 'I know it broke my parents' heart to see me in the newspaper all the time,' Ashling says. She would be in and out of Limerick prison twenty times between 1977 and 1985, when she emigrated.

On her first day in prison, she sobbed loudly in the recreation room. An English woman sat down beside her. 'She shook my hand and said: "My name's Rose." She was very smiley and friendly. When I learned she was actually Rose Dugdale, I nearly died! I knew she had been on the telly a lot.

'I wrote to my mother and father and said: "You will never guess who's in here." I mentioned Rose and Marion. Then I remember being marched down to the officers and the warden, Miss O'Rourke, roaring at me to tear up the letter and that I wasn't to mention anything about any other prisoners in my letters.'

The cells opened at 7 a.m. and were locked up at 12.30 while the prisoners were served lunch. They opened again at 2 p.m., and prisoners were free to roam around the cells and the yard until 7.30 p.m., when they were locked up for the night.

Ashling was in a cell next to Rose's. At night, Ashling would scream until her face was sore, and the other prisoners would complain. Guards would rush in, hold her down and give her drugs – Largactil (an antipsychotic) and paraldehyde (a sedative).

One night the medications made her very sick. Rose made her a concoction from hot water and strawberry jam to calm her stomach and throat.

Ashling found both Rose and Marion kind and sympathetic. For Rose, Ashling was a cause to fight for. 'Rose would say to me: "Are you back in again?" And she would advise me that I was too young to be in prison and that there must be something better for me.

'Marion was very kind as well. We would play table tennis in the recreation room. She was very good at it, but she would let me win.'

The three would walk in the exercise yard, with Ashling in the middle and Rose and Marion on either side. 'We used to have a laugh a lot. They had a good sense of humour. After a while, I got used to prison and, in the morning, when I'd see Marion, I'd call: "Maid Marion!" and she'd reply: "Who made me?"'

Marion began a correspondence course in art history. Rose remembers looking at Rembrandt paintings with her and discussing them together. Every so often, they would call Ashling into their cells for a cup of tea. 'Rose had some really nice biscuits,' Ashling recalls.

Rose did not allow the prison officers to see her chatty, nurturing side. 'I can honestly say that in the whole time I was there, I don't think I heard Rose Dugdale speak once,' Philip Bray says. 'They would be talking away in the exercise yard and then when they were coming close to a prison officer, they would go quiet and start up talking again as soon as they passed you.'

One day while walking in the yard, Ashling recognized one of the soldiers on the prison roof as a man from her home town. 'He shouted down "Hello!' one day and I asked him to throw me down a cigarette, which he did, but he was caught and he got fired from his job.'

Rose and Marion tried to give Ashling a republican education, but they didn't get very far. 'Honestly, I hadn't a clue what they were talking about,' she recalls.

When Ashling's behaviour became very disruptive and she was judged to be at risk of self-harm, she would be taken down to a padded cell in the basement, close to the furnace. 'That was an awful place, it smelled of paraldehyde, and I spent my birthday there. One of the guards said: "Which birthday is it?" and handed in a card from my parents.'

Ashling recalls Marie Murray surging through the women's wing in some private fury, with 'this strange smile on her face. I just didn't warm to her as much. She would walk up and down the corridor with a broom handle, hunting for mice to kill.'

Philip Bray, by contrast, remembers Marie Murray as 'a very soft woman, preoccupied with getting pregnant. She desperately wanted to have a baby with her husband and was willing to start a legal fight over it. As far as we were concerned, she had her political beliefs but she wasn't a subversive in the same way that we would view IRA prisoners.'

Noel Murray, who was being held in Portlaoise, and Marie Murray had begun a decade-long legal battle to have conjugal visits so that they could have a child in prison. Rose would come over to Marie's cell to help her with her paperwork and letters to newspapers.

As soon as Marie's campaign began, Philip Bray was summoned to the governor's office. The governor told him that the prison did not want another baby born in the female wing to a political prisoner. 'He told me to keep a close eye on

Marie Murray during visits so that nobody tried to slip her some of her husband's sperm.' Specifically, the governor told him to be on the lookout for something wrapped in a tissue.

'I tried my best not to laugh and turned to the side,' Bray recalls. 'I think the governor needed a sex-education lesson because I didn't think Marie was going be able to conceive like that.'

Rose and Marion compared notes on Eddie Gallagher and came to the conclusion that Eddie was a player, always looking for the next political and relationship high. They each had a far closer relationship with each other than they'd ever had with him. Still, Ashling noticed that they both had newspaper clippings about him on the walls of their cells. Today, Rose recalls that there was no tension between herself and Marion about Eddie and describes Marion as 'a far greater person than Eddie'.

A strange dynamic developed with Marie Murray. 'Marie would come down the corridor sort of wiggling in her tight jeans and come into Rose and Marion's cells,' Ashling recalls. 'I felt like she wanted something with them, but Marion was more into Rose and Rose was more into Marion than they were into Marie.'

For Rose, Betty was a conduit to the outside world. In 1978, the Year of the Horse in the Chinese calendar, Rose gave Betty a birthday card she had made for Angela Duffin, who had been released the previous year. The card read, 'Happy Birthday. The Year of the Little Horse', with a doodle of an IRA member holding a rifle and an Irish tricolour. On the inside it carried the message: 'Here's the nicest thing I can give you – my playmate, Angela: Lots of Love + Carry On + Fists of Furr + something to brush it with.' Angela says the message 'was probably a reference to my prison-yard protest when Ruairi was sick'.

On their weekly visits to Limerick, journalists interviewed Betty as she was walking Ruairi out of the prison. The Gallagher–Dugdale family was an object of fascination for the Irish public, and Betty had become a prison-gate celebrity. She recalls, 'It never stopped. You'd come out of the prison, and every week they'd say: "Well, how are things this week?"'

On his RTÉ radio programme, Gay Byrne mused about Ruairi's future, with a father in one prison and a mother in another. Listeners were touched, and letters and phone calls started coming in. Someone sent in a toy car and motorbike set and asked that it be passed on to Ruairi. 'Ruairi used to play with it with my own kids on the floor,' Betty recalls. ('I broke it, like I broke a lot of things,' Ruairi recalls.)

Ruairi was treated just like her other two children, says Betty, and the others were trained to take him inside if the media showed up at the house. 'They would look after him, he would look after them. If they saw a stranger talking to him, they would take him by the hand into the house; they knew what to do because it could be a reporter.'

Unlike the other two children, Ruairi had a habit of using swear words. Betty believed it might have come from visiting his father in Portlaoise prison.

'Oh my god, I was so embarrassed. I thought people would think I taught him that language. No matter where he went, he'd use it. Even if we'd stop in somewhere for a meal, he would say: "I want a knife and fuck!" When I would remind him not to swear, he would say: "I did not, I did not!"'

Around this time, according to Betty, John O'Neill was becoming very controlling of her. His passion was céilí dancing, and he and Betty used to travel to dances together; but at some point he started to make up excuses for her not to go. When she became suspicious and asked him why not, she says, he beat her savagely, punching and kicking her down the stairs and dragging her by the hair. Betty was in and out of hospital, even as she continued raising three small children and looking after IRA members.

Rose arranged through her half-brother Simon Mosley for Betty to be paid petrol money and small expenses for bringing Ruairi to her every week. At John's insistence, Rose also bought cars for both him and Betty. After John complained about his car, Betty recalls, 'Rose's solicitor came and paid for a brand-new Ford Cortina 1600, and John traded that in for another car; he had to be even bigger – a two-litre. It was a really big car, well beyond his means.'

During a visit with Betty to Limerick prison, John, perhaps sensing that Rose was a soft touch, asked her to buy them a much bigger house at Rathaldron, just outside Navan. When Betty objected, John pressed down hard on her foot under the table to shut her up. Rose agreed to buy the house for them for £25,000 but insisted that it must be kept in her name. The family moved in within weeks.

The new house 'was too big for us really', says Betty. 'I was very happy in Navan and we had lovely neighbours. When [John] heard she had money he wanted the big house. I was never a day happy in it.'

After the move, Betty says, John became even more violent. Betty, no longer living near her family, was scared. 'He would go to céilís. He didn't have much wages. The times were tough and my mother bought me a beautiful dress for a dinner céilí. I didn't get to the dinner céilí. He destroyed me. He'd go for my head a lot because he knew I had meningitis and it would hurt me more. The rest of my body wasn't as bad, but I was black and blue.

'I often ended up in the hospital. He was very vicious when he started. One time, I was in hospital for a week. I had a terrible [bruised] face on me. The doctor took a garda down to the hospital so that I could make a statement. The doctor told me that if I didn't leave John, I would die. I made a statement to the garda and I never went back to the house.'

Sean O'Neill says he never witnessed his father being violent to his mother, but Ruairi says, 'I can remember the blood on the stairs. It was horrible.'

When she was released from hospital, Betty moved to a bedsit flat on Dublin's North Circular Road. She was a seamstress by trade and found work stitching at a local factory. A friend collected Ruairi, Sean and Andrea from John one day for what was supposed to be a day trip. Instead, the friend took the kids to Betty, who planned to keep them with her in Dublin.

'They stayed with me for a while, but John found out where I was living and he came with a few others and told me to back off, and then they took the three children,' Betty recalls. 'It was a very tough time. I look back now and I think: "How did I make it through that time?" I just don't know, but you have to find the strength, I suppose.'

Betty sent word to the children that Mammy couldn't be living at home but would come to see them. She was still their Mammy. She eventually settled in County Galway.

Ruairi Gallagher and Sean O'Neill both remember John O'Neill as a caring father. But word that something had gone terribly wrong in the O'Neill household made it into the media. On 9 July 1979, the *Irish Times* ran a carefully framed article

headlined 'Woman Caring for Gallagher Boy "Not Missing"',
speculating about the whereabouts of Betty O'Neill.

> Mr John O'Neill, whose wife, Betty, has been rearing the
> son of the kidnapper, Eddie Gallagher, and Dr Rose Dug-
> dale, at their home in Navan, Co. Meath, said yesterday that
> his wife was staying with friends in Monaghan for a few
> days. He denied reports that she was missing and said that
> she would be back soon. He had been speaking to her on
> the telephone, he added. Mrs O'Neill had been suffering
> from an attack of nerves, her husband said, and she felt it
> was better to get away to recover.

Betty could still visit the children under supervision of her
family members and assured them that she loved all three of
them.

The Pope was coming to Ireland in September, the first
ever papal visit there, and the country would be coming to a
standstill. The government announced an amnesty for prisoners in celebration of his visit. Rose saw this as an
opportunity to get out. The amnesty came, and non-political
prisoners due for release that year got an early release in the
hope that the Pope's presence would inspire them to change
their ways.

Through her solicitor, Rose contacted the former government minister Dr Noël Browne and told him about her wish
to take custody of Ruairí as soon as possible. Browne promised to raise the amnesty for her in the Dáil, though this did
not happen until 15 November, after the Pope had departed.
Browne's opposition to the Catholic Church was well known,
and his demand that Rose Dugdale, a fellow Marxist non-
believer, be released as part of a papal amnesty was met with
derision by the Justice Minister.

Browne threw down his papers. 'I suggest that we forget about the Pope and think about Christmas,' he said. 'Will the Minister agree that there are special circumstances in so far as this child is deprived of both parents and, in addition to that, there appear to be difficulties in relation to his present guardianship, and in all these circumstances, in the interests of the child, if not in the interests of the mother, will the Minister consider this case sympathetically?'

The minister made no commitment, and Rose recalls: 'I knew there was no prospect of me getting out.'

John O'Neill, who was by now dating other women, flew into a jealous rage because Willie Lynskey drove Betty and Ruairi to Limerick one day to visit Rose. He suspected, correctly, that Betty and Willie were in a relationship. He convinced two IRA men to come with him to Willie's house, armed with pickaxe handles.

Willie recalls: 'It was September 1980. They beat me so bad that I was in the hospital for at least a fortnight. I had fractures on five vertebrae and my shoulder blades were fractured. I was beaten on my legs and I wasn't able to lift my arms up. I still have the marks on my legs. I was on thirteen weeks' sick leave. I never went back to work for the council after that.'

Willie Lynskey moved to Galway with Betty and they began new lives. The children remained with John in Meath.

Eventually, the prison authorities fixed a date for Rose's release: October 1980. On a visit, Rose showed Ruairi her wedding ring and said that she would give it to him when she got out. She was coming home, and they would soon be together. She was excited, but apprehensive.

'I'd never been a mother before and I wasn't sure how to go about it. I had only been with Ruairi for visits and now I would be his full-time mother for the first time. I had no experience at all.'

John O'Neill, hoping to help Rose avoid the media, asked the prison authorities if they would open the prison's outside gate on the day of her release so that he could drive into the prison grounds. The governor agreed.

On the morning of her release, Rose hugged and kissed Marion Coyle. Outside, the media were gathered at both the front and side entrances.

John O'Neill tried to deceive them, according to a report in the *Guardian*: 'Mr O'Neill and Ruairi left the prison carrying a suitcase and declaring that Dr Dugdale would be freed next Wednesday.'

Inside, the prison guards were ready to give Rose her 'gratuity' – a lump-sum payment from the Irish state that departing prisoners received for 'good behaviour'. Evidently, Rose's serious assault on a garda in the prison, and her general disdain for the prison officers, did not disqualify her from the payment.

'I don't want it! You can keep it, you bastards!' she snapped on the way out. One of the officers joked: 'Well, will you take a cheque, then?'

And those were the final words Rose heard inside. She was released into the prison yard.

Philip Bray looked out of the window. As agreed, the prison gate was opened wide enough to allow John O'Neill to reverse his car into the yard. Rose ran across, jumped into the boot of the car and shut it behind her. The car took off and the media gave chase.

Rose recalls a 'terrible smell of fumes' in the boot of the car. 'I wanted to hold Ruairi so much,' she says.

The chasing media cars lost them temporarily in the streets

of Limerick, and Rose jumped out of the boot and into the back seat. 'It was an unbelievable moment,' Ruairi says. 'I thought it would never come, and here she was with me. I remember holding her hand and thinking: "This is my Mammy."'

John drove Rose at speed to a local guest house, where she stayed for two hours with Ruairi. As she had promised, Rose took off her wedding ring and gave it to him. He was transfixed and put it in his dungarees pocket.

After two hours, they rushed out of the guest house and into the car and sped off, leaving the media behind.

Before they reached Navan, Ruairi had to go to the toilet. John pulled over the car and Rose took Ruairi into the bushes, where he lowered his dungarees and relieved himself. When they got to the O'Neill house, Ruairi reached into his pocket to get the ring and found that it was gone.

He was devastated: the ring was a token of Mammy and Daddy together.

Rose's memory is different. 'Is that what Ruairi said? That's not how I remember it. My memory was that I took the ring and flung it far away, never to be seen again.'

13. The Avenger of Fatima

After getting out of prison, Rose stayed in an apartment in Dún Laoghaire while looking for a place in Dublin. Ruairi remained with the O'Neill family in the Meath countryside.

Asked about why she left Ruairi with John O'Neill, Rose says: 'I had to keep Ruairi's wishes at heart. Ruairi was in school, he had good friends and he told me that John was like a father to him. Yes, there were very great difficulties between John and Betty, but they didn't affect Ruairi and I needed time to adjust to life outside prison before I could take Ruairi. I visited him every weekend and I know that he was happy.'

Ruairi says: 'John was wonderful to me – I never had a problem with him. I had a brother and a sister in Sean and Andrea, and Rose had to get her head together when she got out of prison, so I think everyone agreed, including myself, that I would stay with the O'Neills.'

A senior Garda Special Branch officer called to see Rose in Dún Laoghaire.

'She wouldn't let me in and I didn't have a search warrant,' he recalls. 'I was just at the door telling her who I was and that I wanted to talk to her. I really just wanted to see what her thinking was and with whom she was mixing, but she wouldn't let me in, so I just left.'

Within days of her release, she was back in the national headlines. On Friday, 17 October 1980, the *Irish Times* ran a story detailing how an RTÉ presenter, Marian Finucane, had been prevented from interviewing Rose for the *Women Today* programme about her prison experience because Rose was considered to be an IRA representative. As with RTÉ's decision not to report Rose's court statements when she was sentenced, the row pitted journalists against the government and the management of the state broadcaster.

The *Irish Times* said that the *Women Today* team was 'upset because they did not believe the interview would have been in contravention of Section 31, as Dr Dugdale and others had told them that she was not a member of any of the proscribed organizations'.

RTÉ was not alone in its assessment of Rose's continuing allegiance to the IRA. Another senior Special Branch officer at the time, whom I will call Thomas Connors, believed that Rose would remain with the IRA, even if not as an official member. 'She was radical, she was determined, she had that type of personality that was not going to back down,' he says. 'You could see, even from the people she was mixing with while in prison, that she wasn't just going to go back to her family in England and forget the whole thing.' The *Irish Times* article on the RTÉ row carried a photo of a smiling Rose at a demonstration the night before for Pauline McLaughlin, an IRA woman in Armagh women's prison who was demanding political status.

Rose bought a tiny red-bricked cottage at 13 Eugene Street in the Coombe, a working-class neighbourhood in south inner-city Dublin. It was one of a row of houses in a maze of narrow streets known locally as Munchkin Land. The house was just ten feet wide, and the front door opened directly into the living room. At night, Rose would leave the bedroom door open, afraid of being locked in – a habit she kept for the rest of her life.

She began work for the Sinn Féin weekly newspaper, *An Phoblacht*, writing articles and assisting with printing. The paper – like all the Irish papers – was soon dominated by the hunger strikes undertaken by republican prisoners in Northern Ireland. Rose and the other newspaper staff, including a pipe-smoking German woman named Inga, worked up to twenty hours a day on the newspaper during the hunger strikes.

Over the summer of 1981, ten prisoners in Northern Ireland died on hunger strike – eight IRA members and two members of the Irish National Liberation Army. Belfast erupted in riots every night and the level of violence soared. Sean O'Neill remembers Rose visiting Navan every weekend, 'and she'd still have the black ink on her hands from printing *An Phoblacht*. She would bring me posters – posters with [IRA] lads on streets with guns and masks – revolutionary posters, I would call them.'

Even after Rose's release, Peter Ady and Georgina Moore continued to play a role in the life of Ruairi and the two O'Neill children in Navan.

'At the time, I was into horses, so Peter gave me a present of these off-white riding jodhpurs,' Sean O'Neill recalls. 'They always had presents. Then Peter invited me over to their place in Oxfordshire. I was twelve, I think, it was 1981, and I went over there unaccompanied during the summer. It was my first time being in a plane and Peter was very kind. She and Georgina were well-to-do people but they never looked down on me and they let me ride Peter's horses.'

In October 1981, a year after Rose's release from prison, she and Ruairi met her parents in Wexford, where the wife of her half-brother Simon Mosley was performing at the Wexford

Festival Opera. It was an awkward meeting, but her father, Eric, made the best of it, and dearly wanted a bond with his young grandson. He took out a piece of paper and asked Ruairi to write his name.

'I wrote "Ruairi" and then I stopped,' Ruairi recalls. 'He wanted to see if I was going to call myself a Dugdale or a Gallagher, but I didn't write any more. I didn't know what to write, or I was too stubborn to write any more, I'm not sure which.'

Rose's family still held out some hope that she would leave the IRA and return to England, but she could not even visit the UK, because she was still facing charges for the Strabane helicopter bombing.

Rose's and Ruairi's lives changed in 1983, when John O'Neill moved back to his home town of Coalisland, Co. Tyrone. Rose was concerned that if Ruairi moved to the heartland of the Troubles, his connection to her and to Eddie Gallagher would make him a target for loyalists.

'Even when we were up in the North on visits, Ruairi's name would be kept quiet in case of army harassment or loyalist attack,' recalls Sean O'Neill. Eventually, Rose concluded that she would take Ruairi to live with her in Dublin. 'I can remember the car journey up to Dublin with Ruairi,' Sean says. 'That was a hard, hard day for all of us. Ruairi was crying, he didn't want to leave us, it was a tough time for everyone.'

Ruairi recalls: 'It took a while to settle in, it was a big change but, at the same time, I was finally with my mammy.'

Ruairi was struck by how small the Eugene Street house was. '"The shoebox", I called it,' he says. 'When the tide came in, the walls were damp and the walls were only a single cavity block, no insulation.'

Sometimes Rose brought Ruairi into the *An Phoblacht* office with her; other times, he recalls, 'She would work all night and come home in the very early hours, her hands black with ink, with these big fresh loaves of bread that looked like a shoe, from a place up off Thomas Street that opened very early in the morning.'

At weekends, Rose would bring Ruairi and other kids from the area on fishing trips to the Blackwater and Boyne rivers. 'It was magic, just magic,' says Ruairi. 'We caught trout and they were so slimy and we didn't want to take them off the hook, so Rose would do it for us. I was very happy to be with her. She was like my older sister, she told me everything.'

At a funfair, he was too small to reach one of the shooting games, so Rose got down on all fours and he stood on her back to shoot. A family photo shows Rose on her hands and knees, beaming at the camera while Ruairi aims at the target.

Within Rose's family in England, there were long discussions about what to do for Ruairi. They wanted to support him, but one family member says that they felt that if they sent money to Rose, it would likely be used to fund the IRA.

Eric Dugdale asked his Irish groundskeeper at Yarty, John McGinnis, to travel to Ireland every year to spend time with Ruairi – to take him fishing, which Ruairi loved, and remind him that there was still a family in England who were thinking of him. 'John was such a lovely, kind man,' says Ruairi. 'I really looked forward to his visits and I really loved fishing. I wanted to go over to England to see my relatives, but Rose was definite on that point. She would say: "That's not for you," and she would drop it. She was loving and caring, but I didn't understand why I couldn't know my English family. I was half English after all.'

*

Rose enrolled Ruairi in an Irish-language school, Scoil Chao-imhín, on the grounds of the Department of Education, just off O'Connell Street. It was run by a kindly grey-haired woman named Nora, who made a fuss of Ruairi, the boy who had been born in prison.

One of Ruairi's classmates, Andrew Keniry, remembers that Rose used to climb the steps to a pietà statue in the school grounds and play King of the Castle with the children. 'We would try to push Rose off, but she would grab one of us and swing us down the steps and say: "Not today." She wasn't trying to let you win, you really had to try to knock her off her perch. She was great fun and very different from the other parents.'

On Saturdays, Rose would load Ruairi in the car to visit Eddie in Portlaoise prison. The visiting room was in a cold prefab building.

'There was the chicken wire to the ceiling and, after that, Perspex painted black that was about a foot high to stop you flicking any notes over, and after that another foot-high Perspex wall, and after that more chicken wire, and behind that sat my father. Beside him would sit this prison officer, taking notes of everything that was said.'

Ruairi would tell his father some of the Irish-language words he was learning and Eddie would tell him about the fishing they would do when he was released. At the end of each visit, Eddie asked the prison guards not to handcuff him until Ruairi's departure.

For Ruairi, such scenes were normal. 'As far as I knew, every child did this: you went to see your parents in prison. I don't think I saw my life as different from anyone else's.'

One day, he ran out into the prison yard to pick some primroses for Rose. He picked the most colourful ones, and then turned around to see Eddie being led out into the yard to be returned to his cell. A prison guard saw Ruairi and threw a jacket over the handcuffs, but Ruairi noticed them. Eddie nodded and smiled as he was taken back into the prison building. Over time, Ruairi came to realize that maybe his parents were different, and that maybe other children weren't living like this.

Rose's connection to the republican movement was becoming more official. She worked for *An Phoblacht*, attended meetings at the Sinn Féin office and enrolled Ruairi in Fianna Éireann, the republican Boy Scout group, which had long been a recruiting ground for the IRA. The boys, in their green uniforms and black berets, learned how to march and drill in the courtyard of Sinn Féin headquarters on Parnell Square, and were taught an IRA-inflected version of Irish history.

Fianna Éireann had the same military structure as the IRA. Ruairi's Officer Commanding (OC) was a Dublin boy called Ronan MacLochlainn.

Ronan's mother, Roisin McLoughlin, had been accused of luring British soldiers to their deaths in a 'honey trap' operation in Belfast in 1973. Four British sergeants met two women in a bar who invited them home for a 'party'. When they got to the apartment, a group of IRA men came in and told the sergeants to lie face down on a bed before shooting them all in the head. Three died and one survived, with serious injuries. Roisin McLoughlin fled south, and successfully fought extradition on the grounds that it was an IRA operation and the Republic did not extradite to Northern Ireland for political crimes.

Roisin and Rose became good friends and would take the boys on Fianna Éireann training weekends in the Dublin mountains.

*

In the early 1980s, Dublin was crumbling. Unemployment was at over 20 per cent and the working-class areas of the city were being ravaged by drugs. In part because of global upheaval – the fall of the Shah of Iran, the Soviet invasion of Afghanistan – the West had been flooded with cheap, high-quality heroin.

Young people could be seen openly shooting up on the stairways of Dublin's worst flats – including Fatima Mansions, Dolphin's Barn and St Theresa's Gardens in the south inner city, close to Rose's home. When addicts needed cash, they robbed their neighbours and held up cars. Drivers no longer stopped at traffic lights outside the Dolphin's Barn flats. The gardaí were underfunded and ill equipped to deal with the crime wave.

A new group came together in 1983 through a local priest, Father Jim Smyth, who lived in a working-class flat complex and saw the daily squalor of young people injecting on the landings. He and a group of mothers from the north inner-city flats contacted members of both the Official and the Provisional IRA, including Christy Burke, an inner-city Provisional who had been jailed in 1971 after he was caught at a Dublin IRA training camp.

'Father Smyth and the group of mothers came to me in a republican building, I won't say where,' Burke recalls. 'In the beginning, I wasn't interested. I said: "There is a war in the North. I am a republican, we have other duties." Then Father Smyth said: "Christy, we need your help." I said: "OK, I'll meet you at 1 p.m., but as soon as the state finds out that I am involved, they will say you are being used by the IRA, that it is all for recruiting into the IRA." That was all true – the media went after us for IRA involvement from the beginning.'

At that first meeting, they discussed a name for the new group. Burke recalls: 'I said: "Well, you are all concerned parents. So why not call yourselves Concerned Parents Against Drugs?"'

That very day, the new group, strengthened by IRA muscle, decided to march on drug dealers' homes in the Hardwicke Street flats. 'There was actually a queue after school of kids lining up at a window to buy heroin,' says Burke. 'The money went in a window and the drugs went out. It was appalling.'

Five drug dealers were removed from their flats and a sixth refused to leave. Burke claims that he was a restraining influence on Father Smyth, who wanted to attack the dealer's house. 'I said: "If you attack the house, I'll be blamed because I'm IRA." We eventually got the fella into treatment in Grangegorman, and things took off from there.'

Concerned Parents Against Drugs grew quickly. 'People became obsessed,' says Burke. 'If a person in any flat even had a single visitor, people would come to us saying they must be dealing drugs. It was a huge, huge operation. There were kids in taxis coming into flats to buy drugs, but there were people waiting for them twenty-four hours a day who would say: "There are no drugs for sale in these flats, go on with yourselves."'

Sinn Féin and the IRA became very interested in the growth of CPAD, which seemed to point to a way for the IRA to attract broader support in the South.

Thomas Connors, the former Special Branch officer, says that gardaí were aware of IRA involvement. 'Well, let's just say that there was a certain coincidence of membership between the IRA and Concerned Parents. Were Concerned Parents a front for the IRA? No, but there was a definitely a pattern.'

As CPAD spread, Rose became one of its most prominent figures on the south side of the city. She was soon leading marches and evictions.

'She was absolutely determined, and she really cared,' says Christy Burke. While Burke's preferred method for taking on drug dealers was forced evictions, Rose was pushing for the methods the IRA used against dealers in Northern Ireland: punishment shootings to the knees, and executions if kneecapping didn't make them stop. But the IRA didn't want to bring punishment shootings to the South, fearing a Garda crackdown.

Rose and Burke were not solely focused on the suppliers: they both wanted to help addicts as well. Treatment options for addicts were extremely limited at the time, Burke recalls, and 'The state absolutely wouldn't help us. We were considered IRA and a threat so we had to look elsewhere.'

They found help from Sister Consilio, a nun who set up a treatment centre called Cuan Mhuire outside Athy, Co. Kildare. Addicts who came to CPAD looking for help would be referred to her.

Gerry Clarke, who attended CPAD meetings, remembers Rose as the most committed member on the south side of the city. 'People would say, "That's English Rose" – that's what she was called. We knew that she once dropped bombs on the British from a helicopter, that she had stolen all these paintings from some lord, that she was up for anything. Everyone knew that she was in the IRA so they knew that whatever she did had IRA protection, so people were drawn to her. It wasn't that they were supporting the IRA, it was that the IRA were backing them, and Rose was constantly about escalating the situation, taking it to the next level with the drug dealers, and so people followed her.'

Some families were losing multiple children to overdoses. Sister Elizabeth O'Brien would later tell a trial for vigilantes accused of killing a heroin dealer that the flats were losing an entire generation to heroin. The vigilantes who were driving pushers out of the area were the only recourse that residents had, she said.

Their method was simple – identify the dealers, break into their homes and set up a chain of people to pass along the dealers' furniture to a van outside. The idea was that the gardaí could not place the blame for the theft on a single person.

Two local girls would babysit Ruairi while Rose was working at *An Phoblacht* or busy with anti-drugs meetings. One of them, Martina Brennan, recalls being 'intrigued' by this English woman whose tiny house was filled with books.

'Then, after a few weeks, my dad came around to the house with me to see who was this English woman I was talking about. When we walked away from the house, he said: "You are never babysitting there again." I said: "Why?" and he said: "Do you know who that is? That's Rose Dugdale, she's an IRA woman," and he explained who she was. It was the worst thing he could have said. From that moment on, I was gripped. She was this larger-than-life woman with all of her escapades. I didn't tell Rose what my dad said because I didn't want to hurt her feelings, but I couldn't keep away. I wanted to know more about her. Now, as an adult, I would look at it differently, but at the time I thought she was great.'

Martina remembered being in school on Clanbrassil Street in 1975 when a Sister Margaret Mary led her and the other children in prayer every day for the safe release of Dr Tiede Herrema. Now she was getting babysitting work from the woman whose freedom the kidnapping was intended to secure.

In 1961, Rose Dugdale (wearing glasses) and Jenny Grove disguised themselves as men to attend a debate of the male-only Oxford Union. Women were admitted as members two years later. (Alamy)

TWO girl students disguised as men last night gate-crashed a male fortress—the debating floor of the Oxford Union Society.

It was the first time that women had seen the inside of the society—in which the likes of Mr. Macmillan and Mr. Gaitskell learned their oratory.

Wore wigs

The girls—one a blonde—sat for two hours during a debate on the traditional first motion of the Michaelmas term — "that this house has no confidence in Her Majesty's Government."

The blonde—22-year-old Jennifer Grove—wore a dark wig and her companion an auburn one.

Both had on duffle coats and scarves borrowed from men friends.

Sympathisers also gave them membership cards to get into the debate.

The girls, from the newest Oxford girls' college, St. Annes, are campaigning for the university's 1,200 women to be given the right to join the Union.

Before they went to the debate the girls went for a try-out at their "local."

The landlord, who knows them both, asked: "What will you have, GENTLE-MEN?"

From the *Daily Sketch*, 20 October 1961.

MEN WERE GIRLS!

IT'S happened! Two girls have got into the famous men-only Oxford Union Society and stayed for the whole debate.

Their secret? They were disguised as men. They are seen being made-up in the picture above.

It was the first time the all-male Oxford University fortress had been breached in its 160 years history.

The girls are Rose Dugdale, wearing glasses above, and Jennifer Grove, 22, both of St. Anne's College.

Before entering the debating hall, they called into a public house where they are known. The landlord asked: "What are you having, gentlemen?"

Why did they do it? Miss Grove said: "We gatecrashed to draw attention to our appeal to be allowed to join the Union."

From the *Daily Mirror*, 20 October 1961.

Rose at Oxford, circa 1961. (Jenny Grove)

In October 1963, while studying and teaching at Mount Holyoke College in Massachusetts, Rose (at left, with notebook) covered the campus visit of Dr Martin Luther King, Jr for the college news bureau. (Special Collections Department, Mount Holyoke)

Rose sits atop her MG coupé with a book on European history, having recently submitted her master's thesis, 1964. (Joseph D'Addario/ Special Collections Department, Mount Holyoke)

Rose in London, early 1970s. (Shutterstock)

Rose raises a fist in Tottenham, 1972. Next stop: Northern Ireland. (Alamy)

HAVE YOU SEEN THIS WOMAN?

BRIDGET ROSE DUGDALE
REQUIRED FOR INTERVIEW BY THE POLICE

AGE: 32 YEARS

HEIGHT: 5 FT 6 INS - PROPORTIONATE BUILD - MASCULINE APPEARANCE

FEATURES:

HAIR: LONG FAIR AND STRAIGHT   COMPLEXION: SALLOW   EYES: BLUE/GREY

DRESS:

USUALLY WEARS SLACKS AND SUEDE JACKETS OF DIRTY AND UNTIDY APPEARANCE

SPEECH:

EDUCATED ACCENT OR SOMETIMES ADOPTS AN IRISH ACCENT

ALIAS:

KNOWN TO HAVE A DRIVING LICENCE IN THE NAME OF
MARGARET LINDA CROWTHER

IF RECOGNISED SHE SHOULD BE DETAINED

YOU SHOULD TELEPHONE ANY INFORMATION TO

LISBURN MILITARY (LISBURN 5111) EXT 2214

Issued by Headquarters Northern Ireland

After Rose took part in a helicopter bombing raid on Strabane Barracks in 1974, the RUC hastily issued a wanted poster. (Victor Patterson)

Rose is taken from court after being sentenced to nine years in prison for her part in the Strabane bombing.
(*Irish Times*)

Eddie Gallagher is escorted by police from the besieged Monasterevin council house where he and Marion Coyle had been holding the Dutch industrialist Tiede Herrema captive in autumn 1975, hoping to secure Rose's release from prison. (Press Association)

Marion Coyle leaves prison in 1985 after serving ten years of her 15-year sentence for kidnapping Tiede Herrema. (Shutterstock)

The baptism of Rose's son Ruairi Gallagher was a speedy affair, as his godparents, Martin McGuinness (*left*, holding Ruairi, with his wife Bernadette) and Marion Coyle (*right*), feared arrest for IRA membership. (Andrea O'Neill)

With both his parents serving long sentences, Ruairi was taken in first by Myles and Nora Shevlin in Dublin, and then by Betty and John O'Neill in Navan. (Ruairi Gallagher)

Rose and Ruairi on Abbey Street in Dublin, October 1981. (Eamonn Farrell)

The shoulder-fired missile launcher developed by Rose and Jim Monaghan was known as the 'biscuit launcher' because two packets of digestive biscuits were used to absorb the recoil. (Image below courtesy of the National Army Museum, London; image at right from an IRA propaganda video)

Spear-gun fishing with Ruairi on holidays in Greece in 2001, Rose showed off her familiarity with rifles. (Ruairi Gallagher)

Jim Monaghan pictured with Ruairi Gallagher in Eugene Street circa 1986, shortly after Jim began a relationship with Rose. (Ruairi Gallagher)

Jim and Rose out for a walk in Bray, Co. Wicklow, in 2016. (Ruairi Gallagher)

'Ruairí was a good little boy, very intelligent like his mother, and I tried to keep it secret that I was in the house,' says Martina. Her friend Patricia Green also regularly babysat for Ruairí.

One day, Martina went with her family to a community centre on Donore Avenue, beside St Theresa's Church, to hear Rose speak at a CPAD meeting.

'I remember watching her up there and thinking: "Thank God I am not a drug dealer or a drug user, having to deal with that woman." She would put the fear of God in you, the way she talked about drug dealers and how they all had to be pushed out.'

A young drug addict was brought up on stage by his family to be publicly denounced. 'His family said he had stolen from them and then listed other people that he had stolen from to pay for his habit. People were desperate for an answer and there was a feeling at the time that the drug dealers could just be forced out of the area. Rose was up there giving this huge speech. People knew she was in the IRA so she had this authority. She was really strong up there, denouncing this dealer and that dealer.'

The meetings had an almost religious fervour to them – the sinners brought up on stage to make a public confession, to denounce others, to cry, to beg forgiveness – not from God, but from Rose and CPAD. Sometimes suspected dealers would turn up, get up on stage and explain themselves. If Rose and the community didn't believe them, they would be given twenty-four or forty-eight hours to leave the area or face the consequences.

The militancy of the south-side CPAD operation was causing concern for the gardaí.

In March 1984, it hit national headlines when two men were abducted: Martin 'The Viper' Foley, a heroin dealer; and his friend Thomas Gaffney. Republican vigilantes kidnapped Gaffney on the 11th from the Park Inn in Harold's Cross. He was blindfolded and taken to a farmhouse far outside Dublin. On the 22nd, Martin Foley was taken at gunpoint from his home in Crumlin at 6.45 a.m. His brother, Dominic, and a woman staying at the house were tied up and gagged, and neighbours heard Foley's cries for help as he was bundled into a van.

The abduction of Martin Foley led to an emergency joint operation by the Special Task Force (known in the south inner city as Taskies) and the Serious Crime Squad. Gardaí chased the van across the city for twenty minutes, while a gun battle raged with the kidnappers. They cornered the kidnappers near the Wellington Memorial in Phoenix Park. The kidnappers opened fire on them again and the gardaí fired back with Uzi sub-machine guns. Eventually, four of the kidnappers were arrested after trying to escape. Gardaí recovered a shotgun, a rifle and two handguns nearby.

Later that day, amid a huge Garda crackdown, the kidnappers released Thomas Gaffney in rural County Limerick. He was blindfolded and driven around for three hours before being dumped on a country road. He removed the blindfold and walked for an hour and a half before reaching the presbytery in Abbeyfeale at 1.45 p.m. The gardaí took him to Newcastle West garda station before he was brought back to Dublin, unharmed.

Was Rose involved in the kidnappings? Thomas Connors says, 'She was there or thereabouts.'

Rose, for her part, says: 'It was a fantastic operation. Do the gardaí expect people to just sit around and let drug dealers take over? I'm not saying who was involved, but fair play to them, because so many were dying of overdoses at the time and republicans were left to deal with the mess.'

The episode showed the new militancy of Concerned Parents Against Drugs. The Labour Party, which feared a rise in Sinn Féin support in working-class areas, demanded action from the state. Frank Cluskey, the former Labour Party leader who represented Crumlin in the Dáil, denounced the kidnappings and called for a system in which people could report drug dealers to the gardaí and not to the vigilantes.

The *Irish Times* investigated the links between IRA/Sinn Féin and Concerned Parents Against Drugs, and noted that Rose Dugdale had instructed CPAD members not to speak to the media.

At the UK general election in June 1983, Margaret Thatcher's government was swept in for a second term. Among the new intake of Conservative MPs was Patrick Ground, a barrister who was married to Caroline Dugdale, Rose's sister. On election night, Caroline got up on stage with him at the count centre to the huge cheers of their supporters, who waved Union flags and held up Margaret Thatcher helium balloons and 'Hounslow for Maggie' signs.

Also elected a Conservative MP for the first time was Peter Ady's former student Edwina Currie. Like all newly elected Conservative MPs, Patrick and Edwina were given security tips from the police on avoiding an IRA attack. They were shown how to check for bombs under their cars, and where they should and shouldn't park in the Palace of Westminster. Four years earlier, Irish republicans had killed the Conservative MP Airey Neave by planting a bomb under his car there.

In 1984, the IRA bombed the Conservative Party conference at the Grand Hotel in Brighton, killing five people, including Sir Anthony Berry, the deputy government whip in the House of Commons, and Roberta Wakeham, wife of the chief whip. The Trade Secretary, Norman Tebbit, a close friend of Prime Minister Thatcher, was badly injured and his wife, Margaret, was permanently disabled.

Edwina Currie, who was staying in the Old Ship, a hotel near the Grand Hotel, witnessed Norman Tebbit being extracted from the rubble and taken to hospital. She and her fellow MPs and party activists were all told to go to the conference and put on a brave face. Currie recalls: 'I think we all felt dazed, bewildered, lacking information, with a highly incomplete picture; a kind of incoherence reigned, in which good behaviour was paramount. Call it a stiff upper lip, if you like. We greeted those who had been in the Grand Hotel with hugs and tears, such as Greg Knight MP, my neighbour from Derby, who was still dirty from the dust; he'd been in the bar late. Nobody panicked; anyone who broke down gathered themselves together very quickly. It was important that the press did not take pictures of us in disarray – or the bombers would be winning. When Margaret Thatcher arrived, the conference hall hugely cheered – she was pale but resolute, like most of the delegates.'

Rose was given an apartment above the Sinn Féin office in the Coombe, not far from the Eugene Street cottage. She and Ruairi moved in. Rose would work in the Sinn Féin shop and chair meetings in the office at the back, while they rented out the Eugene Street house.

Ruairi liked the apartment – there was more space, and he could keep pigeons on the roof. There were always IRA people coming in and out of the office below, and everyone patted Ruairi's head – the famous Ruairi who had been born in prison and who was always in the newspapers. 'Ah, the wee Ruairi. How about you, pet? Your mam's a great woman so she is.'

Rose chipped away at the social niceties he had learned from Betty. When he said: 'Pardon me?' Rose would correct him. 'It's not "Pardon me,"' she would tell him, 'it's "Wha'?"'

On Friday, 27 September 1985, Marion Coyle was released from prison, having served nearly ten years. There were no reporters waiting outside – she was told just an hour before to pack her belongings. She was being released three months ahead of schedule after a discussion and vote by the Irish cabinet.

Moments after her release, she knocked on the prison door and was let back in again. Prison officers called her a taxi to get her to the train station.

'It was kind of a forlorn sight,' recalls Philip Bray. 'She was thirty at this point, a lovely young woman, and her entire twenties were spent in Limerick prison.' From Limerick train station, Marion called her parents in Derry to tell them she had been released, then took the train to Dublin, where, at the request of her parents, two Sinn Féin officials greeted her at Heuston Station. She gave a clenched fist and a smile to the waiting photographers.

She met Rose in Dublin and went with her to Ruairi's school.

Ruairi says, 'I can remember her standing outside the school with Rose. She immediately lifted me up and hugged me. Rose said: "Marion is here," but I didn't know who she was, except she was this nice, friendly lady.'

Marion had known Ruairi as a baby, and now he was a schoolboy. She desperately wanted children of her own. She and Rose agreed it was time for them both to find good men.

'I think we both wanted to settle down at that point,' says Rose.

Rose's involvement with Concerned Parents Against Drugs moved to a new level of intensity in 1985. The group set itself squarely against the two main heroin networks in the south inner city: the Dunne Brothers and the Ma Baker group.

The Dunne Brothers were part of a family of sixteen children, and eight of the boys were sent to industrial reform schools. Their parents drank heavily and there was rarely food in the house. A neighbour remembers one of the older boys trying to feed his siblings some stew from a pot in the flat and being unable to cope.

As adults, some of the Dunne Brothers moved from burglary into the drug business, linking up with major heroin dealers in London. When supplies arrived from London, one of the brothers would hire a taxi on St Stephen's Green and go from one grim flat complex to another, dropping off the heroin to small-time dealers.

The Ma Baker network was based in Crumlin, a twentieth-century suburb to which a young Brendan Behan and thousands of other people had been transplanted from the inner-city slums. Ma Baker, the name of an American gangster, was the local nickname for Marie Nolan, who ran the Crumlin heroin business.

Unlike the Dunne Brothers, she had no compunction about dealing from her own properties: one in the inner city, where the family had originated, and one in Crumlin. She was known to keep a fire going all day. At any sign of the gardaí, she would throw the heroin into the fireplace before the police made it up the steps to her flat. Her network was known to give out free samples to get young people addicted.

Rose became obsessed with the two networks, to the point that Christy Burke grew concerned about her single-minded fanaticism. She harassed heroin dealers and organized protests outside their homes, while setting up meetings in which people would come forward and publicly identify the street dealers working for the gangs. If a suspected dealer didn't come down to the next meeting to explain himself, Rose and her supporters would invade their flat, take all the furniture and hand it out to residents or old people who lived in the area. After members of Ma Baker's gang smashed up the cars of Sinn Féin members in Crumlin, the IRA retaliated by smashing the gang's cars.

On 21 October 1985, CPAD held a meeting at the Bricklayers' Hall on Cuffe Street, during which a home on Cathedral View Court off New Street was identified as being used by Ma Baker herself. People stood up at the meeting and said that teen addicts were distributing heroin from the house.

Rose organized a group of over a hundred people to lay siege to the house. They chanted and shouted, and Rose told Ma Baker that she had twenty-four hours to leave the area.

Under huge pressure and afraid of IRA intervention, Ma Baker quickly left her house with her family. Rose and twenty others rushed in and began smashing and removing her furniture, while two hundred supporters cheered outside, including Ruairí. Those inside the house refused to open the door when the gardaí arrived.

The stand-off lasted all day and the gardaí donned riot gear.

Inside the house, the protestors ran upstairs and barricaded the stairs with as much furniture as they could find, including the sofa and kitchen chairs. The gardaí smashed in the front door with a battering ram and pulled down the barricade on the stairs. Rose and the others held out until the gardaí were nearly at the top of the stairs, and then barricaded themselves into one of the bedrooms. The gardaí pushed in the door and grabbed them one by one, beating them and pushing them downstairs and into a waiting police van.

Nine-year-old Ruairí was standing outside the house, looking upstairs. 'I saw a garda with his baton raised over his head beating down on Rose,' he recalls. 'It was a ferocious beating.'

Rose, who had blood streaming down the side of her face, was dragged from the house along with the others and taken to Kevin Street garda station.

Large crowds from the inner-city flats joined parents from Dún Laoghaire and Ballyfermot in throwing rocks at the garda station and demanding the release of the twenty protestors in detention. There were several attempts by the crowd to rush inside the station. Police reinforcements held the line while the arrestees inside were quickly processed and released.

The *Irish Times* reported on Rose's eventual emergence: 'She was greeted with cheers when she emerged from Kevin Street garda station with a nasty cut on the forehead and blood encrusted on her face, which she sustained during the clashes at the house.' She was taken to hospital and emerged early in the morning with her arm in a cast and held in place by a sling.

Ruairí recalls: 'She couldn't even get her coat off because of the size of the cast. I remember she was helping me with my homework and she had her back to the heater and her coat caught fire. I had to run at her and put out the fire myself.'

Asked why he thought Rose undertook such dangerous work for CPAD while she was the sole carer of a young son, Ruairi pauses for a long time before replying. 'You have to understand Rose. It was like when she was in court in front of her father all those years earlier. She told him: "I love you, Daddy, but this is how it has to be."'

'With Rose, everything was rebellion against the rules. I'm not saying that was a good way to be; I learned in some ways how not to be. I remember going up an escalator in a shopping centre and next thing I smelt smoke and I looked around and Rose was puffing away on a cigarette. She was only doing it because it wasn't allowed.'

And yet, within Sinn Féin, her position was increasingly orthodox. She was completely loyal to the party and worked for *An Phoblacht* for a tiny wage. 'She asked the newspaper what was the least they could pay her, so she took £5 a week – and this while some people in Dublin Sinn Féin were making very big money and building very nice houses for themselves,' says Ruairi. She was no longer a maverick within republicanism, like Eddie Gallagher, but a loyal adherent, happy to work within the cogs of a much larger machine.

'Rose was capable of taking orders and working with the system, which is why, over time, she would prove to be a much bigger challenge to the state than Eddie ever was,' says Thomas Connors. 'She was intelligent, and she had that radical socialist streak about her, so she was one of the ones you'd fear, because she actually believed she could change the world.'

14. Love Bomb

A month after the Battle for Ma Baker, Rose was chairing a Sinn Féin meeting in the back room of the Coombe office, just below the apartment she shared with Ruairi. She was still healing from the beating she took from the gardaí, and her arm was in a sling.

Among the people in the room that day was a 40-year-old IRA man named Jim Monaghan who had recently been released from Portlaoise prison. Dublin City Council had given him a flat in St Theresa's Gardens, and he had come to the Coombe office to rejoin Sinn Féin.

Jim Monaghan was originally from Rathmullan, Co. Donegal, on the shore of Lough Swilly. His father, a nationalist from Fermanagh in Northern Ireland, had joined the southern army during the Second World War because he feared a British invasion from the North. The army stationed him in Rathmullan, where he met Jim's mother, Gwendoline. They married and had three boys and three girls. When the eldest was ready to begin secondary school, the family moved to Walkinstown on the south side of Dublin. Jim moved from a primary school in Donegal of about a hundred boys and girls to a vast new Dublin school of nearly a thousand boys. He later attended a technical school on the Clogher Road in Dublin, where he took classes in electronics, maths, physics, metalwork, woodwork, Irish and English.

He was an avid scientist from a young age, fascinated by machines and chemicals. When he was a teenager, he almost blew himself up in a quarry when he dropped a lit bag of nitroglycerine, sugar and fertilizer into a lake, believing it would detonate underwater. The gas expanded and the bag rose to the surface of the lake before exploding.

When Jim learned that his hurling coach had been on active service with the IRA in the Border Campaign in the 1950s, Jim pestered him for stories. According to Jim Monaghan's unpublished account of his IRA activities, the coach told him about an attack on Armagh Barracks. Future IRA army council member Ruairí Ó Brádaigh led a unit in tying up the sentries and clearing out the armoury, capturing large amounts of guns and ammunition. Thus began Jim's interest in the IRA. He went on to read *Guerrilla Days in Ireland* by Tom Barry, about battles against the British troops during the War of Independence in the 1920s, which left a deep impression.

He joined the Republic's local defence force, the FCÁ, which taught teenagers how to use guns. In the evening and weekend training sessions, he learned how to use the Enfield rifle, the Gustav sub-machine gun, the Mills 36 hand grenade, the Bren light machine gun and the Vickers medium machine gun, as well as how to direct small infantry units. In metalwork class, he reactivated an old Luger left over from the War of Independence, by shaping and fitting a new part.

He also gathered a supply of empty 9mm cartridges, filled them with gunpowder and replaced the primer. Later, he made bullets by hammering lead into a bullet-shaped mould. He and a friend knew from their FCA training where the army and police had their firing ranges in the Dublin mountains, and they would travel up there to fire the Luger when nobody was around.

When he finished at the technical school, he went on to

become an apprentice fitter, shaping and welding steel and other metals. He was allowed out of work twice a week to attend Bolton Street college in Dublin city centre to study metalwork. One day in 1966, while he was there, news came through that the IRA had blown up Nelson's Pillar, a statue on O'Connell Street dedicated to British admiral Lord Nelson, and a vestige of British military rule in the South of Ireland.

A debate broke out among the students. Jim argued that it was right to blow it up. Others in the class argued that the British had at least left some beauty in Dublin, and that such statues were now part of Ireland's cultural history. The teacher was delayed because of roadblocks around the bomb site, so the argument continued. Jim remembers being struck by how divided people were and how the legacy of Britain's rule in Ireland was still unresolved.

He became active in political agitation, especially on behalf of housing rights in Dublin – a sphere in which the republican movement was known to be active. He and a friend eventually decided to join the IRA and were sent to a large house in the leafy south Dublin suburb of Rathgar. A man there asked them if they had thought about the hardships of being an IRA member. They hadn't. He told them to reflect on it, and on the politics of the IRA, and come back in two weeks. When they came back, the IRA man told them he was setting up a new unit of young recruits and they were welcome to join. Jim was appointed unit leader, as he was the only one with weapons and military training. They practised with a single Enfield rifle, taking turns firing at a rock sticking out of a lake in the Dublin mountains. If they missed the target, it would cause a splash of water, so they could assess their range. It was amateurish, Dad's Army training for a secret organization that had long run out of energy. Still, Jim persisted, guided by an older IRA man named Frank Driver, who lived in a book-filled cottage in the Dublin mountains.

In 1968, Jim and his friends were watching TV when they saw a nationalist civil rights march being brutally attacked in Northern Ireland. In 1969, he attended a republican commemoration at which the veteran Belfast IRA man Jimmy Steele castigated the IRA leadership for failing to anticipate the brutality of unionist reaction to the Northern Ireland civil rights movement. After the eruption of the Troubles and, towards the end of the year, the schism within the IRA, Jim sided with the new Provisional IRA, which wanted to take on the British state in Northern Ireland with renewed militancy.

Within the IRA, Jim developed a reputation for building bombs from almost anything. He pored over chemistry and physics books and was constantly designing and testing better mortars and fuses.

On 22 February 1974, he led two mortar-bomb teams on an attack at an army border checkpoint in Strabane called the Camel's Hump, which consisted of two towers with anti-bomb netting in between. The IRA team positioned themselves a few hundred yards from the checkpoint in Lifford, Co. Donegal, knowing that the British army had no permission to cross the border.

Jim fired repeatedly from one of the mortars, hitting the checkpoint directly and also damaging a nearby factory, while two groups of four riflemen gave the mortar teams cover, many of them firing from the grounds of a hotel. One of the mortar bombs landed in a Traveller camp and damaged some caravans. Jim's mortar quickly became overheated and his team had to pour water on it to cool it down. Because of the intense heat, Jim had to use his military jacket wrapped around his hand to fire another bomb. The other team's mortar misfired and he told them to bring their bombs over to his team while they continued firing.

In a front-page article the next day, the *Irish Times* reported that the attack had gone on for over twenty minutes, with over four hundred rounds and twenty-five mortar bombs fired. It also noted strident criticism from unionist politicians, who demanded to know why the Irish gardaí and army did not intervene.

Jim was later reprimanded by his engineering department commanding officer, who felt that those designing the mortars shouldn't put themselves at risk of death or imprisonment while using them.

Jim married an Irish-language campaigner named Chris Ó Coisdealbha, with whom he had a son, Donal, and a daughter, Nora.

On 28 April 1975, Jim was caught at a bomb factory and training camp he was operating in a farm in north County Dublin. He was arrested with three others: Joe Reilly, Michael Murphy and John O'Hagan. When gardaí raided the sheds of a farm in Donabate, they found Joe Reilly welding rocket launchers together.

Jim had been teaching bomb-making classes at the farm. Detective Sergeant Eamon Ó Fiacháin would later tell the Special Criminal Court that he found transparencies for a classroom projector showing how to manufacture booby traps, land mines and hand grenades.

All four men were put on trial at the Special Criminal Court. During breaks in the court proceedings, they were held in a cell, and each night they were taken back to the republican wing of Portlaoise prison.

They started working on an escape plan, and they needed as much time as possible to develop it. To slow the trial down, Jim cross-examined witnesses and asked jailed IRA members to come to court as character witnesses. 'I was calling all sorts of witnesses and basically putting up objections to prosecution witnesses until we had the plan in place,' he recalls.

At the time, the IRA was building up a cache of smuggled explosives in Portlaoise prison. He succeeded in delaying the case until the four accused managed to smuggle explosives from Portlaoise into the court building in their underwear. John O'Hagan later told gardaí that he used medical plaster tape to attach plastic explosive to his testicles.

During a lunch recess on Thursday, 15 July 1976, the accused men were taken to their holding cells in the Special Criminal Court, and there they began assembling the bomb. At 1.30 p.m., a guard let one of the men go to the toilet. When he opened the door, O'Hagan threw a bomb into the corridor, and ran in the opposite direction as it exploded. Michael Murphy took a wrong turn in the smoke-filled passageway and ended up in the courtroom, where he was arrested.

The others planted a bomb under a door, which blew apart, and they ran out into the prison yard. At that moment, *Irish Times* journalist Michael Kearney was in the court press room when it was showered with broken glass and debris. 'I was checking my copy when I heard a loud noise,' he told the newspaper later that day. 'I did not immediately associate it with an explosion, but a few seconds later, there was a loud bang and the window of the press room shattered and fell over me.' The ceiling of the court basement collapsed on to the floor, doors in the basement were blown in and masonry fell to the ground.

While the prisoners were running into the yard, an IRA member on the outside placed his backpack against the external wall of the courthouse yard. It contained a bomb that blew open a hole in the wall. Monaghan, Reilly and O'Hagan jumped through the hole, pushing past a soldier, who asked: 'What do I do?' A garda shouted at him to shoot the escaping prisoners, but the young soldier shouted that he had to check with his sergeant. Jim recalls that he and the other two escapees 'went running down the road doing a zig-zag to avoid getting shot', but the soldier never fired.

The three tried to hijack a car, but the driver told them to 'fuck off' so they hijacked a van. The driver who had told them to fuck off followed the van, beeping his horn and flashing his lights to draw attention.

Jim jumped out of the van and on to a nearby bus, where he was arrested. O'Hagan and Reilly were arrested in a shop. Seven people were later treated in hospital for shock as a result of the explosions.

There was a nationwide manhunt for Michael O'Rourke, a Portlaoise prisoner who had appeared as a witness for the defence and escaped. O'Rourke was spirited to the US, where he became a cause célèbre among Irish Americans and was made grand marshal of the New York St Patrick's Day Parade, which finished the Irish government's involvement in the parade for many years.

On 20 July 1976, five days after the escape, Jim Monaghan and John O'Hagan were taken back to the Special Criminal Court, where Justice Pringle, who had suffered the abuse of both Marion and Eddie during their sentencing, jailed them for six years for the Donabate bomb factory. After they were sentenced, Jim told the court that the Ireland he was born into was made for people like Justice Pringle, and not for ordinary people. He said he hadn't intended to make a speech but said that people like him had to go out and sort out the mess that was Ireland. Just as they had blown out the facade of the court the previous Thursday, they would blow out old ideas and replace them with new ideas and new people. Referring to recent fishing and economic disputes, he told the court that Malta and Iceland didn't lie down to Britain, and neither should Ireland. As they were being led away, he shouted: 'There's only thing worse than the landlord, and that's the landlord's agent.'

Later, Jim would be convicted in connection with the escape and sentenced to fifteen years.

Prison time in Portlaoise travelled easily for him. He spent much of his time reading engineering books and pamphlets, and international revolutionary texts. Dáithí Ó Conaill, a former IRA chief of staff, was impressed with Jim's calm manner and encyclopaedic knowledge of chemistry and physics, and made him his deputy leader of the IRA prisoners. Jim was known to walk around the yard designing new mortar systems in his head, and became known as 'Mortar Jim'. He made calculations for new types of mortars using physics he learned in Bolton Street.

'Prison was what you made of it,' Jim says. 'I tried to stay engaged and, sometimes, when the cell door was shut behind me in the evenings, I was looking forward to it because it was a chance to catch up on reading.'

When he was released from Portlaoise in 1985 after serving nine years, a woman from one of the Irish republican welfare organizations got Jim on the housing waiting list in Dublin, and he was given a two-bedroom flat on the second floor of St Theresa's Gardens flat complex. It had a reputation as the very worst flat complex in the city, and the mayhem was hard to avoid. Jim became friends with a neighbouring couple – an ex-Irish army soldier and his wife. One day he came home to find the man lying outside the flats, having been stabbed by his wife. A crowd had gathered around and people were watching him bleed on the ground. Jim picked the man up and took him home to his flat to wait for an ambulance. It was only later that he learned the reason for the crowd's reluctance to help – the flats were riddled with heroin, and the residents were worried about AIDS.

Shortly after moving in, Jim called over to the Sinn Féin office on the Coombe to rejoin the party. There he met Rose, and was immediately enthralled. Ruairi, who was eleven at the time, was at the meeting and recalls, 'It was love at first sight. They talked and talked and talked.'

Rose had a university education, she knew the classics – things that, in a different life, Jim would have wanted for himself. And, like him, she had committed her life to the Irish republican cause.

The attraction was mutual. Rose saw in Jim an intellectual with an almost monastic calm. He was good-looking too, with a shock of black hair, big shoulders and intelligent, piercing eyes. He had a Roman nose, which, while handsome to Rose, earned him the nickname 'Big Nose' from Ruairi.

Jim continued to see both Chris and Rose, while rejoining the IRA's bomb-making department. Some nights he slept in the apartment in the Coombe with Rose, sometimes he stayed in his own apartment in St Theresa's Gardens, and sometimes he was with Chris.

He and Rose talked for hours about revolutionary politics, prison conditions and children, and their hopes for the future. Rose felt that Chris, never having been in prison, didn't understand him like she did. Both Jim and Rose were determined not to go back to prison, but they were also determined to get into the IRA's Northern fight together.

Rose sat Ruairi down one night, he recalls. 'She said, "If you were to have a brother or sister, would it be OK if Jim was the father?"'

Ruairi, who liked Jim, said that he would be fine with it. Rose urgently wanted a baby with Jim; but she was forty-four years old, and they were not able to conceive. They discussed adoption, but with their prison records it was unlikely they would succeed.

Sinn Féin asked Jim if he would lead the party's education department. He accepted, and appointed Rose as his deputy. They were given an office in the Sinn Féin headquarters in Dublin. As head of a committee, Jim was quickly appointed to the party's national executive.

Jim and Rose debated the role and purpose of the education department. 'I told Rose we should teach courses about being the secretary of a cumann and about how to handle finances for the local group,' Jim recalls. 'She said: "You are only talking mechanics, not the politics! What is your aim, why are you there?"'

Rose had ideas about how to talk about sophisticated political theory in a way that would make sense to ordinary people, influenced by Paulo Freire's book *Pedagogy of the Oppressed*. 'Rose distilled it down for me,' Jim says. 'Her whole thing was that people know politics from their own lives and [that we should] try to bring out their own experience and ask what were the structures that led to their life experience. You start with the premise that people already know a lot.'

They travelled around the country, teaching Sinn Féin members how to deal with conflict using Freire's methods. At the time, many people were coming to Sinn Féin looking for IRA back-up in local disputes, having seen CPAD taking on drug dealers. In his book *Killing Rage*, former IRA member Eamon Collins wrote about the depressing regularity with which people showed up at the Sinn Féin office in Newry, hoping that republicans could intervene in petty disputes with neighbours about garden boundaries or noise. Rose and Jim often heard complaints about Travellers moving caravans on to public or private land without permission.

'One of the things we learned from Freire was never to have a table in the room – it creates a boundary between you and the others in the room. So we would sit with people and ask people for their views,' Jim recalls. 'Rose would read from the 1916 Proclamation about equal rights and opportunities and ask if Travellers had the same opportunities. She got people thinking: "Why are those people living that way in standards way below everyone else? What happened in history to create this? What class are these people?"'

Former hungerstriker Tommy McKearney, who was in prison in Northern Ireland at the time, led a project in which prisoners subjected key events in Irish history to Marxist analysis. When the resulting book, *Questions of History*, was published by the education department in 1987, it caused shock waves in the party.

Jim Monaghan's view is that the criticism the book received was directly related to the Provisional IRA's long feud with the Official IRA. On the Provo side, the left was seen 'as a conspiracy within the party, and there was residual hostility that the same thing might happen again'. Rose was seen as having an undue Marxist influence on Jim and on the education department.

The party leadership was most upset about the way *Questions from History* cast doubt upon the republican belief that the 1798 rebellion, in which Catholics and Protestants worked together, was a model for how Northern Ireland could be, if only Protestants would learn their own history. *Questions from History*, according to Jim, cast 1798 as 'almost a planter rebellion' by Presbyterians. 'Wolfe Tone said that Ireland's problems arose from British colonialism. The other side of that coin is that if you ended British occupation, all the problems end, and that just wasn't true.' The book, he says, 'wasn't saying what should have happened in 1798, but asking what were the interests of the different classes involved'.

Jim and Rose started planning a second edition *of Questions from History* that would examine Irish history from 1916 up to the late 1960s. However, Jim recalls, 'The leadership told us there would be no second book.' The dispute, he says, 'really marked the moment when we began to fall out of favour with the leadership'.

Throughout 1986, while working with the education department but before the internal political dispute came to a head, Jim taught Rose everything he knew about bomb-making – recrystallization, stabilization, bonding agents, solvents, strikers, triggers and wiring.

Jim and Rose's role was unique. They were not members of the IRA's engineering department. They were, along with a Mayo man called Danny Campbell, the IRA's research and development unit. Since the early 1970s, Danny Campbell had taken in hundreds of IRA members for weapons and bomb training on his farm in Ballycroy, on the west coast of County Mayo, overlooking Blacksod Bay.

Every month they liaised with the operations officer in South Armagh, but they were not part of the South Armagh hierarchy either. They were their own semi-autonomous unit, and were delighted to stay that way. Whenever a unit in the North needed a specialist weapon, the Northern Command would contact Jim, who would bring out his physics and chemistry books and begin the project.

Jim had a job at a workshop in Dublin, where he repaired things like fire extinguishers and metal gates. On the side, he also did welding for IRA missiles and bombs. Anything created in the workshop was sent to Danny Campbell in Mayo for testing. Initially, the testing was done at a remote farmhouse near Ballycroy, not at Danny Campbell's own farm.

The big project that year, and one that fascinated Rose, was designing a grenade that could be lobbed at passing army or police patrols in Northern Ireland. By then, the security forces were heavily protected, with bulletproof vests, which featured a ceramic plate that took the force out of a bullet and Kevlar strips underneath that would resist the weakened bullet and turn it sideways. Their vehicles all had a centimetre-thick anti-missile reinforcement that the IRA was finding difficult to penetrate. Also, the IRA's shoulder-fired armour-piercing rocket was too difficult to operate: the recoil was too powerful. The operations officer in South Armagh appealed to Jim and Rose for something new that could devastate army and police vehicles.

The first prototype – about 600 grams of Semtex packed inside an empty bean can – took a month to design before it was sent to South Armagh for inspection.

The hand-thrown grenade avoided the recoil problem of the missile launcher. Another advantage was that it did not cover the user in residue that could be traced by police forensics. With training, it could be thrown from a distance of 25 metres.

After testing in the Dublin workshop, Jim and Rose added a

strip of polythene cut from a bin-liner to the tail. This 'drogue' opened out like a parachute to keep the grenade travelling head-first, so that the explosive end would hit the target.

Jim took the grenade to a derelict house in South Armagh, where the local IRA unit was waiting for him. The grenade was placed on its nose vertically over a 2-centimetre-thick steel plate on the floor of an empty room.

He detonated the grenade using a command wire and battery from 100 metres away. Slates jumped off the roof and the glass from the windows flew out.

The grenade had punched a hole in the steel plate big enough to put a finger through. This suggested that the grenade was powerful enough to penetrate the centimetre-thick armour plate on Northern Ireland police and army vehicles.

The strict rule was that an IRA engineer must live-test the weapon before IRA members were expected to use it. And so Rose and Jim drove up to Mayo to test the grenade.

First they made a dummy version and practised throwing it at a haystack. They experimented with different trajectories and throwing methods. When they were satisfied that under-hand was the most accurate, they decided to test the live version, with the explosives packed into the bean can.

They decided to blow up a derelict car on the farm in Mayo. Jim flung the grenade underhand. It sailed silently and, guided by its plastic bin-liner parachute, landed on the car with a ferocious explosion that blew off the driver's door. A huge plume of grey smoke rose into the air.

They walked to the car for a closer look. They could see that each shrapnel hole had a small ring of copper from the bomb's melted copper cone. Jim was surprised to see the spread of the shrapnel holes, as he expected a much more concentrated pattern.

It would take a very calm IRA member to use this new drogue grenade, but it could be a major part of winning the street battle, especially if used against passing military and police patrols in urban areas.

By now, Rose and Ruairi had moved back to Eugene Street. Rose would pick up Ruairi from one of the neighbours' houses, or from Rita O'Hare's home in the outer suburb of Cabinteely, after returning from Mayo. When she wasn't designing weapons with Jim, she was fighting heroin dealers.

Her next target was a member of the Dunne family, Vianney Dunne, who lived in a house on Weaver Square, behind a heroin-plagued block of flats near Rose's house. Rose spoke at public meetings, challenging Vianney Dunne to show up and deny he was dealing heroin. She led groups down to his house and harassed him, shouting through his door, telling him that the IRA would deal with him.

On 27 February 1987, Rose gathered a number of the most committed members of Concerned Parents Against Drugs. They followed Dunne into and out of the house on Weaver Square, and Rose threatened to shoot him. After Dunne left the house, the vigilantes broke in. They were removing his furniture when the gardaí showed up. Rose was arrested along with four others.

Two months later, the state unexpectedly dropped the charges in the Ma Baker case after Ma Baker declined to give evidence and several Garda witnesses failed to appear in court. Rose and the nineteen other defendants walked out of the courthouse to rapturous cheering from their supporters.

In July, as Rose was awaiting trial for the Vianney Dunne case, the new drogue grenade was used for the first time in the North. The target was a military Land Rover on the Falls Road in Belfast. The vehicle was damaged by the grenade, but the soldiers escaped serious injury. Jim wrote that the failure to do more damage was down to a lack of training about how to throw the grenade properly.

According to Brendan O'Brien's book *The Long War*, drogue grenades were used ninety-six times in that first year. The majority of these attacks were in Belfast, but the weapon was also used that year in Toomebridge, Craigavon, Newcastle, Cookstown, Moy, Strabane, Derry, Omagh, Dungannon, Pomeroy, Newry, Irvinestown and Clogher. According to A. R. Oppenheimer's book *IRA: The Bombs and the Bullets*, the IRA used dog-food cans as well as bean cans in manufacturing the grenades.

The first person to be killed by the weapon was RUC officer Colin Gilmore, who was riding in the third vehicle on an armed patrol that came under attack in West Belfast. Gilmore had a 16-month-old son, and his funeral was held at Seymour Street Methodist Hall in Lisburn, where he had been married three years earlier.

Over the next five years, the drogue grenade was responsible for at least two dozen deaths. Gerard Magee's *Tyrone's Struggle*, published by the Tyrone Sinn Féin Commemoration Committee, claims that drogue grenade attacks killed eleven people in that county alone.

When the case of the State *v.* Rose Dugdale and Others came to trial on 13 October, prosecutors announced that the chief witness, Vianney Dunne, would not be appearing in court and that they would be dropping all charges. A member of one of Dublin's most notorious families was apparently too afraid to show up and testify against CPAD. Yet again, Rose

walked free from court, with Jim Monaghan and other republicans cheering her as she left.

The *Irish Times* reported that, outside the courthouse, Rose
'protested bitterly' that she and her co-accused had appeared
in court twelve times before being told the charges were
being dropped. The paper also noted that the Garda Com-
missioner, Lawrence Wren, had ordered an investigation into
why thirty-three witnesses, including up to two dozen gardaí,
failed to show up in court when another group of Concerned
Parents protestors were being prosecuted.

The reason gardaí were failing to appear in court against
Concerned Parents, the investigation found, was that they
feared angering the Dublin public, thousands of whom were
now supporting the vigilantes.

The next important innovation pursued by Jim and Rose was
a device called an 'all-ways striker' for mortar bombs. The
British army had fortified its bases after a series of car-bomb
and missile attacks. The IRA's push now was for technology
that could launch explosives over the blast walls and into the
bases.

IRA members often struggled with the angle and trajectory of mortars. Many times the bombs failed to explode
because they lost their trajectory or simply landed sideways
or upside down. The all-ways striker improved the likelihood
that the bomb would detonate, no matter which way it
landed.

Jim and Rose worked on the striker in Jim's Dublin workshop, and at the end of each day they would dismantle the
pieces and place them around the workshop in case there
was a garda raid. Jim would do the welding, hour after hour
perfecting the design. Ruairí remembers they kept a bottle of

eye wash at home for Jim, because tiny shards of metal would get lodged in his eye.

In November 1987, Rose took Ruairi on a three-day Sinn Féin education committee weekend. The gardaí followed them to a house in Milltown Malbay, Co. Clare. At 8.30 a.m., a large group of gardaí poured into the house and arrested nine people, including Rose and Jim, and took them to garda stations in Ennis and Limerick. Gardaí spent three hours searching the home while Ruairi sat eating biscuits and chatting to the remaining adults in the house. Nothing was found and everyone was released. Ruairi was seeing less and less of Rose as she became more consumed with weapons development and Sinn Féin business.

'I basically looked after myself one weekend after another because of the IRA and Sinn Féin,' he says. 'I was pushed from one family to another family – staying with friends from school and republicans. I would go up to [Eddie's sister] Margaret in Donegal. Rose would drop me up there with Jim and pick me up on the way back.'

While Jim and Rose's stature within the IRA was growing, their reputation in Sinn Féin was plummeting. In August 1987, the education department had set up a small periodical, written by IRA prisoners and their supporters, called *Iris Beag* ('Little Journal'). It included essays on the political development of republicanism, and, like *Questions from History*, it was immediately attacked as a Marxist Trojan horse.

In one of its first issues, an anonymous contributor welcomed criticism of Sinn Féin's nationalist direction. 'If Sinn Féin opts to be exclusively nationalist, it will identify with the class interests of the section of the national bourgeoisie or petit-bourgeoisie that sees its future being advanced by national independence.' This would lead to 'futile strategies of the petit-bourgeoisie – militarism and individualist terrorism'.

In the letters section of *Iris Beag*'s third edition, in November, Sinn Féin's head of publicity, Danny Morrison, strongly criticized the journal for its 'soulless', 'dry' Marxist language, which he said was not understood by ordinary people. In the December edition, some of the left-leaning prisoners on C Wing of Portlaoise prison who wrote for *Iris Beag* responded with a biting rebuke of Morrison: something not normally seen so openly in the party.

'The language of social revolution will not become "soulless", "joyless" or "dry"; on the contrary, Danny, provided it is backed up with political action and agitation, it will assist in the dropping of scales from the eyes of the oppressed,' they wrote.

The party leadership had had enough of *Iris Beag* and of Jim and Rose. At the Ard Fheis, Jim was voted off the ard chomhairle, or national executive – an extremely rare sanction for a head of department. He and Rose were highly regarded within the IRA but absolute pariahs within Sinn Féin, which began to block them from holding education department meetings. The message was clear: keep developing weapons, not political thought.

'We didn't know it at the time, but the leadership were on a course to unite all Irish nationalists, and we were contradicting it,' Jim says. 'Had they come out and said to us, "We are on a course," we could have dealt with that. We weren't doctrinaire in our approach. If they said, "We are working on a strategy of bringing the whole of nationalism together," I don't know how far they would have got, but we would have at least known what was happening.'

Rose took Jim's departure from the national executive far harder than he did himself. 'That was a difficult time,' she recalls. 'I think that the party was looking for a direction and, as far as they were concerned, we were getting in the way of them finding a connection with other political parties and ending the conflict.' In 1989, Rose and Jim would formally leave the party. It would be many years before they rejoined.

In early 1988, Jim was called to South Armagh. A senior member of the IRA quartermaster staff wanted to meet him.

Jim's 100-lb all-ways striker mortars were turning the conflict in rural areas. They were also good for publicity: when mortars are being used, the international media see a conventional war rather than a terrorist campaign. But the IRA was running out of saltpetre, or potassium nitrate, to make the gunpowder that was used to launch the mortars.

Potassium nitrate had been banned in 1972, as the Troubles worsened. Jim told the member of the quartermaster staff that the IRA could make potassium nitrate from a type of German farm fertilizer, by a process similar to recrystallizing ammonium nitrate used in conventional fertilizer bombs.

He and Rose went to Mayo to try to make saltpetre at an isolated farmhouse supplied by Danny Campbell. The crystals they produced from fertilizer were purified and dried. It took a few weeks to design and build the apparatus to get a production line going on a large enough scale. When they tested it, the new saltpetre was as good as the previous version. It was prone to absorbing dampness from the air, but it guaranteed that the IRA could continue launching mortar attacks all over Northern Ireland. Soon, units across the

North were trained on how to make saltpetre using the new German-fertilizer method.

At home, Rose was running on fumes. She smoked sixty cigarettes a day and drank a dozen cups of coffee. 'The kettle was never off,' Ruairi remembers. 'She would go without food for days and then she'd have three dinners at once. She was always on the move and would sleep very little. She would be up all night writing speeches [. . .] or writing articles. Then we'd get into the car and she'd say, "I have to sleep now," and just nap right there in the car before going off to some meeting or to take on the drug dealers.

'I remember she had these friends, Paddy and Marie, who lived out in Crumlin and had a market stand on Meath Street. Rose went out to see them and they had some Christmas cake. She basically ate the whole cake while she was talking to them because she had gone so long without food.'

She used the pseudonym Róisín de Rossa when writing for *An Phoblacht*. She also used the name Josephine when calling government offices.

'People would phone the house looking for Josephine,' Ruairi recalls, 'and I would say: "There is nobody here by that name," and then Rose would come from the other room saying: "Give me that phone."'

Every summer as a teenager, Ruairi would go up to Bally-bofey to work in the slaughterhouse of his uncle Charlie Gallagher, Eddie's brother.

'I had to kill the animals myself. It was too expensive to kill sheep with a gun, so I'd have to go around beating them over the head with a fibreglass mallet. They would fall on the ground and you would quickly slit their throats. The pigs got no mallet, they just had their throats slit. They put up a fight because they knew they were going to die, they could smell the blood. I felt bad for the piggies, because they knew. The cows were shot in the head and fell out of the pen and had their throats cut.'

In 1988, Eddie came home on temporary release, in preparation for full release in two years' time. He had been in prison for more than thirteen years. Relations between Eddie and Rose were strained, and Eddie took Ruairi up to Donegal without her. Father and son went fishing together.

'He took me up to the Finn River. It was a glorious time,' Ruairi says. 'I was with my father, it felt like things just might be normal for a while. I knew all the Gallaghers anyway, so it was easy to be up there with them all.'

When he wasn't fishing, Ruairi's other passion was ice-skating. The skating rink just outside the Dolphin' Barn House flats was one of the few amusements available to working-class children in the area. Aged thirteen, he got a job there, cleaning up and fitting people with their skates. There was a 16-year-old girl named Sheila Bowes who worked in the coffee shop and the skate shop. According to Ruairi, the job came about because the ice-rink owner was a client of her brother Timmy, who – unbeknownst to Sheila – ran a protection racket.

Ruairi, with his father's charm and confident personality, was popular with girls at the rink, and often had long kissing sessions in the medical room, where they kept the bandages for people who slipped on the ice.

'Sheila knew about it, and I think she was jealous or curious,' he recalls. 'I went to her to get the key to the medical room and she just moved in on me and kissed me.'

Sheila, he soon learned, was from a family of twenty in Fatima Mansions. Timmy was deeply immersed in protection rackets and other criminal enterprises. Another relative,

James Bowes, would later be jailed for twelve years when he was caught with 5 kilos of heroin. Sheila liked Ruairi – he was funny and outgoing, and there was this other side to him. His mother had given birth to him in prison and his father was still in prison. His mother had given up a life of luxury in London to join the IRA and was always in the newspapers for fighting drug dealers.

Ruairi invited her home to meet his mum. Rose was warm and welcoming and delighted that Ruairi had found a girl-friend. But when she started to hear from CPAD people that some of the Bowes family were involved in drug dealing, she started questioning Sheila. When Sheila said she didn't know who was dealing in drugs, Rose told her she was lying.

Ruairi tried to intervene, but relations between his mother and his girlfriend only got worse. Rose was trying to extract information from Sheila for what would likely end up a forced eviction or a beating. 'She hated my guts,' Sheila recalls.

Sheila was a teenage girl who wanted to be like any other teenage girl, but every time she called over to her boyfriend's house she had to undergo an IRA interrogation about drug deals she knew nothing about. Every week there was scream-ing and shouting, doors slamming and threats by Rose to separate her from Ruairi.

'It got intense,' Ruairi says. 'On top of that, my dad heard about Sheila and also wanted her gone.'

Ruairi lost his virginity to Sheila. Rose didn't object to the two of them sleeping together, only to the fact that Sheila wasn't answering her questions about drug dealing in Fatima Mansions. 'I think as far as Rose was concerned, if we were going to sleep together, it was better in the house than in the street,' Ruairi says.

Eventually, relations between Sheila and Rose became so bad that for a time Ruairi moved out of Eugene Street and in with Sheila's parents, who had been given a council house on Clogher Road. Sheila's parents had a less permissive attitude there to the two teenagers having sex, but Ruairi recalls that they 'were both slow on their feet by that point. By the time they got up the stairs, you had an hour's notice.'

Ruairi was meanwhile losing interest in Irish republicanism. He was horrified by what was going on in the North. 'It was an awful time – all these bombings and shootings were going on the background.' What had republicanism brought his family? Imprisonment, poverty and tension.

Garda surveillance on Rose and Jim was increasingly evident, and Ruairi sometimes had to open the door to a police raid. 'They would raid the house at least twice a year, and every time Rose went outside the door, the gardaí would come out of nowhere and start questioning her. There was all sorts of surveillance going on – the regular gardaí and the Special Branch. Rose and Jim would do all sorts of things to lose them – drive backwards up streets, change direction. There was always some way to evade them, but it wasn't easy.'

In the evenings, Ruairi would go up to the Fatima Mansions flats, where boys would be gathering with stolen cars. They would pull doughnuts in the yard outside the flats to announce their arrival. Friends would jump in and they would travel around Dublin having a laugh before dumping the car later that night. 'The Fatima Car Company, I called it,' says Ruairi. He was also fencing stolen goods, going door to door to sell them. One day, while he was doing his rounds, a door was answered by Martin 'The Viper' Foley, the drug dealer who had been kidnapped by south-side vigilantes close to Rose, leading to a shoot-out with gardaí. Foley liked Ruairi and soon got talking to him about how he might be able to employ him. 'That's how it all started,' says Ruairi.

Ruairi became disruptive. When Rose organized a trip for inner-city young people to the Dublin mountains for the weekend, Ruairi loved it so much that he poured soil and sand into the petrol tank of the minibus, preventing them from going home.

He grew increasingly resentful of the anti-drugs vigilantes. As far as he was concerned, a lot of them were puffed-up little men looking for trouble and jealous of those they saw getting out of inner-city poverty. 'These fellas, gathered around a barrel at night, outside the flats, looking for dealers – I didn't like them and gave them some lip, and pretty soon they didn't like me. I think Rose was getting concerned about me, and who I was mixing with.'

And still, every summer, Eric Dugdale sent his grounds-keeper to take Ruairi fishing in the rivers and lakes of Ireland. Ruairi was still dreaming of going to England to meet his rich English relatives. But Rose said no: she was as concerned about him mixing with the English upper class as with drug dealers.

Attending school in the working-class suburb of Tallaght, Ruairi was constantly in trouble for shouting at teachers and refusing to work. He was intelligent, but bored. Finally, he was expelled for throwing a hammer at a teacher, narrowly missing him, and smashing all of the fire alarms to force an evacuation of the school.

Because of the expulsion, he wouldn't be able to sit the Inter Cert, the state exam for 15-year-olds – an entry require-ment for even the most basic of jobs and apprenticeships. He got a job with a shop-fitting company in a grim industrial estate on the Robin Hood Road in west Dublin. He hated it – the job was tedious and the location was miserable. He realized he had made a big mistake with his life.

He turned up at St Kevin's School on the South Circular Road. A Christian Brother who worked there recognized Ruairi from an inner-city hurling club and offered him a place in the school. 'Honestly, I think the only reason he took me in was because he knew I was good at hurling, and I was warned – any trouble and I was out. I owe that man a lot – I was screwing up and I was given another chance.'

On 28 March 1990, Eddie Gallagher walked out of Limerick prison a free man, ten months ahead of his official parole date, having availed himself of a government scheme for republican prisoners who were well behaved and showed no sign of returning to a paramilitary group.

He got a lift up to Dublin and went straight to Eugene Street. He had a bottle of brandy with him, a gift from a supporter. Rose was frosty. She said he was welcome to stay the night but that was it.

Eddie was not happy that Rose was raising Ruairi in a tiny house in the inner city, surrounded by drugs and depravation. It might have suited her working-class fantasies, and her desire to take on the drug dealers, but it was his son in the middle of all that.

'Eddie went mental – mental – when he saw where we were living,' Ruairi says. 'He started on the bottle of brandy and kept going. He slept on the couch and, the next day, he went up to Donegal. That was about it for himself and Rose.'

Eddie decided to convert his family farm into a hostel and horse-riding centre for tourists. Soon after the hostel opened, Ruairi stayed for a few weeks to help out – cleaning rooms and helping guests with their bags.

One weekend, Ruairi went with his cousin, Charlie Gallagher's son, to the Mary of Dunloe festival – a popular Donegal talent and beauty contest. Ruairi spent all weekend drinking, sleeping two nights in a church before making his way back to his father's hostel. Eddie woke him up in the morning and said he needed him in the yard to scatter stones that had been delivered by truck. Ruairi said he was hung-over and needed another hour in bed. Eddie told him that he'd better get out of bed. 'If you have time for drinking, you have time for work. Get up now.'

Ruairi refused. Later, he struggled downstairs, still hung-over.

'Right,' Eddie said. 'Go home to your mother in Dublin and don't fucking come back.'

Ruairi went upstairs, packed his bags and left. As he was walking down the driveway, he met one of the local boys who helped Eddie with the horses. Ruairi convinced the boy to give him a lift to Bundoran, 40 miles away. The two arrived unannounced at the family of Bernadette McAliskey, a former republican MP for Derry and one of the best-known political figures in Northern Ireland. As Bernadette Devlin, the youngest woman ever elected to Westminster, she had famously walked across the floor of the House of Commons and slapped the Home Secretary, Reginald Maudling, when he suggested British soldiers had been acting in self-defence on Bloody Sunday. After surviving a loyalist gun attack on her home in 1981, in which she was shot fourteen times in front of her children, she moved across the border, where her family ran a gambling arcade in Bundoran. It was across the road from a pub run by Joe O'Neill, a local IRA leader.

The two boys stayed with the McAliskeys for three months. Ruairi helped out in the amusement park, emptying the slot machines and getting change for customers. 'I had a great summer and, to be honest, was glad to be away from everyone. I was doing my own thing and Rose was doing her own thing. Eventually I went back down to Dublin. It was the usual when I got home – garda were outside the house, Rose was writing for *An Phoblacht* and spending all her spare time with Jim. If she was getting up to her illegal activity, well, that was giving me time to get involved in mine.'

15. The Camp

Flurries of snow fell in soft waves over the forests of Sliabh an Iarainn, also known as the Iron Mountain, a forested area in Co. Leitrim whose rich iron deposits had been mined for centuries. Iron Mountain had long been used by the IRA for training and target practice, and also to hold supermarket businessman Don Tidey when the IRA kidnapped him in 1983. Now, in late 1990, the IRA was facing another crisis in its weapons arsenal, and Jim and Rose had come to this remote place to try to solve it.

The problem was that the quartermaster department was nearly out of nitrobenzene. According to A. R. Oppenheimer's *IRA: The Bombs and the Bullets*, nitrobenzene was a key component in 'ANNIE' bombs – made with ammonium nitrate, nitrobenzene and diesel oil, which was also known as Donegal Mix.

Nitrobenzene had been banned in Ireland, and for eighteen years the IRA had been relying on old stockpiles and smuggled supplies. Now stocks were low, and as a consequence there was a fall-off in large-scale bombings. Some recent bombs had failed to explode because the booster wasn't strong enough.

The quartermaster-general, Mickey McKevitt, instructed Jim and Rose to develop an alternative booster as soon as possible. In the Dublin workshop, they prepared eight different substances for testing on the Iron Mountain. One of them, they hoped, could be an alternative to nitrobenzene.

When they got to the Iron Mountain, the local IRA unit met them and brought them to a small farmhouse. According to Jim's account, Rose prepared and weighed out a mixture of nitrate fertilizer and each of the eight candidate booster substances in a 5-kilo plastic bag. The bags were then carefully labelled and primed with detonating cord.

A waiting car took away the eight bags while Rose cleaned up any forensic traces left in the farmhouse. She and Jim travelled in a 'clean' car, in which there were no guns, explosives or republican paraphernalia, and met up with the other car at an entrance gate to the Iron Mountain forest. There was a tractor waiting to bring them into the mountains. There were several routes out of the forest, and IRA members with radios would tell them if there was anything suspicious nearby.

Rose and Jim climbed on to the tractor behind the driver. They were joined by a local IRA member, who knew the forest well, and an engineer from the IRA's central command, known as the General Headquarters, or GHQ. After half an hour of driving uphill over bumpy, muddy tracks they came to the test area. It was late in the day and flakes of snow were continuing to fall from the grey sky. Rose was where she wanted to be – an IRA woman who commanded the respect of the men, who could tell the younger recruits what she wanted and to whom they owed courtesy and respect.

On the top of the mountain, the GHQ engineer unwound 50 metres of electric cable, running back to a firing point from where Rose would detonate the explosives. Jim handed her the battery set while he and the engineer prepared the booster charges and wrote down which mixture was included in each.

When the first charge was ready, they walked back to the firing point. Rose connected up the battery set to explode the charge.

'Ready!' she said.

'OK – fire!' said Jim.

There was a sharp crack and a small flash from among the pine trees. No explosion.

'OK, we can write off number one mix,' Jim said.

They tried a second booster – it also failed. They tried a third – it failed too. The IRA men further down the mountain came up to have a look.

Jim was starting to feel embarrassed. Nothing was working. In the end, each of the eight mixes failed. All they had to show for the tests were scattered smudges of fertilizer on the forest floor.

After hours of retests, all unsuccessful, they were out of ideas. The GHQ engineer was deeply disappointed and said so. Nobody could even muster a smile in the cold, damp darkness. The local IRA members were deflated and wanted to go home.

As the tractor bumped and lurched back down the rough path, Rose, Jim, the engineer and the local farmer all hung on tightly and said very little. They knew the seriousness of the situation. Failure to solve the booster problem might force a reassessment of the IRA's entire strategy.

Jim and Rose said goodbye to the others and got into Rose's car. As they drove the long distance back to Dublin, they talked over and over about the problem of detonating the booster charges. Jim recalls that Rose suggested a different approach.

'A booster charge is really a big detonator for setting off bulk explosives when an ordinary detonator isn't powerful enough,' Jim quotes her as saying. 'Think of what conditions you need for a detonator to function correctly.'

This led Jim to the thought that maybe the problem with the eight booster charges wasn't the explosive mixes, but rather with the detonating cord. It was a detonation problem, not an explosion problem. 'You're on to something,' he told her.

Two weeks later, Rose and Jim were on the tractor again, heading through the forest and up the Iron Mountain. With them they had the same eight experimental booster explosives as before, along with detonating cord and electric detonators. The detonating cord had been adjusted to carry the explosion more effectively this time.

Again, Rose set up the batteries, and again she pressed the button for each trial. This time, every single 5-kilo booster charge exploded with a loud crash that echoed through the mountains. The best of the eight boosters was a mix of icing sugar and nitrate fertilizer.

On the road back down through the forest there was laughter and talk. Jim was ecstatic, though he tried to hide it. He felt he and Rose had won back the confidence of the leadership.

Jim told the GHQ engineer that they would do more tests to determine the most effective proportion of icing sugar to fertilizer. The engineer could tell the operating officers to continue with operations all over Northern Ireland that required large explosive charges.

Rose and Jim were now focused on finding the best possible booster to detonate bombs all over Northern Ireland. That would require dedicated focus in an IRA safe area, where they could set off explosives without being detected.

Jim turned to his friend Danny Campbell, who invited them to his training camp on the west coast of Mayo.

Danny Campbell's farm overlooks Blacksod Bay on Mayo's Atlantic coast. Close by is a dancehall – an abandoned grey hulk now, with IRA and far-right slogans scrawled on the wall.

Emigration has taken many people away from this rural, isolated patch of coastal farms. The land here is boggy and poor and much of the area has been converted into one of Ireland's largest national parks. Before emigration, there was the famine. In a neighbouring field, just over some bog dunes, there is a makeshift grave for the McGinty family, who couldn't make it to the sea and died of hunger huddled together.

Danny Campbell came from a strongly republican family. After his father died, and needing to raise money to pay an Achill Island undertaker, Danny emigrated to Chicago in 1964. After a year there, he moved to the home of his brother John, who was living with his wife and ten children in Cleveland, Ohio. Danny stayed in the city for fifteen years, working in construction.

He and John were active in Irish American politics, and sent John's children to protest when Prince Charles visited Cleveland in 1977. 'John's wife made the children these royal crowns and drew blood dripping down the crowns as a protest against the royalty. There was uproar when they got to Prince Charles's event. They didn't start it but some of the royalty supporters saw them and threw paint at them,' recalls Danny's daughter Norah.

In 1980, Danny Campbell returned to the family farm in Mayo. He was cycling to Mass when he saw a local woman,

Phyllis Maguire, walking along the road, and offered her a lift to the church on the back of his bike. After that, he invited her to a wedding. That Christmas, they were engaged.

Jim had not been back to the Campbell camp since he was released from prison five years earlier. The area had changed since then. There were new houses and many small roads winding down to the sea. He had to ask a woman walking along the road for directions to Danny Campbell's house. She laughed and asked him to give her a lift.

Once in the car, she said it was also her house – this was Phyllis, Danny's wife, and she welcomed Jim and Rose into her home.

This was Rose's first time to see the Campbell farm. At the end of the road, there was a long, rocky beach layered with brown seaweed that had been used for IRA target practice for years.

Before the booster experiments, Rose and Jim had met with Danny Campbell in other locations around Mayo – to do tests on mortars and the all-ways striker, to find new ways of making gunpowder for mortar rounds, to blow up cars while testing the drogue bomb. Their new project would need more time, and more experiments. They knew that a mixture of icing sugar and fertilizer could replace nitrobenzene as a booster, but they didn't know what the optimum mix would be. And they needed a place to stay so that they could experiment.

Once they had unpacked, they met Danny and Phyllis's five young children: Norah, Thomas, Anthony, Donal and Katie. Jim explained to Danny that he and Rose wanted to make up five charges of the mixture in different proportions. Each 10-kilo bag would be laid on top of a length of iron sheeting. The strength of the explosions would be measured by how much the iron sheet was bent.

According to Jim's written account, Danny's main concern was the noise of the explosions. He said that in order to muffle the sound, they would bury the explosives deep in the beach sand.

Rose and Jim came back up to Mayo two weeks later, on a Friday. It had taken six hours to drive from Dublin and it was after midnight when they came in the door. They were eager to set up the testing.

With Danny, they moved the cattle to one end of the cowshed and cordoned them off with a chain. Now they had a workspace in which to begin grinding down the fertilizer and mixing it with the icing sugar: cows on one side of the shed, a bomb factory on the other.

The improvised ball mill they used was a slow-spinning barrel with ball bearings inside that would crush the fertilizer. It could grind 25 kilos of fertilizer in an hour.

It was 5 a.m. before all the charges were mixed and bagged, then moved to the sand dunes and hidden. The iron sheets and firing kit were waiting in a 40-gallon plastic barrel that Danny had buried in the dunes.

Light was just about to break when they finished their preparations. They returned to the house. Jim and Rose curled up together, exhausted. They slept through Saturday morning and afternoon then ate with Danny and waited for nightfall. Two local farmers showed up to help with the experiments. The five returned to the dunes. They had only moonlight to guide them.

While the men dug holes five feet into the sand, Rose and Jim prepared the test charges. When all five charges were ready Rose unrolled the electric command wires and connected them first to the charge with the lowest proportion of icing sugar. She made sure everyone else was safely behind the firing point before connecting the battery pack to the command wires.

'Ready?'

'Fire!'

Huge mounds of sand shot upwards in the moonlight while the ground shook with the vibration. Jim remembers that hundreds of sea birds rose squawking into the air. The sand fell back to earth with a pattering, thudding sound. In the faint moonlight, no smoke could be seen.

The crater was about two metres across and a metre deep. Using a small electric torch and carefully shielding the light with their hands, they looked into the crater. On the bottom, almost covered in loose sand, was the bent length of sheet iron.

Rose set off another explosion, then another, then another. Each time, the huge mounds of sand lifted into the air with a whooshing sound and came back down to earth with a loud thud.

It was nearing dawn on Sunday when all five tests had been completed. The final task was to compare the bent iron sheets. Jim felt the fourth test had produced the best result, judging from the bend of the iron. Rose said that she thought the third was the best. They agreed on a mix that would be halfway between the two. The Ballycroy 3–4 mix had been created.

They were happy on the walk back through the sand dunes, talking in low voices about the results. They had buried the bent iron sheets on the beach and the two farmers went home. Danny, Rose and Jim got back to the farmhouse as dawn was breaking.

The IRA now had an alternative booster explosive to replace nitrobenzene. It would prove to a decisive moment in the development of IRA bomb technology.

Rose and Jim were soon sitting around the table with Danny and his wife, eating a big meal. Rose adored the Campbell children. They were polite, they were being brought up as republicans, and they lived in the wilds of the Irish countryside.

'Rose and Jim became like an aunt and uncle to us,' says Norah, who was about six years old when they first started coming to the farm. 'They really became part of our family and Rose was always interested in what we were doing. They would always come with gifts and Rose would always ensure the gifts were educational. They gave us a Commodore 64 computer at a time when nobody had computers, and then they came with all these educational games for us. They were always asking us maths puzzles and, after they were out there firing mortars or testing guns, they would come in for dinner; and afterwards, they and Mam and Dad would sit down for a chat about politics. Jim and Rose would talk about countries we'd never heard of and discuss what should be done there, and they would have these big debates.'

Norah remembers a number of garda raids on the farm over the years, but her father was good at hiding the evidence of training camps and weapons testing. 'He even planted a set of trees across the road from the house because the gardaí used to watch the house from a hill on the common-age bog across the road,' Norah recalls. 'Rose planted her own tree in there as well.'

Danny Campbell had two key assistants. One was a former fisheries officer. The other was a local farmer who had a reputation for secrecy. 'Even now, he still speaks in code. It's like we are still in the mid-1980s,' says Norah.

The Special Branch officer Thomas Connors, who raided the house, backs Norah's view that the Campbell farm was difficult for the police to penetrate. 'I would assess Danny as a very deep thinker and a very solid kind of man. He was very, very secretive, which made it difficult to catch him. There was a garda station in Ballycroy who were relying solely on local information, which takes time to build up. You are talking about an area that was very remote, low population density and a long history of republican sympathy. I'm not just talking Sinn Féin now. I remember interviewing an IRA man who had trained there and he said that many, many houses in west Mayo could be relied upon as safe houses.'

Danny's farm had been used as a safe house for a long time. In 1983, the IRA unit who had kidnapped Don Tidey fled for Danny's farm after a shoot-out with security forces.

'They were only about a mile from Danny's when they were stopped on the road by two gardaí, including Sergeant Des O'Rourke from Ballycroy garda station,' Thomas Connors recalls. 'The IRA stripped the gardaí of their uniforms, tied them up in the bog and fled for Castlebar. Our intelligence was that they were to be taken by fishing boat to Northern Ireland, but they were rumbled in Castlebar and fled again. But it showed where Danny was in the scheme of things.'

Another Campbell daughter, Katie, recalls Rose and Jim coming and going without notice. 'You wouldn't be told when they were coming. You would just see Rose driving in as fast as Michael Schumacher and they would suddenly pull up and you'd think: "OK, they have landed."'

From an upstairs window of the family home in Ballycroy, Norah points to the spot where Rose, Jim, Danny and the local farmers would carry the components of heavy mortar tubes and shoulder-held rocket launchers in backpacks down to the shore. They would then walk to a firing point two miles down the rocky beach, where they would fire missiles and mortar bombs into the sea.

'In the winter, Daddy, Jim and Rose would go out there on to the shore at dusk and maybe go until 10 p.m. In summer, they went out there much later and they would go all night and come back in the morning for breakfast. But there was often very heavy equipment to be brought out there, so it would be Jim, Rose, Dad and a very small group from Bally-croy that Daddy completely trusted.'

Norah was trained to identify Special Branch cars. If a strange car didn't give a flash of its lights as it approached, she would shout to her parents, who would hide explosives and spirit IRA members out the back.

In 2011, Rose wrote about the farm for a Sinn Féin 'Cairde' night in Belfast honouring Phyllis Campbell for her contribution to the IRA. 'The struggle has been one of endless and personal sacrifice, which goes back through generations of Campbells in Ballycroy, who scraped a livelihood by the sea, on a few fields with a few cows, and who kept a whole community alive to the struggle,' Rose wrote.

She recalled how the Campbells would prepare for a camp. 'There was transport; hot food; warm, dry clothes; gloves and boots for all – all were difficult. At every stage the camp could be uncovered by a careless move,' she wrote. Even bringing in loaves of bread for a large group of IRA members could raise suspicion. Sometimes they were delivered to the back door and hidden in the cot with the baby, Rose recalled.

Rose also recalled spotting Sergeant Des O'Rourke, who had been stripped and tied up by the IRA during the Don Tidey kidnapping. He had called to the farm to see what Danny was doing.

'One day, I remember Sergeant O'Rourke drove up, stopped at the house and was looking to see Danny. They were all waiting in the house, waiting to go out. We had the loaves hidden everywhere, even in the bath, beneath the blanket that was steeping in the bath.'

She also recalled that Brian Keenan, who brought the IRA bombing campaign to England, had trained at the Campbell farm, as had the IRA bomber (and later MEP) Martina Anderson, IRA army council member Bernard Fox, and Monaghan IRA leader Pat Treanor.

Norah recalls helping Treanor, a close friend of Jim's, climb out a back window while gardaí were coming through the front door. 'Another night, Pat was coming from an operation and, in the darkness, he walked right into a garda car parked outside our house. He had to hide in a ditch for hours until they were gone.'

16. Bombs and Poetry

'Can anyone tell me what Patrick Kavanagh is trying to evoke in this poem? Anyone?'

Rose looked around the classroom at her students.

Outside the school, Special Branch officers had been sitting all morning in their car, waiting to follow her when she left.

Ian Tims, one of Rose's students, remembers her asking the class: 'Is that car still out there?'

'Yes, miss.'

He throws his head back laughing as he remembers. 'There was nothing like her,' he says.

Rose had begun a new job in St Kevin's Community College in Clondalkin, west Dublin, in 1991, teaching English and Environmental and Social Science.

It was a tough school, and some of its classes seemed like nothing more than a dumping ground for some of the department of education's most intractable charges.

She had applied for the job as Rose Gallagher, and the students called her Miss Gallagher; but they knew who she really was. Students brought newspaper articles about her to school.

'They all used to slag her about it,' recalls Patrick Donohoe, one of her English students. 'They would shout. *Tiocfaidh Ár Lá!* in the corridor and, one time, when she came into the classroom, someone had written: '"Up the 'RA"'. She just rubbed it off and got on with it.'

Donohoe himself was from a strongly republican family: when he was seven, his house was raided and his father grabbed a bag, jumped over the back wall and fled to the home of an IRA supporter named John McCann, who agreed to hide the bag for him.

'I told Rose who my dad was and then she was really nice to me and would ask how my father was doing, so it was useful,' says Donohoe.

She was the only teacher he knew who swore in class. Once, when one of the students reacted to a poem by an American poet and criticized Americans, Rose snapped, 'Well, the English have been pushing down the Irish for centuries and most of you have done FUCK ALL about it!'

John McCann's son, Bernard, remembers her as willing to take on disruptive teenage boys.

'There was this fella in our class who was quite brainy, but one day starts giving a lot of lip to Rose, and he is standing up in class, he's at least a foot taller than she is. She used to wear these hiking books in class so she just walked right up to him, put her boot on his toes and pushed him over, and he fell backwards on the ground. Everyone just burst out laughing. No other teacher would do that.'

'He didn't complain to the principal about her. Nobody did. You wouldn't dare because you knew she was IRA and nobody wanted to mess with that.'

One pupil asked bluntly: 'Miss, did you go to jail?'

'Not for anything that concerns you,' she said. And yet everyone had a theory on why she was missing the top of a finger, which she would hold up and show them when asked.

The explanation for the damaged finger was not very exciting – she had cut it on a door on Eugene Street, according to Ruairi – but dramatic rumours circulated in the school.

Patrick Donohoe heard that she had cut it off in Limerick prison during the Tiede Herrema kidnapping, as some sort of signal of how serious she and the kidnappers were. Bernard McCann heard that she had done it to defy her family when she was younger.

Bernard's sister Marlissa, who used to get a lift home with Rose, said that Rose was happy to cultivate an aura of mystery. 'She gave one explanation for her finger in one class and another in the other class. She was like that. Great teacher. Eccentric, though!'

Patrick Donohoe remembers Rose's keen interest in developing the students' essay-writing skills. 'If she didn't like the end of your essay, she just said it straight out and you'd go off and try to think of a better argument. She wasn't so much into imaginative composition, she was more into – do you have an argument and how are you going to defend it?'

On the morning of 7 February 1991, the British Prime Minister, John Major, was beginning a cabinet meeting. At the cabinet table with him were Foreign Secretary Douglas Hurd; Defence Secretary Tom King; Chancellor of the Exchequer Norman Lamont; Attorney General Sir Patrick Mayhew, and the Chief of the Defence Staff, Sir David Craig.

The meeting had just begun when there was a huge thud and the windows smashed in. A 4.5-foot-long IRA mortar bomb, packed with 40 lbs of Semtex, had crashed into the garden of 10 Downing Street and exploded.

'We were in the midst of a meeting, discussing the Gulf War,' Major would later tell journalist Peter Taylor for a BBC/PBS documentary. 'Suddenly there was this tremendous explosion, and then an aftershock, and then what seemed like a second explosion. And it took just a fraction of a second to realize what it was. And then, suddenly, the windows all caved in. Everybody ducked down under the table.'

The attack had been launched from a Ford van parked off Whitehall, 250 yards from Downing Street. Police said two men were seen fleeing from the van before the mortars fired.

Peter Gurney, the most senior bomb-disposal officer in the London police, recalled to Taylor that the van was 'burning furiously'. 'Hanging out the back, there were some blankets. And I thought these, if I could get them out, would make good forensic evidence. I couldn't get them out. The heat was too much. Through the flames, I could see three mortar tubes.'

He assessed that the cabinet were 'extremely lucky' not to have been seriously injured or killed in the attack.

Two other mortar shells fell near the Foreign Office. The head of the Metropolitan Police Anti-Terrorist Branch, Commander George Churchill-Coleman, told the Press Association that those two mortar bombs caught fire but did not fully explode and that some windows shattered at the Foreign Office. The Press Association reported that three mortar tubes could be seen bolted inside the van, and part of the roof had been crudely cut away above them.

The Queen, who rarely speaks on current events, had a message for the attackers in a speech at the opening of a London hospital. 'I would like to take this opportunity to remind them that they will not succeed,' she said.

Jim Monaghan wrote: 'The mortar bombs were the older "heavy mortar" design which fired from a cut-off oxygen cylinder. Each bomb was carrying about 40 pounds (18 kg) of Semtex. A minute or two after the driver had left the van, three heavy mortars fitted with all-ways strikers were fired through a camouflaged hole cut in the roof.' He concluded that the all-ways strikers had done their job in the Downing Street attack, but the detonators had not.

As the bombs landed, Rose and Jim were in an IRA safe house in the Dublin mountains, assembling detonators for bombs with two other IRA members. On a table, they had assembled most of the components and had set a target of assembling fifty detonators for the day.

They were on a tea break when the old man running the safe house, identified in Jim's manuscript by the pseudonym 'Michael', came rushing into the room with news of the Downing Street attack. Despite the ultimate failure of the attack, Jim records that there was a sense of jubilation in the safe house that it had come so close to wiping out the British cabinet.

After the Downing Street attack, surveillance of Rose intensified. Special Branch officers followed her to and from school, they followed her to Jim's workshop, and to the home of their IRA-supporting friend John McCann. Before going to Mayo, Rose and Jim would leave their cars at a Dublin train station and switch to a rental car supplied by the IRA.

Their powerful new explosive, Ballycroy 3–4, was used for the first time in conflict on 31 May 1991. At about eleven thirty in the morning, a Mercedes truck drove into a field overlooking a British army barracks at Glenanne in County Armagh. The truck contained the largest bomb ever employed in the Northern Ireland conflict, packed with 2,500 lbs of Ballycroy 3–4. The South Armagh unit didn't want to just damage an army base, they wanted to annihilate it.

The truck stopped at the top of a hill and, with its engine off, began to roll down the field. The driver jumped out.

The Glenanne barracks normally accommodated fourteen Ulster Defence Regiment soldiers. This morning there
were forty people gathered for a social event. The truck
crashed through the perimeter fence and came to a halt. Two
soldiers who had been playing pool rushed out to investigate.
As they approached the lorry, they heard shots. The back of
the truck had been fitted with a metal plate that would cause
the bomb to detonate if it was hit with a bullet. One of the
IRA members fired at it from the top of the hill. The truck
exploded with such ferocity it could be heard 50 miles away,
and left a crater 200 feet deep.

Both of the soldiers were killed instantly, along with
another soldier inside the barracks. Eleven more were seriously injured, and the other twenty-six occupants of the
base received less serious injuries. The shock killed cows in
nearby fields and scattered debris 300 yards in every direction. The damage was so great that the base was never rebuilt.

The IRA had shown that it could destroy a heavily fortified
barracks. And it had done so using home-made explosives
developed by Jim and Rose and tested on a remote beach in
Co. Mayo.

17. Antisocial Behaviour

Ruairi is in a taxi on his way up to the border. His destination is a British army checkpoint.

He knows the taxi driver well: they grew up in the same neighbourhood.

Scottish squaddies are ahead of them on the road. There are blast walls and concrete blocks to deflect a car bomb. From positions above them, army snipers peer down.

The taxi pulls up at the checkpoint. A soldier looks in. He has seen Ruairi plenty of times before but doesn't know his name. He has no idea that he is the son of the famous Rose Dugdale.

The soldier gives Ruairi a bag, and Ruairi gives the soldier a roll of money.

The taxi drives up the road and back down through the checkpoint and returns over the border to Dublin. Ruairi opens up the bag. It contains hundreds of ecstasy tablets.

In the early 1990s, rave culture – fuelled by ecstasy – was at its peak. The drugs Ruairi was handling were imported from the Netherlands, via England. There were many people on the supply chain, and everyone needed a cut. Ruairi was making about £1 a tablet: a margin that was worth the risk only at scale: 'You were doing hundreds at a time.'

Just like his mother, Ruairi was constantly switching cars, constantly dodging the gardaí.

Coming from an IRA family had its advantages: if Ruairi didn't come up with payments in time, he got extensions.

He and his friends abhorred heroin and crystal meth, and considered themselves a superior breed of drug dealer. Ecstasy was a party drug taken at the weekends by people with lives.

'It was rave at that time, and thank god it was, otherwise it could have been heroin that everyone was on or crystal meth – that would have left everyone wrecked and ruined. We took pride in not getting into heroin, we saw ourselves as a level above that,' he said.

Despite his mother's militant anti-drugs activism, Ruairi didn't see anything wrong with what he was doing. The IRA represented violence and martyrdom. Didn't he already have enough of that in his family? And as for going to prison – he was born in prison, his parents had been in prison, everyone he knew had been in prison.

Rose heard that Ruairi was dealing ecstasy, and she continued to suspect – wrongly – that Sheila was involved as well. Sheila was working in St James's Hospital at the time, and walked the short distance to and from work. One day, a car approached her from behind and swerved towards her, almost hitting her. The driver was Rose.

Sheila took it as a warning: stay away from my son. Shaken, she told Ruairi about it: 'That crazy bitch tried to run me over. Do something.'

In the early 1990s, Rose bought a two-storey house on Kilworth Road on the western edge of Drimnagh in west Dublin. Ruairi says she made the move in the hope that it would 'get me away from the people I was mixing with'. The new house, though modest, was much bigger than the cottage in Eugene Street – but Ruairi couldn't take to the suburban streets of Drimnagh. 'I don't think I spent more than a night there, despite Rose's best efforts. I was over in

Sheila's, I was looking for a place, I was doing my own thing.'

In the hope of coaxing Ruairi, Rose threw a housewarming party, inviting Eddie, Jim and all her republican friends. Eddie made the trip from Donegal. As the guests drank in the front garden, Rose told Ruairi a story about an Italian woman. The woman's son was selling drugs and had damaged her honour. She couldn't accept it, so she murdered her son to teach all the other youths of the town a lesson.

Eddie was standing at the garden wall, listening with rising anger. He stepped up to Rose: 'If anything happens to that boy, if anything fucking happens . . .'

Others separated them and told Eddie to calm down. Rose went into the house. She was not threatening Ruairi, she insisted; she was just pointing out how another woman had reacted.

The incident shocked Ruairi, and it is one of the few subjects on which he is in complete agreement with Eddie. 'If Ma had her way, well, I'm sure I could have ended up in trouble,' he says. 'Fair play to the old man, he put his hand into the fire for me.'

At one point, when Ruairi was facing a series of charges, Eddie showed up in court to tell the judge that he was taking Ruairi up to Donegal. That seemed to please the judge. Ruairi committed himself to Donegal – to slaughtering animals in Uncle Charlie's abattoir, fixing up the farm and working in Eddie's hostel. But still, the old problems between himself and Eddie lingered.

'We are just too alike,' says Ruairi. Both were charming and intelligent but easily angered. Eddie felt that Ruairi never listened. Ruairi felt that Eddie was always lecturing him. After a few weeks, he packed his bags and left without a word. He made his way back to Dublin, where he stayed with Sheila and other friends.

In the early 1990s, the Irish National Liberation Army, or INLA – a nominally Marxist republican paramilitary organization – was beset by internal feuding. By that point, the INLA was increasingly a front for drug dealing and other forms of criminality. As a result of the internal conflict, some of its leaders moved to Dublin, and with them came drugs and a great number of guns.

The INLA chief of staff, Gino Gallagher, was living on Cork Street with his mother. The mustachioed Gallagher was a good-looking man, popular with the ladies. Ruairi remembers Gallagher 'coming to Rose and begging her, absolutely begging her, to help him – that the IRA was after him and that she must help him out, put in a good word for him, he was trying to stay out of trouble, all of this.'

Gallagher tried to appeal to Rose as a fellow revolutionary socialist, but she wasn't convinced. It was ridiculous to her that the INLA could spout Marxism while selling drugs. Still, she said she would do what she could.

Gino was no sooner out of trouble with the IRA than he was threatening Ruairi and his friends while trying to expand his drugs network in Dublin. 'I couldn't believe this,' Ruairi says. 'He's over with Rose, begging for his life, and then he turns around and he's telling me that I'm a dead man? But that was the INLA – always trouble.'

The INLA was involved in dealing heroin in Dolphin's Barn at the time. Ruairi, who was starting to lose contemporaries to overdoses, increasingly recoiled from that world.

'There was a hole in a wall that people climbed through to get into Dolphin House, and the drug dealers would gather to sell to the junkies coming through the hole. There was dirt and piss there, junkies with AIDS. Any weekend you'd see junkies walking up and down the road outside the hole, looking inside cars and doing a smash and grab at the traffic lights then going straight to the hole to get that fix, anything for that fix. You'd see kids with handkerchiefs over their faces, after robbing a jeweller's or something, running up the road to the hole, there was something every day. It was horrible, absolutely horrible. I didn't know how to get out of there, but I had to.'

Rose and Jim's next big weapons-development project had its origins in a meeting in 1990 with the operations officer for South Armagh, who told them that the British had greatly improved protection around their armoured cars and military barracks. The IRA wanted a shoulder-fired missile launcher with missiles that could pierce the latest generation of British armour. The missile launcher would have to be easily constructed from household and farm implements, and any non-reusable parts would have to be readily obtainable. Its warhead had to be at least as powerful as an impact grenade, and it had to be easy to use, even for someone without much training. Also, the IRA didn't want to have to build an elaborate bunker to store it, so it would need to be simple to assemble and dismantle. The operations officer also told them that the complete weapon could not be longer than 65 centimetres, so that it would fit into the standard plastic barrel used by the IRA for underground arms storage.

Jim and Rose worked on this new weapon for months in Dublin and Ballycroy. It had a crucial feature: digestive biscuits.

'We remember the packets of biscuits,' says Norah Campbell. 'You would see them lying around the place, they were noticeable. We couldn't be seen with boxes of them, but they would be laid out in individual packets, ready for Rose and Jim.'

In order to minimize recoil on the missile launcher, Jim and Rose used two 400-gram packets of digestive biscuits at the back. The biscuits would absorb the recoil after the missile was fired and disintegrate harmlessly.

Norah Campbell remembers her father loading up heavy backpacks with Rose and Jim before walking two miles along the coast at night to fire dud missiles into the Atlantic. Once Jim and Rose were satisfied with how it tested, the Biscuit Launcher was ready for mass production. It was packed with 600 grams of Semtex and fitted with a 'squash head' warhead that could penetrate armour. A squash head was designed to flatten on impact and then detonate, penetrating the 10mm armour mounted on British personnel carriers and armoured jeeps.

During training, it was discovered that, instead of using the projectiles Jim designed expressly for the missile launcher, they could be replaced with large beans or dog food tins, packed with explosives.

For the gardaí, the arrival of the cheaply made Biscuit Launcher was a concern. 'At first it was a mystery to us why we were finding large amounts of digestive biscuits on IRA training camps,' says Thomas Connors, the former Special Branch officer. 'At first, we assumed it was because biscuits can last a long time as food supplies, but then it became clear that it was being used for a shoulder-held rocket launcher. It showed a certain innovation and understanding of physics that few would possess.'

The physics might have been sophisticated, but the DIY manufacturing of the missile launchers was sometimes imperfect. In one of the first Biscuit Launcher attacks, on the streets of West Belfast, a young IRA man fired from close range at a giant army troop transporter. The missile flew out behind him and exploded into a wall, and the crushed biscuits fell out in front of him: the weapon had been assembled with the trigger facing the wrong way. From then on, operating officers were instructed to make sure there was an arrow painted on each Biscuit Launcher to show which way the trigger should face.

In May 1991, the Biscuit Launcher was used in an attack on an RUC armoured vehicle travelling along Mica Drive in West Belfast. Three RUC officers were badly injured and one, Sergeant Stephen Gillespie, died a few days later. Sergeant Gillespie, who lived in Ballygowan, Co. Down, was a father of two. He was a sportsman who had won medals in the British Police Games. He was known as a quiet man who loved his family and had recently suffered the loss of a child.

Robert Gibson, then the mayor of the local council, remembers calling to the Gillespie house to offer his condolences to Stephen's crying family. 'At that time, our area was considered relatively safe, so a lot of police moved here. Stephen's family moved out soon after his killing. There was a lot of killings going on in the early 1990s. I'm afraid to say that attending funerals became a way of life.'

18. Someone is Listening

The IRA's next munitions crisis started in 1991, with the breach of a concrete wall in an underground bunker in the west of Ireland. The bunker filled to the top with water. It was the IRA's main storage bunker for Libyan detonating cord, detonators and fuses.

'It was so serious,' recalls Thomas Connors, the former Special Branch officer, 'that [Quartermaster-General Mickey] McKevitt and his wife, Bernie, travelled down there to inspect the damage. When they opened the bunker, it was like a swimming pool in there. We knew the IRA was in trouble as a result. We were hoping to stop them from getting any more cord, and [Libyan dictator Muammar] Gaddafi was unlikely to resupply them at that point.'

Gaddafi was making overtures to the British government in the hope of ending international sanctions against his country and was no longer supplying the IRA.

Jim got a message to report to the South Armagh brigade as soon as possible. He took the day off work to go to the meeting. When he got there, he noted the worried looks on the faces of the operations officer for South Armagh and the brigade quartermaster.

The operations officer told Jim that, as a result of the damage caused by the bunker flood, the IRA had only three months of detonating cord left before the entire bombing campaign in the North would grind to a halt. Later that week, Jim and Rose travelled to the Campbell farm to address the question of how to replace the lost supply of detonating cord. The farm would be theirs for as long as they wanted.

Detonating cord, by Jim's definition, is a length of plastic tubing filled with an explosive that could carry a detonation wave. The tube is usually 4 or 5 mm in diameter.

Jim's first idea was to use nitrated starch as the explosive in the detonating cord. They set up a device in Danny Campbell's shed to nitrate starch, but when the starch was drying it spontaneously caught fire. Next, they manufactured picric acid, an explosive used by the British in shells in the Boer War and the First World War.

They made up a batch of picric acid in the Campbells' cowshed: it took the form of a mass of bright yellow needle-like crystals. They would have to dry the crystals indoors and, at Jim's request, Danny kept the shed warm. When the picric acid was ready, they packed it into the plastic tube. As they were packing it, Jim and Rose both sensed a bitter taste, although neither of them had put crystals near their mouths. Micro-crystals were floating in the air.

Danny gave them painters' face masks to protect their lungs from the micro-crystals. When they walked outside the shed and into the sunlight, Rose and Jim could see each other's hands and faces were turning yellow from the crystals in the air.

When they tested the picric-acid-filled plastic tube on the sand dunes, it exploded near the detonator and then fizzled out. Starch hadn't worked, and neither had picric acid. Rose, Jim and Danny were sitting around a table discussing the problem when Rose made a suggestion.

'Why not start with what we have?' Jim quotes her as saying in his memoir. 'We know that Semtex is a mixture of RDX and PETN explosives with a binding material. Could we extract the explosives from it using a solvent?'

Rose and Jim returned two weeks later with several different solvents, and quickly found the one that worked best on Semtex. That weekend, they were able to design and build a lab in the cowshed for extracting, purifying and drying the powdered explosive. Jim filled a 5-mm plastic tube with the white extract.

Jim, Rose, Danny and a local farmer went out to the dunes and buried a 300-mm length of the new detonating cord in the sand. Rose took up the battery firing set and connected the wires. When she flicked the switch there was a sharp thud and the sand flew in all directions along the entire length of the detonating cord.

They now had their own home-made detonating cord. Semtex was a very safe explosive to handle. The problem was that it was valuable and scarce. In order to use as little of it as possible, they wanted to find a way of using shorter lengths of detonating cord, while delivering enough power to set off an explosion.

Outside a corner shop in Dublin, Jim stopped the car while Rose went in to buy cigarettes. As he waited, Jim watched a tiny fly circling near the dashboard. It was so quiet he could hear the buzz of its minute wings. Then he heard a metallic click from somewhere in front of him. It sounded like an audio tape coming to an end.

He got out of the car. Rose was coming out of the shop and Jim put a finger to his lips. They walked some distance down the street before Jim told her that he thought the car might be bugged, and that when they got in they should talk about 'anything except army business'.

That evening, Jim unscrewed the dashboard and found a battery pack and a circuit board bound up in yellow PVC insulating tape. He very quietly replaced the panel and tightened the retaining screws. He then brought his tool kit over to Rose's house. They moved her car to a secluded spot and Jim searched it. Once more he found a battery pack and circuit board wrapped in yellow tape.

Jim called the electronic engineers in the South Armagh brigade to tell them what he had found, and he arranged to have both cars brought to their bomb-making garage. He and Rose drove their cars over the border and into a large barn made from corrugated-iron sheets. As a British army helicopter circled the area, an IRA man drove them to a safe house, where they waited half an hour until an IRA member collected them. Making sure that the helicopter was out of sight, they drove their cars out of the shed and back to Dublin.

At a debriefing after the electronics had been examined, they were told that the circuitry was very advanced and included electronic chips that the IRA engineers had never seen before. There were no obvious clues as to who had bugged the cars. It was likely that it was the Garda Special Branch, but there were other possibilities to be investigated. Jim and Rose were warned that they were 'red hot', a term of art in the IRA for people under heavy surveillance, and that they were to halt all experiments or testing of new weapons. The IRA interrogated them separately about whether they had talked about the research unit while travelling in the car. Both knew better than to lie. They both said they talked all the time about the bomb-making and missile technology they were developing.

The questions flew at them, testing to see if there were any inconsistencies. Some double agents in the IRA had been known to 'find' bugging devices, with the cooperation of their handlers, as a gambit to bolster their credibility.

What had they talked about in the past days and weeks? How long could the bugs have been there? How could the cars have been got at? What opportunities would the eavesdroppers have had to change audio tapes and battery packs? (When asked if the Garda Special Branch was behind the bugs, Thomas Connors says: 'Absolutely no comment.')

Jim wondered if the yellow PVC insulating tape was a clue. Sometimes technical experts liked to leave their own signature on their work or had their own code for telling their agents about the device.

The IRA eventually traced the security breach to a large car park beside the Dublin railway station where Jim and Rose habitually left their own cars and got into hired ones for trips to Mayo. Now they had to rethink their security and their routines.

Jim continued researching in the Dublin workshop, but he worked on the assumption that it was being watched and probably bugged. He and Rose would no longer use the workshop to make prototypes.

At around 9.30 p.m. on 10 April 1992, the day after John Major was re-elected prime minister, most people working in the financial district had gone home, or had gone out for the night in other parts of London.

A white Ford Transit van was parked in front of the Baltic Exchange building in the City. The driver got out and walked down the street. Some minutes later an IRA unit phoned a warning to police. Before the bomb-disposal units got to the van, it exploded. A thousand kilograms of Ballycroy 3–4 turned into white-hot gas under tremendous pressure. The gas shot outwards in all directions.

The resulting blast was funnelled down the streets between

the high buildings. The shock wave in the ground spread through the foundations of the buildings and the underground infrastructure of water, gas, electricity, communications cables and sewage pipes, destroying them all. A second later, the vast ball of hot gases cooled and contracted, leaving a vacuum in the streets above, sucking thousands of windows outwards. A cascade of 500 tons of broken glass fell into the deserted streets.

The bomb killed three people: Paul Butt, aged 29, who was walking nearby; Thomas Casey, 49, a Baltic Exchange doorman; and 15-year-old Danielle Carter, who was in a car close to the bomb site. Another ninety-one people were injured, and the bomb caused £800 million worth of damage.

After the bombing, MI5 and Sir Patrick Mayhew, now Secretary of State for Northern Ireland, began sending out overtures to the IRA leadership. An MI6 member named Michael Oatley, code-named Mountain Climber, was tasked with setting up the communication channel. It went from the British government to Oatley to a community activist and chip-shop owner in Derry named Brendan Duddy, to Martin McGuinness, vice-president of Sinn Féin and a member of the IRA's army council.

Even as these very sensitive overtures were being made, the IRA army council took the view that one more massive bomb in the London financial district could force the British government into formal talks – something the British government had repeatedly said it would not do without a permanent end to the IRA campaign.

Secret talks between Sinn Féin leader Gerry Adams and John Hume of the Social Democratic and Labour Party (SDLP), which had commenced in 1988, were ongoing, and the IRA was continuing to communicate with the British government through the Mountain Climber channel. Both sides were anxious to change the dynamic of the conflict.

Patrick Mayhew issued a statement in December 1992 saying that Sinn Féin could take part in peace talks only after an IRA ceasefire. The IRA and Sinn Féin claimed that a ceasefire would lead only to futile talks with unionists, who would drag it out for years until the IRA fell apart.

In March 1993, IRA bombs in Warrington, England, killed 3-year-old Jonathan Ball and 12-year-old Timothy Parry, and injured fifty-six people. The agony of Warrington led to an outpouring of rage in Ireland. Peace activists organized mass rallies in Dublin, which attracted huge support.

On 10 April, Hume and Adams met in Derry, and two weeks later they issued a joint statement for the first time. Hume was heavily criticized in the Dublin and Belfast media for talking to Sinn Féin, especially after the Warrington bomb.

On 24 April 1993, just over a year on from the Baltic Exchange bombing, a 30-ton blue Ford tipper truck carrying a construction team arrived at the extensive security cordon that had been established around London's financial district. Police verified that the truck belonged to an approved building company.

In fact, the truck was a 'ringer' – it had been made to a likeness of the original, with the same registration number. It contained 1,500 kilograms of Ballycroy 3–4, with booster tubes connected to the deconstructed-Semtex detonation cords that Rose had conceived. It parked outside 99 Bishopsgate, then the UK headquarters of the Hong Kong and Shanghai Bank. As the driver and the passenger got out, they set the bomb's timer and switched on the truck's hazard lights. An accomplice in a car outside the security perimeter then drove them away.

The IRA put through eight warning calls to the London police from a phone box in Forkhill, South Armagh. The police were already approaching the suspicious-looking truck when the bomb warnings came through. They immediately began evacuating the streets around the truck.

A *News of the World* photographer, having heard of the IRA warning, evaded the police cordons and approached the truck to get a close-up snap. As he took his photos, the truck exploded. The photographer was killed instantly, and forty-five other people – security guards, builders and office workers – were injured. The war was far from over.

If you visit the National Army Museum in Chelsea, you can see one of the IRA Biscuit Launchers that were developed by Jim and Rose. Rose's childhood home is visible from the window of the museum's Northern Ireland section.

Before it became a museum piece, the captured launcher was analysed by the British army, along with the remains of missiles that had been fired from the launchers. The missiles were engineered to explode just after impact, so army engineers mounted hard chipboard a few inches out from the armoured plates on the sides of army vehicles. They calculated that this outer surface would cause the warhead to explode before it hit the armoured plate.

By this time, Jim and Rose had already modified the device, replacing the digestive biscuits with packets of long-grain rice, which did a better job of absorbing the recoil gas.

'I remember well when rice replaced the digestive biscuits because there was any amount of rice in the house,' says

Norah Campbell. 'We had so much rice to eat that it kind of put me off it.'

The operations officer for South Armagh now wanted them to find a way to defeat the extra layer of armour on British army vehicles. Jim and Rose began testing a new copper cover on the missiles to penetrate the chipboard and allow the explosive charge to reach the police or army vehicle.

Tension was brewing between Ruairi and Martin 'The Viper' Foley, who believed he had been shortchanged on a drug deal. Ruairi went one night with a friend up to the Red Cow in west Dublin to talk to Foley. They agreed to follow Foley there, but he broke a red light and they lost him. Ruairi later came to believe that Foley might have intended to shoot him that night.

As Ruairi accumulated an ever-growing list of people to fear on the street, he concluded that he had to get out of Ireland. In the summer of 1994, he emigrated to Germany, where many Irish were working in construction. He said goodbye to Sheila. The two of them had started dating when he was thirteen. Now he was nineteen and they were finally breaking up.

He got work with a roofing company, and quickly met a German woman called Angelika. 'I was only going to try Germany for a few months, but there was no going home after that,' he says.

Ruairi went on to set up his own construction company, and he and Angelika bought a big house in Regensburg, in eastern Bavaria that needed to be completely renovated. Just as Rose had come from a huge house and was now living in a tiny one, he had grown up in one of Dublin's smallest homes and dreamed of living in a palace. Ruairi spent a year on the house, redoing the roof, the floors and the walls. Eddie came over to help him with the roofing. When not working on building contracts, Ruairi was travelling all over Germany to source materials and fittings for the interior of the house. He found an antique piano for the living room, along with lights, beds and kitchen worktops. Soon, Ruairi and Angelika converted their home into a guest house. Ruairi had learned the rudiments of hospitality from Eddie's hostel in Donegal, and took to it immediately. 'I was a workaholic at that point,' he says. 'The stress was mounting but it was a very different stress to the one I had in Dublin. I never wanted to go back'.

Talks continued between Sinn Féin/IRA and the SDLP and, in the deep background, between the IRA and the British government, via Michael Oatley. Speculation mounted in the Irish media that an IRA ceasefire was coming. By August 1994, it was understood to be a certainty – the only questions were when it would happen, on what terms, and whether or not it would last.

On 31 August 1994, RTÉ broadcast an audio cassette supplied by the IRA. The voice of an unnamed woman announced 'a complete cessation of military operations'.

When the ceasefire was announced, Jim and Rose were in Mayo testing the 66-mm armour-piercing Rice Launcher. With Danny Campbell and other local IRA men, they discussed the ceasefire. Jim's belief was that it only meant a halt to 'attacks on the Brits' and did not rule out research and development. 'We'll continue our work unless ordered to stop,' he said. Rose, who didn't think the ceasefire would last very long anyway, was also in favour of continuing.

On 7 March 1995, Patrick Mayhew made a speech in

Washington laying out three conditions that the IRA would have to meet before Sinn Féin could take part in all-party peace talks. He said that there must be 'a willingness in principle to disarm progressively', a 'practical understanding' of how to decommission weapons, and the actual decommissioning of some weapons.

Jim and Rose met with Danny and his small inner circle to discuss the implications of Mayhew's speech. All of them were sceptical of the UK government's bona fides and opposed to weapons decommissioning – and such views were widespread within the republican movement.

On 1 September 1995 the IRA issued a statement saying that there was 'absolutely no question of any IRA decommissioning, either through the back door or the front door'. Establishing decommissioning as a precondition for talks was 'a new and unreasonable demand'.

The army council told the South Armagh brigade to begin preparing for another major bombing in London. It would take months to put together.

On the evening of 9 February 1996, a flatbed truck was parked about 70 yards from South Quay station on the Docklands Light Railway in London. A box had been welded into place under the truck's flatbed trailer. It contained 3,000 lbs of Ballycroy 3–4, in sacks. Interspersed among the sacks were metal booster tubes packed with Semtex. Attached to these booster tubes, according to Toby Harnden's book *Bandit Country: The IRA and South Armagh*, 'were lengths of improvised detonating cord made from plastic tubing filled with PETN and RDX, the two constituent elements of Semtex'. This was Rose's work: she had been the first to suggest that they use PETN and RDX for detonating cord.

After the truck pulled up a South Armagh IRA man named James McArdle made the warning calls.

The bomb detonated just after 7 p.m. The blast and the tremors could be heard and felt across London. Two men in a nearby newsagent's – owner Inam Bashir (29), and employee John Jeffries (31) – died after they were blown through two walls and their bodies were buried by the rubble. More than a hundred people were hurt, mainly by broken glass. Most of the injured were staff from nearby office blocks.

Zaoui Berrezag, his 17-year-old son and 14-year-old daughter were injured as they waited in their car, 40 yards from the bomb, after finishing a cleaning job. His son suffered facial injuries and a perforated eardrum. Another victim, Barbara Osei, required three hundred stitches to her face and suffered shrapnel penetration to her right eye.

A second explosion, caused by a gas leak, hampered rescue efforts. Three buildings – the Midland Bank, and South Quay Plaza I and II – were destroyed. The South Quay train station was also severely damaged, and travel on the line was disrupted for months.

John Grieve, head of the Metropolitan Police's anti-terrorist unit, described 'a scene of utter devastation . . . like a scene from the Apocalypse'.

When the bomb detonated, Jim and Rose were on their way to Ballycroy for another test of the shoulder-held Rice Launcher. They stopped off for a meal in a little town on the way. It was a cold night and neither the heater nor the radio in the car was working. They were glad of the warmth of a café and a break from the long drive west. While eating they heard on the radio news that there had been a huge truck bomb in London's Docklands.

When they arrived at Danny's farmhouse in Ballycroy around midnight, the mood was celebratory.

Danny told them: 'I was losing faith in the army council. It's good the IRA put a stop to that messing around.'

Jim records Rose as saying that while the British were picking up the pieces of their financial centre, they could think back on why they're known around the world as 'Perfidious Albion'. 'Negotiating in bad faith was always their strong point,' she said.

Jim's view was that the British had been 'playing us along', but that 'if we keep hitting the decision-makers where it hurts, they'll be back to the table before long'.

Danny's wife, Phyllis, was the lone voice of dissent. She was exhausted from the long war, tired of seeing so many people suffer. Jim records her saying: 'It's a pity the talks broke down. I'd hoped that they'd succeed this time, and that there would be no more people killed or sitting in jails. It's twenty-seven years since the war started.'

19. Rabbits and Rendezvous

Even as Gerry Adams was telling the world that the IRA wanted peace, Rose Dugdale was working on a new weapon to cut through police and army flak jackets.

A month before the London Docklands bombing, Jim had been summoned to South Armagh. The IRA needed a long-range sniper rifle. Sniper teams in South Armagh had killed a number of soldiers and police officers, causing such terror that some soldiers falsified patrol log books while staying in the safety of their barracks. The snipers had been using a US-imported Barrett rifle, but smuggling the Barretts from the US was difficult. Mickey McKevitt and the quartermaster team had long hoped for an IRA-created replica.

Through 1996, Jim experimented at his workshop in Dublin. The key element was the rifle barrel: Jim spent a long time working out how to drill a long, straight hole in a bar of shock-resistant steel. Eventually he succeeded in a process that produced a good-quality 12.7mm barrel that could fire fifty to a hundred rounds before it had to be replaced. Jim and Rose decided to use iron sights instead of a telescopic sight so the entire weapon could be manufactured in IRA workshops, and on the beach at Ballycroy they successfully tested a prototype with a propellant gas that pulled the weapon forward with each shot, to counteract some of the massive recoil.

Late one night, back in Danny's house, they all got round the table and drank a toast to the new 12.7mm sniper rifle.

The gun itself was by then hidden inside a dump Danny had built specially for it, where it would wait until Jim and Rose arrived back in Mayo for a series of new experiments. Further tests would be conducted many miles away, deep in the Mayo mountains.

Jim reported to GHQ about the success of the sniper tests. The problem now was that he and Rose had laboured for many months on building and testing one prototype. The IRA needed to start mass-producing the sniper rifle and getting it into the hands of units across Northern Ireland.

GHQ told Jim that they had appointed a new IRA man to their research and development team. His name was Mick and he was known for his precision metalwork. He also had good contacts with other skilled workers and workshops.

He would work separately from them, and meet for testing and new design ideas. His first project was to make a barrel from shock-resistant steel. It had to be drilled, then reamed to produce a mirror surface and breech, and then rifled, so that the bullet would move effortlessly through the barrel and allow an accurate shot. He would also create his own reamer, using tungsten-carbide-tipped tools.

When the day arrived for the final test, Rose, Jim, Mick, Danny and a member of the South Armagh sniper team went to an isolated valley deep in the Mayo mountains. The gun and ten rounds of ammunition had been brought there separately.

The rifle had been 'bore sighted' – the sights were not yet set for distance. The sight had three fixed apertures or small holes in a vertical line to sight through – a design that was first used on the shoulder launchers. The range for each aperture would have to be found by a series of test shots.

They selected a position on top of a small rise that

overlooked a pool in a little stream about 200 metres away. They decided that Rose, who was known to be skilled with a rifle, should have the first shot. She was to fire at a rock visible in the pool.

Rose lay down and pulled the butt of the huge sniper rifle into her shoulder. She aimed carefully, breathed out, and gently squeezed the trigger.

The rifle gave a ferocious roar; the muzzle blast kicked up a cloud of leaves and debris. The black-tipped armour-piercing round bounced off the water a bit short of the target and grazed the rock.

The South Armagh sniper, who had several kills to his name, asked them to put a white 5-litre plastic can filled with water on a gravel path 200 metres away. He took up a firing position and shot off a round. The gravel flew up with the strike of the bullet, a little to the left and a little high. He reloaded and retook his firing position. When he squeezed off his shot, the 5-litre can exploded in a spray of water.

Norah Campbell, who was sixteen years old at the time, remembers asking her father if she could fire the rifle. 'I think first they were shocked when I asked, but Rose was delighted,' Norah recalls. 'The gun was a big, huge size and we tested it against a sand bank.'

As each Campbell child passed into teenage years, Rose taught them how to drive – starting on the tractor, Katie Campbell recalls, 'because that's how she learned on the family farm in Devon. She often talked about the farm and how much she loved it there.'

Norah says: 'Dad had learned to drive an automatic in America, and had taught Mam on an automatic. Rose was just better at the gears, so she taught us how to drive. She would really help us with schoolwork also. If we were struggling with maths, Rose would set aside one evening to sit down and help you understand it.' She also coached Norah and Katie's brother, Donal, through preparation for a French exam.

Discussions about allowing Sinn Féin into formal talks with the British government continued through 1996. In late November, the IRA released a statement suggesting a renewed ceasefire, after which Sinn Féin would be immediately allowed into talks, but without weapon decommissioning.

John Major responded in the Commons on 28 November 1996, saying that the British government would not talk unless there was 'an unequivocal restoration of the ceasefire' and an assurance that Sinn Féin would sign up to the new Mitchell principles on democracy and peace, created by former US senator George Mitchell.

The IRA's response, from the beginning of 1997, was to step up its attacks on military and RUC targets, mostly using mortars and shoulder launchers. Still, the IRA was showing signs of long-term fatigue. Its former head of intelligence, Kieran Conway, would tell the BBC that he believed the IRA was losing or had already lost its war and that it was time to 'cash in its chips' in negotiations.

The operations officer for South Armagh told Jim that key IRA personnel had got full-time jobs during the 1994–6 ceasefire and it would be difficult for them to return to the conflict. It was hard to get back into the mindset and the level of organization required to keep up a sustained campaign. A lot of operations had gone wrong or were ineffective. Resupply of mortars and shoulder launchers was taking time.

In May, the new British Prime Minister, Tony Blair, said

that getting a permanent IRA ceasefire was a priority, and he flew to Belfast within days of taking office. Most parties in the Irish Republic and in Northern Ireland, he said, were committed to peace. 'The one glaring exception is Sinn Féin and the republican movement.'

Pressure was mounting on the IRA from the London and Dublin governments and from all the political parties on both sides of the border. Sinn Féin was excluded from talks and politically isolated. Two months after Blair's speech, the IRA army council announced 'a complete cessation of military operations' so that Sinn Féin could enter talks.

The republican movement, which had long demanded a complete British withdrawal from Northern Ireland, now sought a 'level playing field' – power-sharing under continuing British rule. After over 3,500 deaths and 50,000 injuries, it was openly acknowledging that its campaign was not going to bring about a united Ireland.

A friend of Rose's, Jackie Kaye, remembers: 'At the time, people were being cautious and not saying much, but not Rose. She wanted everyone's view and she wasn't shy about asking for it. "Tell me what you think." "How is this going to work?" "How is that going to work?"'

Jim records Rose recalling something Gerry Adams had said: that when conditions gave rise to conflict, then you needed to change the conditions to resolve the conflict. A level playing field could now be created, in which a united Ireland could come about through democratic means.

Rose and Jim remained loyal to Gerry Adams and the leadership. With the approval of the IRA army council, which wanted a quick return to war if there was a breakdown in talks, they continued their weapons work.

One day as they were walking back through the sand dunes

following a rocket test, Jim spoke of his own misgivings about the peace process. 'Are we burning our bridges regarding a return to armed struggle?' he asked, and argued that there was no guarantee that inequalities could be removed in Northern Ireland. He records that Rose replied that if the ceasefire was wrong, then the next generation will 'either have to accept British rule or try a different strategy to end it'.

In April 1998, as the peace talks reached their final stages, Tony Blair flew to Belfast and the Taoiseach, Bertie Ahern, drove up from Dublin. After years of talks, the Good Friday Agreement established that Northern Ireland would remain part of the UK unless and until a majority voted in a referendum for a united Ireland. There would be a number of new human-rights bodies, including a parades commission to reroute the hated Orange Order marches, and there would be a release of all IRA and loyalist prisoners over time. Most importantly, there would be a power-sharing assembly in which unionists and nationalists would always be in coalition together.

Not everyone in the IRA was behind the agreement. After a stormy army convention in Falcarragh, Co. Donegal, the hawks gathered around the quartermaster-general, Mickey McKevitt. This was a perilous situation, because McKevitt was in charge of all IRA weapons, and he had the support of much of the southern IRA.

The IRA leadership warned McKevitt that he was not to interfere with weapons or remove them from their bunkers. McKevitt removed Semtex from bunkers to use as a booster for fertilizer bombs, and handguns, but otherwise he largely left the IRA arsenal intact. He was, however, very interested in Jim's home-produced sniper rifle. He told David Rupert, his main US fundraiser, that he had a team working on producing their own version, using a workshop in Cork. McKevitt did not know that Rupert was working as a spy for both MI5 and the FBI.

Liam Campbell, an experienced Provisional IRA member from South Armagh, became McKevitt's second-in-command in what became known as the Real IRA. A senior South Armagh IRA figure loyal to McKevitt recalls a tense stand-off between Campbell and the South Armagh Provisional IRA leader, Sean Hughes. 'There was a meeting and [Liam Campbell] brought his own people to it to show support, and from that moment on, there was a compromise in South Armagh. The Provisionals didn't want a conflict either.'

One of the Real IRA's first operations was to rob a security van coming from a bank in Wicklow. A group of armed men set up a roadblock and threatened the driver. Armed gardaí rushed through the traffic. A garda shot one of the Real IRA men in the head, killing him instantly. When they took off his balaclava, they discovered it was Ronan MacLochlainn: Ruairí's Officer Commanding in Fianna Éireann when they were boys.

In late 1998, Sinn Féin approached Jim, who had not been a member of the party for nearly ten years, to ask if he would rejoin and take an official role in a new organization called Tar Isteach, helping the hundreds of republican prisoners being released under the Good Friday Agreement to find jobs. Jim's willingness to engage with Marxism was no longer seen as a threat within the party, and his organizational skills were needed. In addition, he was respected within the IRA and would give a voice of authority to the prisoner operation.

'The first thing I did was get Rose involved,' Jim recalls.

Although they were no longer in the education department, 'my vision and Rose's vision was that it was still education'.

Bernard McGinn, a member of the IRA's South Armagh sniper unit who had received multiple life sentences, found himself out of jail less than three years later, having tea and cake with Rose and Jim. Some newly released prisoners were asked to talk about their prison experiences for a video series that Rose recorded on taxpayer-funded cameras.

Still, Rose and Jim thought of themselves as armed revolutionaries. While some of their comrades now aspired to be local councillors or members of the Northern Ireland Assembly, they missed the war.

Through Basque friends, Jim had made contact with FARC, the Colombian Marxist group. FARC, which was awash with cash from the cocaine trade, was gaining ground every day against the Colombian government from its jungle base in the south, and now it wanted to expand its arsenal of bombs and mortars to launch attacks on military positions and cities. Through an intermediary, talks began between Jim and FARC.

Jim contacted an IRA member named Martin McCauley, who had worked with him and Rose on projects in Ballycroy, including the long-range sniper rifle. In 1982, when McCauley was a teenager, the police shot him and another teenager, Michael Tighe, at an isolated farmhouse near Lurgan, in an assault to recover IRA weapons. McCauley survived, but Tighe was killed. The event was captured on an RUC police recording, but investigators were unable to recover it during the Stalker Inquiry into police and army shootings in Northern Ireland. Years later, McCauley was convicted of weapons possession and jailed.

The IRA put Jim Monaghan and Martin McCauley

together with Sinn Féin's representative to Cuba, Niall Connolly, who spoke Spanish fluently.

Through those months, the Northern Ireland Assembly was in turmoil over allegations that the IRA was gathering lists of targets and holding on to its weapons. Nobody knew it then, but a massive political crisis was about to erupt in Ireland, and it would come, not from South Armagh or West Belfast, but from the southern Colombian city of San Vicente del Caguán.

20. The Export Market

It was summer in the jungle and the air was humid and dense. The Irishman travelling under the name Edward Campbell was known in San Vicente del Caguán.

Following peace talks between FARC and the Colombian government, San Vicente had been declared a demilitarized zone. This created an opportunity for FARC to bring in external help for its military campaign. FARC wanted to obtain better mortar technology, as it believed the peace talks were likely to break down soon and it had plans to lay siege to the Colombian capital, Bogotá.

British intelligence was following Edward Campbell's path out of Ireland very carefully. They knew that Campbell was really Jim Monaghan, the head of the IRA research unit. According to Norah Campbell, the fact that Jim was using the surname Campbell 'was probably not a coincidence'.

A source familiar with the operation says that Jim had asked Rose to stay at home, against her objections, because Colombia was so dangerous and he felt he needed to figure it all out before bringing her in.

By Jim's own account in his book *Colombia Jail Journal*, based on the diary he kept at the time, he met with FARC leaders and over several days they discussed the Irish peace process and how such a process might be used in Colombia. However, none of the three men in Jim's group had any experience in peace talks. What FARC wanted was Jim Monaghan's ability to take bin-liners, packets of biscuits, long-grain rice, plastic drainpipes, icing sugar, fertilizer and a soldering iron and turn them into weapons.

After a week in a guest house at FARC's invitation, the three Irishmen flew back to Bogotá on 11 August 2001. Their plan was to travel on from Bogotá to Ireland. All three were travelling on false passports.

According to Jim's book, when he got to the passport control window, the officer looked at him and then at his passport. He asked Jim and the others to come to a room for some routine questions. But they did not go to a room in the airport. Instead, thirty armed soldiers flanked them and led them out of the airport and into three waiting trucks.

They were driven to the barracks of the 13th Brigade Military Police, where they were separated and fingerprinted. Jim could hear Niall Connolly being processed in another room. The three men didn't know how much the military police knew.

A man in a black jacket began speaking. He told Jim to empty his pockets and place all the items on the table. Then he was told to strip naked, which he did. They made sure he was not carrying any weapons, identification or notes. Jim was told to get dressed, and the man in the black jacket began the questioning: 'What were you doing in San Vicente? Were you dealing in drugs?'

Jim said he would not answer any questions until he had seen a lawyer.

Was he being paid in drugs?

He would not answer any questions until he had seen a lawyer.

The man in the black jacket said that someone from the US embassy would test Jim's belongings for drugs and explosives. An hour later, according to *Colombia Jail Journal*, someone from the embassy came into the room carrying a briefcase. He identified himself as Molloy. He swiped the emptied contents of Jim's rucksack with white cloths and placed the cloths in sample bags.

Jim's account was later confirmed in court by appeal judge Jorgé Enrique Torres, who said he failed to see the need for having a 'special adviser' from the US embassy to perform 'illegal' tests on the men.

Suddenly, the man in the black jacket and the soldiers ran outside, as if startled by a sound. Jim felt it might be a trap to get him talking to McCauley, who was standing at the door of the room. He told McCauley: *Lan ar aghaide ag caint* – continue talking – as the two of them searched the furniture for bugs. McCauley found one under the interrogation table. He was able to say in Irish that he was OK and so was Connolly.

All three were taken to a hospital under army escort for a check-up to prove that they hadn't been beaten during interrogation. A nurse examined them, and then they were taken to another room. The man in the black jacket, who had been friendly until now, became annoyed at Jim's refusal to answer questions. Eventually, he took Jim out into the corridor and told him that unless he started talking, he would be placed with right-wing paramilitary prisoners, whose lives revolved around killing FARC members and their supporters.

News of the arrest of the men who became known as the Colombia Three was a major international story, and it sent an earthquake through the Northern Ireland peace process. The US State Department launched an investigation, as did the CIA. FARC had been killing US soldiers and officials for many years. If the IRA were involved, then the IRA too was a direct enemy of America.

A spokesman for the US State Department, Philip Reeker, told a press conference in Washington that the department was investigating alleged collaboration between FARC and the IRA. 'We have been in touch with Sinn Féin on this subject,' Reeker said. 'We will continue to monitor the situation closely. But I think all I can reiterate is that no one should have any doubts about the seriousness with which we would take collaboration with the FARC by any individual or organization.'

Sinn Féin was scrambling to contain the situation. Spokesman Mitchel McLaughlin said the party had 'demonstrated to the satisfaction of the American authorities' that it continued to support the peace process and was 'confident that we can resolve the outstanding problems'.

'Sinn Féin also denied the men were members, although Mr McCauley and Mr Monaghan were formerly prominent figures in the party,' the *Irish Times* reported. The party's claim about Jim Monaghan was false: he had rejoined Sinn Féin with Rose when approached to work with Tar Isteach in 1998.

The Al Qaeda attacks of 11 September 2001 only intensified American anger about the Colombia Three. At a meeting that day, the US envoy to Northern Ireland, Richard Haass, met with Gerry Adams. According to a report in the *Observer*, Haass snapped as he listened to Adams's usual talk about the peace process inching forward.

'If any American, service personnel or civilian, is killed in Colombia by the technology the IRA supplied, then you can fuck off,' he shouted. 'Don't tell me you know nothing about what's going on there, we know everything about it.'

Colombia was developing into a huge headache for Sinn Féin. Since the Good Friday Agreement, the IRA had insisted it would never decommission. Now, in late October 2001, it finally announced that it would send a representative, believed to be Brian Keenan, to meet John de Chastelain, the retired Canadian general overseeing the decommissioning of Northern Ireland paramilitary groups.

'The discovery of the [Colombia] trip was the lever America needed to push Adams towards last week's historic announcement that the IRA had agreed to decommission some of its weapons,' the *Observer* reported. Until then, it pointed out, Brian Keenan had been arguing that the British army should be decommissioning, not the IRA.

It wasn't just Haass. Bill Flynn, chairman of the Mutual of America Financial Group and a supporter of Sinn Féin, told the *Observer* that he'd told Adams, post-Colombia, that the only way for the IRA to rescue its reputation in America was to begin disarming. 'They listen to me because I am a strong supporter of what they are doing to unite Ireland,' he said.

Years later, Flynn, a conservative Catholic, told me that he warned Adams that, with bad publicity in Colombia, he needed to get rid of the 'Bolshevik shit' if it wanted to retain US support.

While trying to appease the US government and US supporters through engagement on decommissioning, Sinn Féin stuck to the line that Jim Monaghan was in Colombia for peace talks. The party insisted that he had been committed to peace since his release from prison in 1985 and had not been arrested since.

New graffiti appeared on the walls of Belfast's loyalist areas: 'Gerry Kelly Can FARC Off.' Gerry Kelly had been one of the Old Bailey bombers in London, along with the Price sisters. Rose had stolen the Russborough paintings to have Kelly and the others transferred to Northern Ireland.

Now Kelly was a Sinn Féin member of the Northern Ireland Assembly and one of its negotiators in the peace process, and he was being tarnished by the Colombia Three debacle.

News came through shortly afterwards that the US House of Representatives would be holding Colombia Three hearings. I was a reporter with the *Belfast Telegraph* at the time. I told my editor that I wanted to move to America as US correspondent, and the newspaper sorted out a visa.

A week before the hearing, I had lunch with a British official working as a liaison to the White House. This official wanted to know my thoughts on the Colombia Three. A few days later, an Irish official called me and asked for a drink. He told me that the British official was an MI6 spy and I should be very careful what I said.

The Irish government was trying to downplay the Colombia Three, fearing that the crisis could derail the Good Friday Agreement. The British, meanwhile, saw the affair as an opportunity to undermine the IRA in the eyes of its US supporters. Two officials from the Northern Ireland section of the British government met me for dinner and handed me a brown folder containing all the anti-Colombia Three articles that they had managed to get into the US media.

The hearing was held on 24 April 2002, under the title 'International Global Terrorism: Its links with illicit drugs as illustrated by the IRA and other groups in Colombia'.

The Republican chairman of the House International Relations Committee, Henry Hyde, opened the hearing and immediately made it clear where he stood: claims that the three men were in Colombia to help peace talks were 'an insult to our intelligence', he said. The IRA had 'significantly enhanced the FARC's campaign of urban terrorism, which can already measure its success in thousands of casualties'.

The head of the Colombian armed forces, General Fernando Tapias, had flown up from Bogotá for the hearing. He told the committee that the three were involved in training FARC guerrillas in the use of mortars, explosives, intelligence and combat techniques. General Tapias insisted that Jim Monaghan was the IRA head of engineering and McCauley was his deputy. The general insisted the men were operating with IRA sanction.

The State Department's deputy coordinator for counterterrorism, Mark Wong, testified that the dramatic increase in the FARC's bombing technology could be related to IRA help and that the use of secondary explosions to kill those gathered at the scene of a first blast was a 'known signature IRA urban terror tactic'. He also had a message for Sinn Féin: 'If we were to discover evidence of any such ongoing [IRA] support, it would raise fundamental questions for US foreign policy. We also remain concerned about the potential of any past relationship between the FARC and the IRA to affect stability in Colombia as well as US interests there.'

An accompanying report by the committee said that FARC's effectiveness was greatly enhanced as a result of IRA mortar training. It said innocent people had been killed by FARC because of the IRA and that US interests were 'badly damaged' as a result of FARC/IRA cooperation.

In June, the *Irish Times* ran a story citing British security sources as claiming that the Colombia Three had been authorized by two of the IRA's most senior members. 'The revelation, which is sure to inflame unionist concerns over the peace process, was denied by the IRA this evening,' it reported.

In Dublin, the government was under pressure from opposition parties to crack down on the IRA. Senior Special

Branch officer Thomas Connors was among those who organized a massive raid on Danny Campbell's farm in Ballycroy in 2002. Connors says that the raid was done because he had to draft a report on the state of the IRA's ceasefire. Were they serious about peace? Had Jim, Rose, Danny and Co. been developing weapons?

Norah Campbell says that the Campbells were regularly tipped off to raids: the phone would ring once the night before. They knew that the caller was a sympathizer at a Mayo garda station. 'So on the night before the big raid,' she says, 'the phone rang once, and we knew.'

The next day, a Sunday, the gardaí began a major house-to-house search in Ballycroy. Norah recalls: 'They were idiots, they searched every house in the village and finally came to us – like we didn't know it was us they were targeting.'

Jim had sent hand-painted postcards to the family from his prison cell in Colombia. Just as the gardaí approached the farm, Phyllis Campbell remembered the postcards.

Norah recalls: 'Mam had them stored in the top drawer of this big wardrobe we had. She was crying as she burned them in the fire, but she had no choice, the gardaí were coming down the road at that moment.'

The raid, Norah says, went on for a week and was, at least on the face of it, sophisticated and well resourced. 'They had dinghies along the shore. The tide is so shallow you could walk across, but they still had dinghies. They drilled into the floor in the cowshed, they threw every bit of a turf stack apart and didn't put it back together. They stopped every delivery van and mobile shop and postman.'

Thomas Connors says that the Special Branch had received a tip-off about 'where to find the stuff in the bog'. The searchers, Connors says, found detonators, mortars and anti-tank weapons – as well as prototypes for various kinds of weapons: evidence of 'development of weapons for fifteen years or longer'.

The gardaí found the stash on commonage bog, which was shared by over twenty farmers, so it was difficult to link it back to Danny Campbell. He was eventually arrested and questioned in Castlebar, Norah says, 'about some burned plastic milk carton they found'. But there was nothing they could pin on him.

For Ruairi, Jim's arrest, and the enormous international fallout, was the cause of great disquiet. When Ruairi's drug dealing had got him into huge trouble with the vigilantes and republican paramilitaries, Rose had refused to intervene because those were the rules. Now, it appeared that Jim was doing work for people who funded their campaign via cocaine production on a vast scale.

'I was very upset about it,' Ruairi says. 'He wasn't down there on holidays. All of these guys standing around barrels in Dublin outside the flats – and this stuff is going on in Colombia? . . . Jim was like a father to me, but I was going to raise it with Jim when he got back.'

For her part, Rose stuck to the party line – that the Colombia Three were innocent and that Jim must be supported.

When Jim was in prison in Colombia, Rose went to South Africa on holiday with Ruairi and Angelika. On safari, the guide warned them to switch off their phones, so as not to startle the lions. Rose forgot to switch hers off. As they observed a pride of lions, her phone rang. She picked it up. It was Jim calling from prison. 'Jim!' she said loudly. 'How are you?'

*

In December 2002, I flew to Bogotá with a group of reporters to cover the opening of the trial of the Colombia Three.
The mood in the city was tense. Grim-faced soldiers raced
up and down the streets in troop transporters and all foreign
guests were warned not to leave their hotels unaccompanied,
because kidnapping was so common.

We all stayed at the Hotel Tequendama in the centre of
Bogotá, which, as we later learned, was owned by the Colombian military. There was a sign at reception telling guests not
to go outside alone. When I ignored this advice, one of my
fellow guests followed me down the street, urging me to
come back. This was Paul Hill, who had been wrongly convicted of carrying out the IRA's 1974 deadly bombing of a
pub in Guildford, Surrey. Hill was in Colombia to show support for the three IRA men and was a flurry of energy
around the hotel, telling prison stories to journalists waiting
around until the trial began.

The danger outside the hotel was real. A reporter for the
Los Angeles Times was kidnapped by FLN, the right-wing
paramilitary group. Two weeks after we left the hotel, FARC
planted a suitcase bomb in one of the hotel's function rooms,
injuring over thirty people attending a Christmas party.

I wondered what prison conditions must be like for the
three. Some reporters had tried to get into La Modelo prison,
where they were being held, but were denied entry. I went by
myself and met a delegation of Sinn Féin members and
human-rights activists who were on their way in. They handed
me some papers and I followed them into the prison, though
I was not able to get upstairs to where they were meeting the
prisoners. La Modelo was a dank, dangerous place. A female
reporter who tried to interview a paramilitary leader that year

was abducted in the prison, beaten, raped and dumped in a rubbish heap outside.

While Jim was in prison, Rose sent him news articles about Ireland and Colombia. He spent much of his prison time painting, and so Rose sent him art books, including a hardback collection of Monet paintings. Jim placed the book on top of the steel springs of his fold-down bed, as a makeshift easel.

The case would drag on for more than another year. In March 2003, a court in Medellín, Colombia's second city, heard evidence from a former FARC member, 19-year-old John Alexander Caviedes, who said he had received bomb-making and mortar-assembly training from three men who, he was told, 'belonged to a revolutionary group in Ireland'.

In July 2003, the three defendants made their final speeches to the court. 'In the summer of 2001, we travelled to Colombia principally to see the peace process but also to enjoy a holiday,' Jim Monaghan told the judge. All three denied being IRA members.

In April 2004, the Bogotá court acquitted the three of aiding terrorism but convicted them of travelling on false passports. Although they'd all been convicted of the same offence, Jim Monaghan was jailed for forty-four months, McCauley for thirty-six months and eighteen days, and Connolly for twenty-six months. The varying sentences were seen as reflecting the depth of their perceived involvement in the plot with FARC. The judge lifted the custodial sentences, released the three upon payment of fines, and ordered their expulsion from Colombia. But prosecutors appealed against the terrorism acquittals, and so the three were compelled to remain in the country pending the appeal. They soon disappeared into FARC-controlled areas.

In December 2004, while they were still on the run, the appeal court convicted them of terrorism charges and handed down seventeen-year prison sentences. Although their passports had been taken from them, they managed to get out of Colombia and eventually, by the summer of 2005, they made it back to Ireland. Jim Monaghan has never disclosed how they did it.

Jim and Rose wanted to get back to weapons testing as quickly as possible. Despite the damaging fallout of the Colombia Three affair, Jim claims they had the full support of the IRA army council for this, but they had to be discreet. They established themselves in a new farmhouse whose location, unknown to the gardaí, Jim still refuses to disclose.

He and Rose set to work on a project that Jim had been working on for six months in Colombia: making fertilizer explosives more effective. They hoped to eliminate impurities that slowed the explosive chain reactions. Jim used computer modelling to plot a graph of the energy output of bombs against fertilizer ingredients. His hypothesis was that one of the ingredients was hindering, rather than adding to, the power of the explosions.

He and Rose zeroed in on limestone – a key constituent of many fertilizers. They found that limestone added mass and absorbed heat energy while being raised from normal temperature to bomb temperature, slowing the chain reaction. Jim asked one of the IRA research team to bring them a kilo of fertilizer and some weighing scales, so that they could extract the limestone and run a heat test on it.

When the man returned, he was without the fertilizer or the weighing scales. 'You're to stop work now,' he said. 'The war is over.'

On 28 July 2005, Séanna Walsh, an IRA member who had served eighteen years in prison, was recorded on video reading a formal statement from the IRA leadership announcing the end of the armed struggle. 'All IRA units have been ordered to dump arms,' he said. 'All volunteers have been instructed to assist the development of purely political and democratic programmes through exclusively peaceful means. Volunteers must not engage in any other activities whatsoever.'

Rose and Jim went to Ballycroy – which they reckoned to be safe for Jim, now that the war was over. With other members of their R&D unit, they gathered around the TV to hear the news being made public.

Jim records that Rose gave a little speech that she had prepared for the moment. 'Those members of the IRA who want to, can join Sinn Féin and continue the struggle by political means – and it will be a long, hard struggle,' she said.

After the Provisional IRA disbanded, Rose was now free to be seen openly with republicans.

Danny Campbell was gravely ill following a stroke on 14 March 2005 and was in Beaumont Hospital in Dublin. His children stayed with Rose at her house in Drimnagh while they were visiting him.

'That would never have happened in previous years,' says Norah Campbell. 'Not only could we stay with Rose, but we could have our photo taken with her and with Jim, which we never did before because the gardaí might confiscate it. We stayed with Rose and she was fantastic. She offered to cook and we thought: "Oh god, no," because we knew she was a terrible cook, but she made dumplings and it was fine. We got to see her chickens, which she kept out the back as well.'

Katie Campbell says: 'The chickens were named Ophelia and Rafael and classical names like that. Their names were out there. With Rose, the chickens were never going to be called John and Tom and Mary.'

On 5 August, word came through that the Colombia Three were back in Ireland. The *Irish Independent* reported: 'News of the men's return began seeping through the corridors of power after 4 p.m. One official in the Taoiseach's office heard the news through a journalist.'

That afternoon, RTÉ reporter Charlie Bird was taken by van to a secret location to meet Jim Monaghan. Bird pressed Jim about whether he had been helping FARC in Colombia.

Jim replied: 'I didn't go to train the FARC, I went because of the peace process, because of our own involvement in the peace process. I was delighted to go to Colombia and . . . I have no regrets about it.' When asked what he thought of FARC and their tactics, he replied: 'I haven't got an opinion on the FARC and their tactics and I'm not going to get into a kind of condemnation . . .'

He declined to say where the three had been for the sixteen months since they had jumped bail, except that they had had help from people in several countries. He did not specify how long he had been back in Ireland.

Unionists in Northern Ireland immediately backed a call by Colombia's vice-president, Francisco Santos, to extradite the men back to Colombia. But this was never a real possibility, as there was no extradition treaty between Ireland and Colombia.

The next day, 6 August, the *Irish Times* devoted a full page to political reaction from correspondents in Belfast, London and Dublin, along with a transcript of Jim's RTÉ interview.

The Sinn Féin MP for Newry and Armagh, Conor Murphy, a former IRA prisoner, said that the return of the three would be 'a huge relief to their families and to all those who supported the Bring Them Home Campaign over the past four years'.

The SDLP's policing spokesman, Alex Attwood, said the three had done 'huge damage' to the peace process and that they were 'clearly up to no good' in Colombia.

The next day, Sinn Féin President Gerry Adams said he was 'delighted' by their return. 'This is not causing a crisis in the peace process,' he told RTÉ radio. 'What is causing a crisis in the political process is the refusal, or the failure, by the unionists to share power with the rest of us at this time.'

Through 2006, debate raged among republicans about whether to support the Northern Ireland police. With Sinn Féin's popularity soaring among nationalists in Northern Ireland, they had a real chance to enter government the following year.

In advance of the Sinn Féin Ard Fheis, Rose put her name down to speak in support of a resolution supporting the reformed Northern Ireland police force, called the Police Service of Northern Ireland, which replaced the old Royal Ulster Constabulary.

Rose had contributed to the death of many police officers; now she would tell delegates the time had come to support them.

There was tension outside the RDS in Dublin, where the Ard Fheis was taking place on the last weekend of January 2007. Some members of the dissident group Republican Sinn Féin shouted 'Traitor!' at Sinn Féin deputy leader

Martin McGuiness, and one shouted, 'Here comes the chief constable!'

Rose got up on stage to loud applause. Of the historic resolution to support the police, she opened with the remark: 'I want to support this revolution . . . sorry, resolution . . .' The slip brought laughter from around the room.

The resolution was passed by a comfortable margin. During the Troubles, 319 RUC officers had been killed and almost nine thousand injured in paramilitary attacks, mostly by the IRA. Now the IRA's political wing supported the Northern Ireland police.

Rose was a member of Sinn Féin's All-Ireland department, a wonkish committee established to push for greater North–South integration in the post-Troubles times.

The All-Ireland department's motions were the first to be discussed at the 2007 Ard Fheis, with all the department's most prominent members – Rose, Jim, Martina Anderson and the chair, Sean Oliver – addressing the delegates.

Rose used her position in the All-Ireland department to tell the Ard Fheis about the campaign against a Shell gas pipeline in Mayo. 'Dugdale told delegates that the Shell contract is invalid and '"needs to be renegotiated on behalf of the people of Ireland"', *An Phoblacht* reported.

Her motion was passed, but behind the scenes there was turmoil in the All-Ireland department. Following elections to the Northern Ireland Assembly in March 2007, Sinn Féin entered government with Ian Paisley's Democratic Unionist party in May. A party that had done everything it could to bring down the Northern Ireland state was now ruling it. Ian Paisley became First Minister, and former IRA Chief of Staff Martin McGuinness became Deputy First Minister.

Of Sinn Féin going into government, Rose wrote to

Domhnall Ó Cobhthaigh, a fellow All-Ireland department member and a councillor in Fermanagh: 'Strange times – got the backwoodsmen to play ball. Amazing. But still does it leave big gaps? The idea of peeling away the unionist establishment, it seems to me, has not been effective – they are still there and dominating the paradigm.'

Rose was concerned Sinn Féin was becoming too middle class and servile, and she let it be known at the All-Ireland department meetings. At a tumultuous and angry department meeting that month, she was refused permission to present her left-leaning economic paper on North–South integration, which was backed by Jim.

Afterwards, she wrote a 2,300-word analysis for Domhnall Ó Cobhthaigh, whom she accused of being among those who had ignored her and her economic paper. 'That was a very bad meeting yesterday,' she wrote. 'It was a crazy, ill-considered decision' to hold the meeting, 'which took no account whatever of the stuff me and Jim put up: no pre-discussion of what was needed in the "presentation" or whatever we were to do.'

She ended the long letter with an attempt at conciliation: 'Sorry if this is a diatribe, sorry that you had to be the object of it. But hope you too can pick up on my angry complaints and take them forward a bit. That might make for greater clarity in my head, not to mention my presentation of it.'

In *An Phoblacht*, too, Rose was finding herself shut out. She felt the paper was becoming less militant, hoping to make Sinn Féin appealing to undecided voters. In March 2008 she wrote to a friend: 'A bit sadly, I don't write any more for [*An Phoblacht*] –'cause I think the editor didn't want stuff – nor does the paper want the type of political/investigative journalism that I tried to practise.'

She was also part of the short-lived Unionist Engagement Department of Sinn Féin, as it was hoped that an upper-class British woman of Protestant background might be able to talk to unionists; but it soon fizzled out and the department was wound down.

Having spent many years on the radical fringe of the republican movement, and then a few years largely in sync with the party leadership, Rose increasingly felt herself on the outside again. To a friend, she wrote in March 2008:

> What do I do? Not much. Local cumann, hope to get video political programme on DCTV [Dublin Community TV], tie in a bit with Unionist Engagement shortly to meet its demise, I guess, and did tie in with All-Ireland Agenda, until it met its demise, recently! Write the odd speech, and meet the odd person, who is more central and operational than I! A thin canvas, but then you can, at your leisure, go frenetically around, telling everyone what should be done – and the hope of getting them to do it is vacuous!

Rose, though still a stalwart of the party, was finding herself increasingly isolated in the new, peacetime Sinn Féin.

21. Reuniting

In August 2008, Rose flew to Regensburg to see Ruairi, Angelika and her two grandchildren. She also hoped to meet her brother, James, who had inherited the family estate in Devon and the double townhouse in Chelsea. They had not seen each other in many years. James, who was living in Paris, came to Regensburg with his son, Leo.

Ruairi recalls the family reunion as being 'fabulous'. 'James was a lovely man, we all got on really well and I could see that Rose really loved being in his company,' Ruairi says. 'He was very kind to us and the kids and it didn't look to me that there was any bad feeling from the past.'

Rose missed her flight back to Ireland and had to arrange another. After she got back to Dublin, she wrote to James:

Was again very good fun to talk with you, in Regensburg, and I am extremely glad that you were able to meet Ruairi and Angie. Very nice of you to come down. Hope indeed that we can repeat such encounters again – always find it enjoyable and provocative to meet myself coming backwards! Very entertaining, especially as the company is so good.

Writing back, James spoke with similar warmth about the Regensburg holiday; but he was less enthusiastic about the prospect of a broader family reunion:

Obstinate, perverse, impulsive and inconsiderate (in my case slow-witted and often obtuse), there is not a single member of my family that qualifies for the description of good company. When I've spent next weekend with Caroline, I'll tell you if there's reason for a change of mind. I don't expect, though, to do much analysis of scenes of childhood or linger among the ruins. Rather it will be navigating the incomprehensible delusions and compulsions that make us so inexplicably unhappy and dissatisfied.

Jim and Rose remained heavily involved in the campaign to stop the Shell oil company from building its natural gas pipeline from a gas field off the Mayo coast to a refinery at Bellanaboy, a short distance north of the Campbell farm.

In September 2008, a pipe bomb was planted outside Shell's Dublin headquarters. Two months later, gardaí carried out a 6 a.m. raid on Jim's home in Killester in north-east Dublin, where he lived with Chris and their family, and found an imitation pipe bomb. The area was sealed off and the army bomb-disposal team was brought in.

Jim and his teenage son, Donal Ó Coisdealbha, were both arrested. Neither of them said anything in the garda station and they were released without charge.

At the time of the arrest, Jim and Rose were hosting Iñaki de Juana Chaos, one of the leaders of the Basque separatist group ETA. In August, de Juana Chaos had been released from a Spanish prison after serving a sentence of twenty-one years for twenty-five murders.

Fearing re-arrest, he had flown to Ireland the day after his release, and he flitted between Jim's house in Killester and Rose's in Drimnagh. The same week that Jim was arrested for the replica pipe bomb, a Spanish court issued an arrest

warrant for de Juana Chaos after he failed to appear in court
on new charges.

In December, Rose wrote to James to wish him a happy
birthday. She began with some jocular references to the
global financial crisis that was unfolding at the time, before
getting more serious:

*Ah, the arrogance of those who said they saw it all coming . . . In
2015 the world will have reached irreversible global warming – find a
nice spot on a hill and grow organics!! Crazy world . . . Have a
happy birthday with many good friends and a pleasant Christmas in
climes that are warmer than ours. I am visiting the children over
Christmas, but hope to be back (here) at the end of the month,*

Lots of love,
Rose

The next day, James wrote back. Like Rose, he was nostalgic
for their childhood in Yarty, his memories returning to their
days hiding from the London Blitz during the Second World
War, a time when Italian prisoners of war were working on
the estate.

*I did find myself, as the snow fell in Paris, thinking how the day must
have been at Yarty with you and Caroline sheltering from the London
bombing raids and the mother and child enjoying the cooking of
Olivia Rampagni and the Italian prisoners of war.*
  *Ruairi told me you were going to him for Christmas and he very
kindly asked me too, but I leave for Africa next weekend. He told
me there was no recession in Regensburg; but banks in these days do
have an unpleasant habit of calling up further collateral, which can be*

troublesome when prices are falling. I hope your resources are proof against these.

In 2009, while Rose and Jim were attending a protest at the spot on the Mayo coast where the Shell gas pipeline comes ashore, a group of protestors tried to pull down some security fencing and fought with gardaí. Seven men were arrested and charged with obstruction, criminal damage and public order offences. The *Irish Independent* noticed the 'the protest was attended by a number of senior republican activists', though it added that neither Jim Monaghan nor Rose Dugdale 'was involved in the clashes'.

In July of that year, Rose made an extended trip to the Basque country, where she met ETA members. From there, she travelled to Regensberg, where she and James had planned a tour of stately gardens.

The trip was not a success. James wanted to address Rose's past, but she didn't want to talk about it. She wanted everything to be happy between them, and to enjoy her time among family. She was also feeling stressed about health problems.

In late August, she wrote an apology to James for her behaviour in Germany:

> *I was unhappy at the way we left things between us when you were in Regensburg. It was so nice of you to visit, and lovely going off to Munich and Passau together.*
>
> *Feel very bad at my lazy attitude to your questioning and reluctant attitudes to engage in discussion of different issues. It has been a bit of a hard time, for reasons I don't want to go into in the least!!*
>
> *But I hope they will resolve themselves in the coming weeks! Meanwhile, I just ask you to forgive me for appearing very rude, which was not at all meant. Will be in touch at greater length soon, I*

REUNITING

*hope – let you know that all is well!! And hopefully meet again soon,
with an entirely different approach, at my end, to chat together –
which was an amazing and really enjoyable event, which I would look
forward to again soon, I hope.*

*Meanwhile, all the very best – thanks for coming to Regensburg,
and your generosity with lovely presents that you brought the kids,
and forgive me for my lack of generosity when we were together.*

Hope to meet again soon,

Love,
Rose

In October 2009, Rose wrote to Domhnall Ó Cobhthaigh, who had recently left Sinn Féin to join the Socialist Party. The two had previously sparred, but now they found common cause as left-wing republicans.

Rose thought Sinn Féin lacked revolutionary drive, and felt this tendency was epitomized in a book called *Sinn Féin and the Politics of Left Republicanism*, by a rising star in the party, Eoin Ó Broin. She described the book as 'part of the new fashion/ way which amounts to denying the armed struggle and the role it played over 40 years – though of course in a way wanting to claim its martyrs and heroes all over the place'.

In November 2010, Martina Anderson, now a member of the Northern Ireland Assembly and soon to be a junior minister in the power-sharing administration, wrote to Rose for her opinion on how Sinn Féin could inspire people. The two had served together in the party's All-Ireland department, when Rose had found herself at odds with the others. Anderson wrote, 'Suspect that much of [your reply] will be about what "we" are not doing right but always appreciate your thinking and do take it on board . . . if you can go easy on the finger wagging and more on the way forward based on where we are at – it would be great to hear where your wee head is at.'

Rose replied that Sinn Féin

are irrelevant to the huge turmoil which is happening in Ireland now . . . too much dirty water (theirs) has gone under the bridge. The bank bail out is in place. We have to bring the governments (hopefully several in succession) down. Neither we, nor any other group, is waiting in the wings.

Sorry, Martina, hard times. No ready answers.

Hope to see you soon perhaps.

Much love and respect as always,
Rose

Rose and Jim remained regular visitors to the Campbells in Ballycroy.

'Rose was still an absolutely mad driver and she would come tearing up here,' says Norah Campbell. 'We knocked down the old house and built our current house in its place, but Mam wanted a table, rather than an island, in the kitchen because that is how Jim and Rose would sit and have big discussions with the family. They were always debating – the Church, the state. The abortion debate had come up again and Jim disagreed with the proposed law and Rose shouts: "That's because you'll never have to have one, Jim!" Outside of that, it was unthinkable for us to have a wedding or any big family event without them. They came to two of my brothers' weddings and they were like celebrities. Everyone wanted to shake hands with them.'

Rose's nephew and godson, George Mosley, grand-nephew of Oswald Mosley, was now an accomplished opera singer. In May 2013 he was performing in Dublin and invited Rose to hear a performance and to have dinner.

*Oh, great to hear from you. [*she wrote on 23 May*]. I would love to come to* La Traviata, *it would be lovely, and also to meet up together.*

We could meet Sunday, maybe before the performance if that is good for you, maybe lunch time suits you? And could happily entertain you for lunch in the early afternoon, or maybe you need to make it a light lunch, so that you can sing beautifully that evening!

Lovely that you got in touch.

I am really so grateful. Great to see you.

Peter Ady had died, aged ninety, in 2004, but her partner, Georgina Moore, a magistrate and active member of her parish council outside Oxford, stayed in contact with Rose, and she came for visits with her son, Zander. In August 2014 they had dinner, along with Jim, at the Gresham, one of Dublin's most beautiful old hotels. It was an incongruous ménage – two members of a paramilitary organization that had killed several British judges sitting with their old friend, the English magistrate. Georgina sometimes wore a blue silk square that Rose had sent to Peter as a present.

In a letter to Georgina, Rose referred to having 'awful thoughts'.

Would so love to be able to talk to Peter about such thoughts, one to one – thoughts about death. Find them ever so hard to deal with.

Did you EVER *talk to Peter about death? I wonder. Love to hear what she said.*

The gardaí were watching Jim's son, Donal Ó Coisdealbha. He had been arrested with his father in 2008, and they knew he had links with the Real IRA.

A good-looking, clean-cut and intelligent student, Donal was working on projects at Dundalk Institute of Technology and at a business incubator in Maynooth. Like his father, he used all the tools around him to experiment.

The Special Branch discovered that he was meeting with Seamus McGrane, the director of training and research for the Real IRA. The pair would meet at the Coachman's Inn near Dublin Airport, and officers bugged the snug where they plotted.

Prince Charles and his wife, the Duchess of Cornwall, were coming to Ireland in May 2015 to lay a wreath for Charles's great-uncle and mentor, Lord Mountbatten, who was murdered by the IRA in Sligo in 1979, along with four others. The Real IRA were plotting to set off a bomb while Prince Charles was in Ireland: they wanted to show that they were continuing the fight that had killed Mountbatten.

A week before Prince Charles's visit, as the gardaí listened, Seamus McGrane and Donal Ó Coisdealbha talked about their plan to bomb a First World War memorial in Glasnevin cemetery in Dublin. Donal already had an untraceable motorbike for the bombing and had been up and down to Wexford to meet with other Real IRA members.

McGrane warned Donal to be careful. 'I don't like surprises,' he said.

Then the two started talking about missiles. McGrane asked if Donal still had the plastic balancers for the missiles. Donal replied that he had them, and could supply them.

McGrane told Donal he had a bunker on his farm where they could be stored, and that he had some good shoulder-held missile launchers and a large quantity of weapons.

In the days before Prince Charles's visit, Donal was arrested at the business incubation lab in Maynooth. In his locker, police found bomb-making equipment. McGrane was arrested at his farm in Dromiskin, Co. Louth. Gardaí hired a contractor to dig up his land. To avoid exposing the contractor to Real IRA reprisals, gardaí removed the digger's licence plate, and the operator wore a balaclava while he worked. For three days, the army cordoned off the fields until they had unearthed all of the containers of guns, explosives and rocket launchers. It was the Real IRA's largest stockpile.

When I went to attend Donal's trial at the Special Criminal Court, in front of me in the queue to enter the courtroom were Jim Monaghan and Chris Ó Coisdealbha.

Everyone had to sign in. Chris refused to give her name in English and answered every question in Irish. The garda outside the court was not able to answer her and called for back-up. The second court garda was also unable to speak Irish (though fluency in the language is a stated requirement of the job), and they had to get a commanding officer. Behind them, the queue grew long. It took several minutes before it could be sorted out, with Chris defiantly refusing to use English.

Inside the courtroom, Jim waved at Donal, who waved back.

Donal was sitting beside McGrane. At the back of the courtroom sat Donal's girlfriend.

I looked at him, and then at McGrane, with his 1970s moustache and big belly. He had joined the IRA in 1969 and now here he was, over forty years later.

Afterwards, I sat with Chris and Jim in the court café. It was my first time speaking to Jim. We talked about Colombia, and about Donal's case. Chris would only speak to me in Irish, so we switched over. She talked at length about the British landlord system in Ireland and how it had displaced our old tribal ways and led to the conflict we see today.

During the trail, Chris and Jim went to court to see Donal; Rose and Jim stood outside the Dáil demanding his release. The two women rarely spoke.

In December 2016, Donal was jailed for five and a half years; a year later, McGrane was sentenced to eleven and a half years.

On Saturday, 28 November 2015, Rose, Jim and the Campbells attended Sinn Féin's annual 'Dublin Volunteers' night at the Gresham Hotel, honouring IRA members, with Jim as 'special honoree'. The announcement of the event in *An Phoblacht* was accompanied by a full-page interview with Jim and Rose. Tickets cost €50. The event was hosted by Mary Lou McDonald, the future leader of Sinn Féin.

Sinn Féin had negotiated a deal so that IRA 'on-the-runs' like Rose would be allowed to enter the UK without fear of arrest, and Rose found a new delight in taking the train to Belfast to see friends. She no longer had to worry about being arrested for the Strabane bombing, or for arms importation in the 1970s.

One day, while using the bathroom of the train station in Newry, Rose fell. She was rushed to hospital. She would later deny it to Ruairi, but she had had a stroke.

While visiting Ruairi and his family in Germany, she fell again and had to be airlifted to hospital; and she had chronic low blood pressure and fainting spells. Several times while she was visiting the Campbells in Ballycroy, they had to call for a doctor when she felt faint.

In December 2014 she was taken to St James's Hospital, where she reported that she had not eaten in three days. She also complained of confusion and pain. After conducting tests, doctors determined that she might not be able to look after herself.

In February 2015, the HSE approved Rose for state-funded nursing-home care. After talking it over with Ruairi and Jim, she agreed.

There were no socialist republican nursing homes. Where would she fit in? Ruairi and Jim spent a number of weeks looking for the right place.

The Poor Servants of the Mother of God have a nursing home in the Dublin suburb of Chapelizod, close to where baby Ruairi began his post-prison life at the home of solicitor Myles Shevlin. The nursing home is called Maryfield, and Rose is one of the few residents who is not a retired nun. As a retired revolutionary, her entry into Maryfield was met with a mix of curiosity and apprehension.

Everyone knew who she was. Some looked the other way when she came down the corridor, but most welcomed her as a conversation refresher during family visits.

Once when I was visiting her, I overheard an exchange in the lobby between a nun and her visiting family. 'Do you know who is here, now?' the nun said. 'Rose Dugdale.'

'From the IRA?'

'Yes. She's just down the corridor.'

Sister Sarah Crowley, a retired nun who taught in Italy for over thirty years, is a particular friend of Rose's and often drops in for a chat and to admire family photos.

At the back of the nursing home, the River Liffey meanders slowly by. It is a beautiful spot for a walk in the summer. Outside the main door is a statue of the Virgin Mary in a pristine white cloak and blue Marian dress, looking serenely downward.

The first time I visited Maryfield, in 2018, I noticed that Rose's door was the only one open. It was a legacy of prison life: she always hated closed doors.

Rose, a fan of Roger Federer, was watching the tennis. Her bookshelf and windows were piled high with non-fiction, mostly on international politics and Northern Ireland. Gerry Adams's face smiled brightly from the cover of one. Jim Monaghan's *Colombia Jail Journal* was there too. Marion Coyle came most Sundays. Like Rose, she had thrown herself into the Dublin anti-drugs scene when she got out of prison, and now, like many republicans, she was working for a government-funded drug-awareness programme.

Rose had had a bad fall in 2016, two years before our first interview, and often used a wheelchair. Some days when I went to see her, our conversations went nowhere. We just watched nature documentaries and ate chocolate biscuits. I discovered that bringing in books in which she is mentioned was a way to get the conversation going – so I brought *Last Curtsey* by Fiona MacCarthy; *Janey and Me* by Virginia Ironside; and Philip Bray's *Inside Man*, an account of working as a prison officer in Limerick prison.

Rose was still married to Eddie Gallagher, though they hadn't spoken in years. Occasionally, cheques arrived at the nursing home: income from family property and shares.

This July 2018 letter from her cousin Simon Dugdale, a solicitor, was fairly typical:

Dear Rose,

I enclose a cheque for £1,663.73, which is your share of the proceeds of the sale of ground rents in Burnley, which belonged to the Abbey Pension Fund. This is capital. I don't have any idea how tax works over there, but I am treating my share as a capital gain. No tax was paid previously because it was a pension fund.

It was great to speak to Jim yesterday and sorry we did not speak to each other. Very best wishes and love from Sam.

On a warm, sunny morning in 2017, Ruairi was helping Eddie to drive stakes into the ground at Eddie's equestrian centre in Donegal. The two had gone six years without speaking but had been reconciled in the last year and a half.

Ruairi's task was to hold the stakes in place while Eddie knocked them into position with the bucket of a digger.

Eddie brought the bucket down and gave a tap on the stake a moment earlier than Ruairi had expected. Ruairi thought that Eddie had done it on purpose, as a joke.

Eddie did it again. He was smiling; it was a light-hearted moment for him.

Ruairi said to his father: 'Fuck off with that digger. You bang it again without me being in place, I swear to God . . .'

It happened again.

Ruairi shouted: 'You do that one more time, I'll rip your fucking head off. I'll have you, I'll have you!'

When Eddie refused to get out of the digger for a fight, Ruairi shouted: 'Come on, get out of the digger, I'll have you. Come on, get out!'

Eddie moved to get out of the digger.

Ruairi: 'You get out of that digger, you will NOT be getting back in, believe you me.'

They did not finish driving the stakes into the ground. Ruairi, not for the first time, left Donegal abruptly.

In September 2019, after many hours of video interviews between Ireland and Germany, I met Ruairi for the first time in person at the West County Hotel in Chapelizod, near Rose's nursing home.

He was friendly and warm, full of ideas and business plans. He laughed easily and, like his father, he was charming and mischievous.

I looked around the hotel. It was here in 1986 that Ruairí Ó Brádaigh led his supporters after they walked out of Sinn Féin's Ard Fheis to set up Republican Sinn Féin and the Continuity IRA.

Ruairí was in Ireland to visit Rose and to set up a new export–import business. He told me the plan was to set it up with his father.

I put down my beer. I pointed out that he hadn't spoken to Eddie in two years, and I asked him why he would want to take on the drama and conflict that would inevitably arise.

'Yeah, I know,' he said. 'But I need it. I need to bitch at him. I need it.'

I looked at him across the table and, for the first time, I saw Rose: that attraction to conflict as a source of energy.

Jim visited Rose in the nursing home nearly every day. He was soft spoken and patient with her, wheeling her out to the garden so she could have a cigarette. He told her about deaths, marriages and births of IRA comrades. Once I arrived to find them working on a jigsaw puzzle of a pride of big cats that he had brought her. Despite my protests, Jim insisted on clearing the jigsaw aside to let Rose focus on my visit.

One day, while we were watching *Peppa Pig* on television, I asked Rose if she had regrets. She paused for at least ten seconds and looked directly at me. 'No, I cannot say I do regret it. There was no way, after a certain point, that I would turn back.'

'She couldn't turn back,' Ruairi would tell me later. 'You have to understand Rose's personality. She was all in or nothing, so it just wasn't in her nature to turn around and stop.'

At one point while researching this book, realizing that I knew more about Rose's family than about my own, I started digging in archives, going through family papers and interviewing relations. I learned about how my ancestors fled Cork during Cromwell's genocidal purges and made their way as refugees to Clare; how the area where they resettled had the worst workhouse death rate, and how they had participated in the Land War in the late nineteenth and early twentieth centuries, culminating in my grandfather joining the IRA in 1919. He moved explosives to blow up Scarriff police station in September 1920 and supplied the guns that killed six RIC men in an ambush in Glenwood near Sixmilebridge.

By pedigree, the task of bombing the Six Counties into a united Ireland would seem to have been likelier to fall to me than to Rose Dugdale, but I never felt the urge. Coercing a million outraged Protestants into a Catholic-majority state always seemed like an exercise in futility.

Rose, from her very different background, came to a very different conclusion.

The British press in the 1970s tended to assume that Rose was acting out of anger towards her family arising from some unseen wound. But the more I looked into it, the less power this sort of explanation seemed to have. Her mother was maybe misguided in her insistence on order and conformity at all times, but Rose was far from the only child of her generation to be brought up in that way. Rose's sister, Caroline, grew up in the same home, married a Tory MP and remained a Conservative all her life. I have been able to find no event or specific family dynamic that explains why Rose took such a different path.

Rose's zealotry was still evident in our last interviews. It was what led her to give away much of her fortune; to become involved with Eddie Gallagher and participate in two of the most spectacular and quixotic republican operations of the entire Troubles; to conceal a pregnancy in prison; to fight drug dealers on the streets of Dublin (and to turn on her son when he became one of them); and to devote years to developing weapons that caused an untold number of deaths and injuries, not only of UK security forces but of ordinary civilians.

If the zealotry was a constant, so too was her attractiveness to others. In my interviews with dozens of people for this book – colleagues in Tottenham, fellow inmates in Limerick, students in Clondalkin – not one of them ever questioned Rose's sincerity or her kindness.

At the time of writing, in early autumn 2021, Rose Dugdale is eighty years old. We had concluded our interviews by the time the Covid pandemic began, though we spoke on the phone a few times after visits to the nursing home were banned. Rose herself contracted Covid earlier in 2021 – but, in spite of everything, she survived.

Note on Sources

I was drawn to the story of Rose Dugdale for many reasons: a fascination with 1960s radicalism and 1970s urban guerrilla groups, an interest in the history of Northern Ireland and, most of all, a wish to break through the silence that surrounds the Provisional IRA more than twenty years after it ended its armed campaign.

The IRA's political wing, Sinn Féin, is now the largest political party in Ireland. The IRA, once the senior partner in the republican movement, has disbanded. As the years pass, so much history and personal experience is dying away without being recorded.

Rose Dugdale was in no way a typical member of the IRA. Apart from being an English heiress who came to Irish republicanism through radical left-wing politics, she was never based in Northern Ireland. But her story – which she and key people around her have been willing to share with me – gives us rare insight into the working of the IRA from the early 1970s to the mid-1990s. Rose's paramilitary actions in the 1970s were reported, sometimes luridly, by the media, but after that the reporting went almost completely silent.

The most important sources for this book are new. Rose Dugdale agreed to be interviewed and did not seek editorial control of any kind – but she said it would be up to me to find other sources. I made many, many visits to Rose in her nursing home. In these interviews she was sometimes guarded, and mostly refused to speak about IRA operations, but she gave me valuable new information. I also conducted hours of interviews with her former partner, Eddie Gallagher, with her son, Ruairi Gallagher, and with her partner of recent decades, Jim Monaghan. I also drew on Jim Monaghan's unpublished memoir, which no researcher had ever seen before.

The world has long known of Rose Dugdale's spectacular acts of the 1970s. But Jim Monaghan's manuscript revealed the previously unknown, and immensely consequential, second chapter of her paramilitary life: her extensive collaboration with him in the development of mortars, rockets, explosives and sniper rifles for the Provisional IRA. Locating the Mayo farm where much of this work took place became my all-consuming passion for several months until a casual conversation with one of my interviewees led me to the family of Danny Campbell in Ballycroy.

While I found Jim Monaghan to be a very reliable narrator, I needed other sources to corroborate the details contained in his manuscript. Crucial in this was the cooperation of a very senior Special Branch officer, who spoke to me on condition of anonymity. (I call him 'Thomas Connors'.) This officer had conducted surveillance on Rose and Jim, visited the Campbell farm and personally inspected the weapons developed there. Danny Campbell was no longer alive, but I received the assistance of members of his family, who corroborated Jim Monaghan's account. Another key corroborating document was a copy of the speech Rose Dugdale gave on the occasion in 2011, when Sinn Féin honoured Phyllis Campbell, Danny Campbell's wife, for her work on behalf of the republican movement. Another very useful document was the *An Phoblacht* obituary of Danny Campbell, which was written by Jim Monaghan with the approval of the Campbell family.

This book tells of many people who love Rose: unnamed family members; college friends; those who worked with her as she gave away her fortune to the poor of north London; her partner, Jim, her devoted son, Ruairí. And there are also those who have good reason to despise her – such as the former mayor of Limerick Thady Coughlan, and Gerry Pollard, whose family was held hostage by Rose during the Russborough raid.

The two sides of Rose, the extraordinarily generous and the disturbingly brutal, were evident in my conversations with her. She exuded the energy of someone who was very kind to children, to animals and to the poor, but she showed little empathy for anyone she regarded as being on the wrong side of class politics. In our first ever conversation, she was completely dismissive of the terror and physical harm she and her accomplices caused to the Beit family, saying they deserved it for the beatings suffered by black people in apartheid South Africa. She also seemed indifferent to the suffering of the Beits' servants, some of whom struggled with life-long trauma after the raid.

And yet, she so vividly understood suffering. She spent her family fortune buying clothes for poor children and gave her flat to a homeless couple she found sleeping in a cemetery. In prison, she offered shelter to the most painfully marginalized, yet she had no compunction in disfiguring a police officer by flinging a basin of boiling water into her face. This book presents no prescription or diagnosis, but I hope it offers insights into a complex personality.

I am grateful to the many sources who helped make this book possible – the ones I have named in this note, others named in the source notes below, and others who asked not to be named. In particular I want to acknowledge the invisible hands running through the first few chapters of the book, family members whose contributions have helped me to explain things previously mysterious – such as the precise sources of Rose's fortune and the sums she drew from these sources at key junctures – while offering valuable insights into her early years.

Source Notes

Where possible, sources are indicated in the main text. Here, I provide details that could not be included there.

Prologue

Interview with Meg Poole.

For details of the debutante ball, I have drawn upon Fiona Mac-Carthy's *Last Curtsey: The End of the Debutantes* (Faber & Faber, 2006).

1: The Perfect Candidate

Interviews with Rose Dugdale, Meg Poole and Virginia Ironside.

For information on the marriage and divorce of John Mosley and Carol Mosley (née Timmis), I have drawn upon divorce records from 1936, held in the National Archives, Kew.

Information on Eric Dugdale's income comes from a statement he made to police in 1974.

Fiona MacCarthy's recollections are from *Last Curtsey*.

Details of Rose's travels in 1957 are from a CV held in the Mount Holyoke College Library.

Una-Mary Parker's recollections are quoted in Tom Mangold's article 'The case of Dr Rose Dugdale', *Encounter*, February 1975.

2: *Clandestine Love*

Interviews with Rose Dugdale, Jenny Grove, Jill Paton Walsh and Devaki Jain.

Recollections of Peter Ady by June Knowles, Tim Gardam and Maurice Scott, and details of documents held in the Peter Ady archive at St Anne's College, are from speeches given at a memorial held at Oxford University in 2004.

Details from Iris Murdoch's diary are from *An Iris Murdoch Chronology*, edited by Valerie Purton (Macmillan, 2007).

3: *The Secret*

Interviews with Rose Dugdale, Barbara Lloyd, Virginia Ironside, Peter Ayrton and Edwina Currie.

Details of Rose's analysis of the Radcliffe Committee, and her work in the UN, come from her CV held at Mount Holyoke College and from the March 1962 edition of the *Banker Magazine*.

Details of Mount Holyoke press releases and photographs, as well as Rose's thesis, are from Mount Holyoke library.

Rose's comments on her first visit to Ireland are from an episode of the TG4 series *Mná an IRA*, first aired in January 2012.

4: *The Revolutionary Philanthropist*

Details of Rose's trust fund come from a statement made to police by her father, Eric, in 1974.

Interviews with Rose Dugdale, Wally Heaton, Nettie Pollard, Jenny Grove and Jill Paton Walsh.

Details of Wally's criminal record and the arrest of Rose and Wally at the dockers' protest are from declassified police documents held at the National Archives, Kew.

Eric Dugdale's recollection of meeting Wally, and of Rose's trust fund and sale of shares, are from his 1974 statement to police, and from Melvin J. Lasky, *On the Barricades, and Off* (Routledge, 1988).

Details of the Yarty burglary, and the subsequent court case, are from court reports in *The Times* and the *Guardian*.

Details of the Angry Brigade members' sentencing come from J. D. Taylor's essay 'Not that serious? The investigation and trial of the Angry Brigade, 1967–72', in *Waiting for the Revolution: The British Far Left from 1956*, edited by Evan Smith and Matthew Worley (Manchester University Press, 2017).

Details of Rose and Eric's exchange of letters are from Mangold, 'The Case of Dr Rose Dugdale'.

Details of Rose's conviction for driving on a footpath were reported in the *Guardian*, November 1973.

5: The Spark

Interviews with Eddie Gallagher and Mervyn Johnston.

Details of the Pettigo bombing are from Eddie Gallagher and from *Irish Times* court reports.

Details on the Strabane bombing are from Rose Dugdale, Eddie Gallagher and *Irish Times* court reports.

The quotation from Major Richard Earle is from Mangold, 'The Case of Dr Rose Dugdale'.

6: The Heist

Interviews with Rose Dugdale, Eddie Gallagher and Gerry Pollard.

Details of the Kenwood House theft are from reports in *The Times*.

Details of the Beit family history are from Matthew Hart, *The Irish Game: A True Story of Crime and Art* (Walker & Company, 2004), reports in the *Irish Times* and my interview with Gerry Pollard.

Details of the Russborough House robbery are from Rose Dugdale, Eddie Gallagher and reports in the *Irish Times*.

Details of the search for the thieves are from Rose Dugdale, Matthew Hart's *The Irish Game* and the *Irish Times*.

7: The Most Guarded Woman in Europe

Interviews with Rose Dugdale, Philip Bray, Ruairi Gallagher, Betty O'Neill, Eddie Gallagher and Angela Duffin.

Details of Rose's and Angela Duffin's court appearances, and Eric Dugdale's quotes to Irish reporters, are from the *Irish Times*.

Iris Murdoch's letter to the Beits is held in the manuscript collection of the National Library of Ireland.

8: Born in Captivity

Interviews with Rose Dugdale, Angela Duffin, Betty O'Neill, Philip Bray, Jenny Grove, Willie Lynskey and Eddie Gallagher.

Details of the birth of Ruairi Gallagher, and of subsequent debate in Limerick Council, are from the *Irish Times*.

For my account of the Ferenka factory in Limerick I have drawn on coverage in the *Irish Times*.

9: The Kidnappers

Interviews with Rose Dugdale, Eddie Gallagher, Willie Lynskey, Betty O'Neill and Thady Coughlan.

Details of the kidnap plot are from *Irish Times* court reports.

10: All the World is Watching

Interviews with Eddie Gallagher, Pearse McCorley and Deric Henderson.

Tiede Herrema's recollections are from the *Irish Times*.

The recordings of the hostage negotiations are held in the Tiede Herrema collection, Glucksman Library, University of Limerick.

Details of Eddie Gallagher's court appearance are from the *Irish Times*.

11: Barbed-wire Live

Interviews with Rose Dugdale, Angela Duffin, Betty O'Neill, Philip Bray and Eddie Gallagher.

Details of Eddie Gallagher's court appearance, and of the Limerick female prisoners' attack on a garda, are from *Irish Times* court reports.

Wally Heaton's court appearance was reported in *The Times*.

Iris Murdoch's letter to Irish ambassador, and the ensuing correspondence, are held in the Irish National Archive section of the Cain Collection at Ulster University.

Gordon Hayes's statement was quoted in the *Irish Times*.

12: Steel-bar Wedding

Interviews with Philip Bray, Betty O'Neill, Willie Lynskey, Pearse McCorley, 'Ashling', Ruairi Gallagher and Sean O'Neill.

Details of the wedding are from Betty O'Neill and the *Irish Times*.

Details of Rose's sharp exchange on leaving prison are from Philip Bray.

13: The Avenger of Fatima

Interviews with Rose Dugdale, the senior Garda Special Branch officer Thomas Connors, another Special Branch officer, Andrew Keniry, Christy Burke, Gerry Clarke, Martina Brennan, Edwina Currie, Ruairi Gallagher and Philip Bray.

Sister Elizabeth O'Brien's testimony was quoted in the *Irish Times*.

Details of the Foley/Gaffney kidnapping, and Frank Cluskey's comments, are from the *Irish Times*.

Background on the Dunne and Ma Baker gangs are from articles in *Magill* magazine (November 1983 and March 1984) and the *Irish Times*.

Details of the Ma Baker house occupation are from Ruairi Gallagher and the *Irish Times*.

14: Love Bomb

Interviews with Jim Monaghan, Rose Dugdale, Ruairi Gallagher and Dieter Reinisch.

Details of Jim Monaghan's family background and early IRA activities are from his unpublished memoir.

Details of the bombing of the Special Criminal Court, and of the subsequent court case, are from the *Irish Times*.

Details of rocket and mortar development are from Jim Monaghan's unpublished memoir, and are confirmed in broad detail by Thomas Connors, who later seized prototypes from various stages of their development from Danny Campbell's bunker in Ballycroy, Co. Mayo.

Details of the Vianney Dunne court case are from the *Irish Times*.

15: The Camp

Interviews with Rose Dugdale, Jim Monaghan, Norah Campbell, Katie Campbell, Thomas Connors and Ruairi Gallagher.

Details of explosives development are from Jim Monaghan's unpublished memoir. Details have been confirmed by Thomas Connors, Norah Campbell, Katie Campbell and Rose Dugdale.

16: Bombs and Poetry

Interviews with Ian Tims, Patrick Donohoe, Bernard McCann, Marlissa McCann, Thomas Connors and Norah Campbell.

The listing of Cabinet members present on the day of the Downing Street bombing is from the *Irish Times*.

Jim Monaghan's recollections of his and Rose's bomb-making in the Dublin mountains, and of the Glenanne bombing, are from his unpublished memoir. Details of the scale of destruction from the Glenanne bombing are from the *Irish Times*.

17: Antisocial Behaviour

Interviews with Ruairi Gallagher, Thomas Connors, Norah Campbell and Robert Gibson.

Jim Monaghan's recollection of the development of the Biscuit Launcher is from his unpublished memoir.

18: Someone is Listening

Interview with Thomas Connors.

Jim Monaghan's recollections of bomb and weapon development, and of his and Rose's movements on the day of the 1996 London Docklands bombing, are from his unpublished memoir.

Details of the Baltic Exchange and Bishopsgate bombings are from the *Irish Times* and *The Times*.

Details of the Docklands bombing are from the *Irish Times* and the BBC.

19: Rabbits and Rendezvous

Interviews with Norah Campbell, Rose Dugdale, Jim Monaghan, Jackie Kaye and a senior Real IRA figure who cannot be named.

Details of weapons development are from Jim Monaghan's unpublished memoir and corroborated by Thomas Connors and Norah Campbell.

Details of peace discussions among the Ballycroy group are from Jim Monaghan's unpublished memoir.

20: *The Export Market*

Interviews with Jim Monaghan, Rose Dugdale, Ruairi Gallagher, Bill Flynn, Norah Campbell and Katie Campbell.

Jim Monaghan's recollection of his arrest in Bogotá is from his book *Colombia Jail Journal* (Brandon, 2007).

Details of the US Congressional hearing are from my own reporting for the *Belfast Telegraph* and from the *Irish Times.*

Details of the Colombia court hearings are from my own reporting for the *Sunday Independent* and *Belfast Telegraph,* and Deaglán de Bréadún's reporting for the *Irish Times.*

Interview with Thomas Connors.

Jim Monaghan's recollection of the Ballycroy group's meetings to discuss peace is from his unpublished memoir.

Rose Dugdale's correspondence is from her personal collection.

21: *Reuniting*

Interviews with Ruairi Gallagher, Norah Campbell and Katie Campbell.

Details of the Seamus McGrane bomb plot are from my own court reporting for *The Times.*

Rose Dugdale's correspondence is from her personal collection.

Acknowledgements

My sincere thanks to Rose Dugdale, Jim Monaghan, Ruairi Gallagher and Eddie Gallagher. Without their help, there would have been no book and I am very grateful.

Rose never turned down an interview. Some days her memory was good, other days she struggled, but she was always generous with her time.

I am deeply grateful to Jim Monaghan for his insights and patience, and for facilitating interviews with other people.

Ruairi Gallagher spent many, many hours in conversation with me, never showing any impatience and always offering valuable insights.

Eddie Gallagher opened up about his relationship with Rose for the first time, and I am very grateful for his hospitality.

I was also fortunate to receive the assistance of people who knew Rose as a girl and young woman in England. Virginia Ironside invited me into her home and was an excellent interviewee with wonderful insights. My warmest thanks to Jenny Grove for her extraordinary patience in telling me of Rose's Oxford days, and for her valuable insights and brilliant research. Meg Poole's account of Rose's debutante presentation before Queen Elizabeth left me in awe of a theatre director's ability to tell a great story. Jill Paton Walsh provided invaluable context for Rose's life in Oxford, and shed light on the background of her cousin Peter Ady. Special thanks, too, to Devaki Jain for her wonderful recollections of Rose's Oxford days.

Barbara Lloyd was hilarious in her recollection of Mount Holyoke in the 1960s, Peter Ayrton offered great insight into Rose's time in Cuba and in radical academic circles in London, and Edwina Currie showed great patience in explaining both her confrontation with Rose and her friendship with Peter Ady.

Wally Heaton and Nettie Pollard offered great insight into Rose's Tottenham days, and I am very grateful to both of them.

Mervyn Johnson and Robert Gibson gave powerful accounts of what they and their neighbours suffered at the hands of the IRA, and Gerry Pollard shared valuable recollections about life in Russborough House and the aftermath of the heist.

Thady Coughlan, the former mayor of Limerick, wonderfully described his dealings with Rose following the kidnapping of Tiede Herrema. Retired army officer Pearse McCorley and journalist Deric Henderson also offered great insight into the kidnapping from very different perspectives.

Former prison officer Philip Bray gave me a vivid account of life in Limerick prison in the 1970s. Angela Duffin and the woman I have called 'Ashling' were brilliant guides to prison life with Rose. Angela deserves special praise for her kindness and for explaining the intricacies of republican politics in the prison.

I will always be grateful to Betty O'Neill and Willie Lynskey for inviting me to their home, and for their wonderful insights into life with Rose and Ruairi.

Sean O'Neill offered a very different perspective, and for that, too, I am very grateful.

Other people offered great insight into Rose's post-prison life in Dublin, especially the former Special Branch officer I call 'Thomas Connors', who did several interviews and helped corroborate key information while offering his own memories and perspective.

Andrew Keniry, Gerry Clarke and, especially, Martina Brennan offered valuable memories of Rose's Dublin life, as did her former students Ian Tims, Patrick Donohoe, Bernard McCann and Marlissa McCann.

I will be forever grateful to the Campbell family, especially Norah Campbell and Katie Campbell, for their hospitality and their insight into weapons development and republican life in Mayo.

Also, a special thanks to Jackie Kaye for her insight into republican politics in London.

Several librarians and researchers deserve special thanks. Deborah Richards, the college archivist at Mount Holyoke, was so kind and generous with her time, and I am very grateful.

Katarzyna Kamieniecka at the National Library of Ireland got me out of a tight bind during lockdown and was also very kind. Seán Cafferkey at the Glucksman Library at the University of Limerick said yes to me when others said no and I will always be grateful to him. Dieter Reinisch, an encyclopaedia of knowledge on Irish republicans, also helped with finding written sources.

Finally, I am so very, very grateful for the patience, kindness, insight and editing skills of Sarah Hale, without whom I wouldn't have been able to finish this book.

Index

Campbell, Danny 223, 224, 231
America
emigrates to 244
returns home from 244–5
arrest 295
assistants 248
celebration of London
Docklands bombing 277
characterization of 249
children 245
death 322
illness 299
marriage to Phyllis 244–5
republican background 244
Campbell, Donal 281
Campbell, Edward (aka Jim
Monaghan) *see* Colombia
Three: Edward Campbell
Campbell family home
farm 244
raids on 248–9, 294–5
as a safe house 249
RD and Jim Monaghan
Campbell children and
RD 248
as guests 248, 249, 310
training camp 244
booster testing 245–7,
249–50
detonating cords 265–6
preparations for 250
sniper rifles 278–80
surveillance of 251
Campbell, John 244
Campbell, Katie 249, 280
on RD's chickens 300
Campbell, Liam 284

Campbell, Norah 244, 287, 310
on digestive biscuits 262
fires sniper rifle 280
on garda raid 294
on garda tip-offs 294
helps friends avoid gardaí 251
as a lookout 250
RD and
on being taught to drive by
280–81
on driving style of 310
on Jim Monaghan and 248
on staying with 299
on weapons training 250
Campbell, Phyllis (née Maguire)
245, 277
honoured by RD 250
postcards from Jim 294
Caola, Frank 8
Card, Thomas 60, 63–4
Carr, Robert 61
Carter, Danielle 270
Casey, Thomas 270
Castle, Barbara 41
Caudwell, Sarah 32, 35
Caulfield, Justice 171
Caviedes, John Alexander 297
Charing Cross Hotel 8
Charing, Gaby 51, 53, 69
Charles, Prince 244, 312–13
Chelsea Bird (Ironside) 40
Chelsea Hospital chapel 21
Cherwell 34
Churchill-Coleman, Commander
George 255
Civil Rights Union 74
claimants union 48

de Chastelain, John 291
de Juana Chaos, Iñaki 306–7
debutantes 3–6, 20
decommissioning of weapons 275,
    281, 291
Derry city 53–4, 58, 143
diamond industry 90–91
Dignam, Thomas 72, 73
dockers strike 55–6
    arrest of Wally Heaton 56
    people's roadblock 55
Doherty, Sean 130
Dolphin's Barn, Dublin 199, 233,
    261–2
Donnelly, Michael 54
Donohoe, Patrick 252–3, 254
Dorchester Hotel 16
Doyle, Mrs 115
Driver, Frank 215
Dublin, drug problem 199–202
    Concerned Parents Against
        Drugs *see* Concerned
        Parents Against Drugs
        (CPAD)
    confessions 203
    dealers 200, 201, 202, 203
      abductions 203–4, 205
      Dunne Brothers 208, 226,
        227–8
      garda beating of protesters
        209–10
      Ma Baker group 208, 209–10,
        226
      RD's injuries from the gardaí
        210–11
      RD's obsession with 209–10
      RD's operations against 204

      shootout 204
    Hardwicke Street flats 200
    meetings about 203
    overdoses 202
    treatment for addicts 201
    vigilantes 202, 204, 205, 226,
      228, 236
Duddy, Brendan 270
Duffin, Angela 122–3, 124, 127, 128
    birthday 184–5
    on drills in prison 165–6
    organizes protest 131–2
    RD and
      Christmas present for 169
      excluded by 139
      meets in prison 124–5
      on support from 171
      on solitary confinement 169
Duffy, John 123
Dugdale, Carol (mother of RD)
    7, 17
    dinner parties 17
    early life 7–8
    Eric and
      introduction to 9–10
      marriage to 10
    fashion 17
    John Mosley and
      divorce from 8–9
      marriage to 8
    marriage proposal from Eddy
      Sackville-West 9
    post-partum depression 10
    RD and
      ambition for 19–20
      visits in Limerick prison
      125–6